M000105673

BOUND FOR ROQUE ISLAND

Sailing Maine and the World

by

R. J. RUBADEAU

Bascom Hill
Minneapolis, MN

Copyright © 2010 by R.J. Rubadeau.

BASCOM
HILL

Bascom Hill Publishing Group

212 3rd Avenue North, Suite 290

Minneapolis, MN 55401

612.455.2293

www.bascomhillpublishing.com

All rights reserved. No part of this publication may be reproduced, stored in a retrieval system, or transmitted, in any form or by any means, electronic, mechanical, photocopying, recording, or otherwise, without the prior written permission of the author.

This book is printed on acid-free paper.

ISBN - 978-1-935098-33-1

ISBN - 1-935098-33-0

LCCN - 2010908046

Cover Design by Alan Pranke

Typeset by Sophie Chi

Cover photograph: *HOMEFREE* at Roque Island, completing her 2006-7 voyage to Cape Horn and return, by R. J. Rubadeau.

Printed in the United States of America

CONTENTS

ACKNOWLEDGEMENTS

Long night watches at sea bring out the storyteller in all of us. The stories grow and gain importance in the retelling as the water hisses by, and the boat tracks down the miles to the next port. My first attempts at putting many of the experiences in my life into words were given to an audience of natural, unrestrained critics who had no where to hide. You quickly learn how to tell a story that moves along or you become mute. My thanks to those who let me experiment and talk it out onto the page.

Kudos to Randal Peffer, writer, novelist and friend, who read early drafts and gave needed encouragement. Thanks to my editor Ken Kane who kept my feet to the fire on the specifics. Interior Design created by the talented Sophie Chi. A special appreciation goes to Herb McCormick, Mark Pillsbury, Elaine Lembo, John Burnham, Andy Burton and the rest of the folks at *Cruising World Magazine* and other great boating publications that I have worked with over the years. I learned that good writing is mainly about those words you are able to leave off the page.

A special shout out to those icons of the international yacht racing scene in the late sixties and seventies who were passionate about the boats and the experiences and never gave a thought to how they might make a buck off the effort. It was a rare and special time in the history of yachts and the folks who love them. I was lucky to have been a part of it.

To Mary, Skye, and Tristan
the finest shipmates ever
and
To *Dog Star,* a remarkable companion

In order to be a sailor you have to go to sea.

Peter Pye, sailor

*When a man comes to like a sea life,
he is not fit to live on land.*

Samuel Johnson, author

PREFACE

Bound For

Maine dares you to try and love it. The sun is a precious commodity come December and a shy visitor most other times of the year. Daily life on the rugged Acadian coast is tide-scrabble hard. It is not a place for the timid or those who like to run around naked. Geographically, Maine is the rest of New England, north of where the cartographers once wrote *terra incognita*, the "unknown land." Vikings found the whale-backed rocks and wind worn fields to their liking centuries before Columbus shipwrecked onto the tropical sands of the Bahamas. Henry David Thoreau called it "America's Great Wilderness." Maine is still chronically misunderstood. Those who sail here for fun are determined, resourceful, and stubborn.

A favorite joke I share often, while waxing noxious with my enthusiasm for cruising Down East, is the answer to the question: "What do you do in Maine in the summer?" The answer: "If it comes on a weekend, we have a picnic." This is a Mainer's joke, and it demonstrates a self-deprecating style of welcoming you to their world. It is understood that Maine has more homespun opinions per square mile than anywhere else on earth. Each Mainer you meet is as real as a dime.

You learn quickly that Maine offers a sailor no apology for its weather or much else. The air here is reliably wet, overcast, and ruled by sharp winds. A hundred shades of fog curtain the coastal and inland byways. Damp morning mists tumble in knee-deep blankets down every creek bed. Bamboo congested evergreens thickly settle the ancient round hills, where shorelines drop down to slick gray granite ledges that are battered silly by endless Atlantic rollers of cold purpose.

Because of all these challenges, the few crisp clear days sailing on this sharp-fanged coastline, when the sun riots and all the worlds align, easily stand out in my mind as the most unforgettable moments of a long life spent around boats. A perfect clear-blue windy day in Maine, etched in brilliance on a simple sailor's brain, is called a "sparkler." This coastline is a magical place where I practice the graceful art of cruising.

It is only two hundred and fifty air miles from the tip of Cape Cod to Passamaquoddy and Canadian territory, yet the Gulf of Maine's magnificent inter-tidal perimeter rolls out for over three and a half thousand coastal miles, and includes some three thousand islands, many uninhabited. For most New England sailors the distant goal of Roque Island, up near the town of Machias on the wild northern edges of our nation's coastline, is still the cruising man's Holy Grail. Not much has changed at Roque, as far as amenities for yachts, since the first "damn fool yachtsman and his flapper" sailed for fun past Schoodic Point heading just north of east for the signature white crescent beach of this far off island.

On a cold day in April, two miles high in the Rocky Mountains, I set the Great Beach at Roque Island as this coming summer's family sailing goal. The hitch in the giddy-up of this perfect plan is that, with the notable exception of cash, my grown children are no longer dependent on me in any way, and ordering them around doesn't get the same results as when they were five. I am also facing the twin life-altering events of becoming a grandfather in a few months and sending my youngest child off to college in the fall. These facts have created a variety of age and maturity-related

gut checks that have done little for my seasonal mood swings. I
feel adrift as time flies by. This is a worrisome state of affairs for a
guy who still thinks he's full of pickles. In the ongoing process of
trying to get a grip on my new maturity, I mistakenly opened forty
years of my journals and sailing logs. The ghosts were let out, and
they speak volumes about my serial co-dependence on beautiful
sailboats and deep ocean water.

I was barely out of my teens when I sailed my first dinghy in 1969;
by 1974 I found myself bringing the world famous 73' Maxi-Class
ocean racer, *Ondine,* as her captain, into San Diego . This followed
a line honors victory for the U.S.A. in the Sydney-Hobart Race and
a crossing of the Pacific Ocean from Australia via Pitcairn Island
and Acapulco. These were the golden years of offshore racing with
the likes of Ted Turner, Jim Kilroy, Huey Long, Ted Hood, Sir Peter
Blake, Holland, Snaith, Sir Ted Heath, Nye, Alan Bond, and dozens
of other enormous international egos spending millions to race
criminally expensive sail boats for tin cups and, more importantly,
bragging rights at the bar. With well over a hundred and fifty thousand
blue water miles under my keel, I have my share of juicy anecdotes.
Why not tell a good story? The statute of limitations should be up by
now.

Dredging through four decades of hard won prejudices in the
care, navigation, and hands-on management of sailboats, I found
a few things that seem to work all right in a variety of situations
most of the time. These I'll share. I'll throw in an observation or
two about the special care and preservation of a classic wooden
vessel. *Dog Star* is my family's Philip Rhodes designed double-
ended ketch. She turned seventy-five this exciting summer, proving
again her pedigree as a stable and seaworthy cruiser. She has come
under my care for the last thirty years. We are growing more mature
together.

Like most sailors, I also have strong opinions on everything
from anchoring to dinghy docks, from the essential cruising rules

of social behavior to rowing. I include, at no additional charge, a rigorous course on swearing, along with insulting ethnic hand gestures, in four Romance languages. You are trained to use them as a response to powerboat operators leaving gunnel-washing wakes.

As with all voyages, long or short, this summer's odyssey found the unexpected vagaries of wind, weather, and chance pulling us off course. The resulting disasters, barely avoided, gave our crew much to reckon with before it was over. This is why all vetted navigators never state that they are "going to" a certain destination or harbor; "bound for" is the proper entry. Failure to achieve the goal is only by never leaving port. This lack of clarity is vexing for those well appointed captains and their land-comfortable guests on the yacht club veranda. These are the folks who race around buoys or run off to Nantucket on a schedule and a tight timeline. The reality is that the simple act of taking a boat out on the water includes the not-so-odd chance that we are far more likely to end up somewhere other than where we had planned when our time runs out. I think this common sense observation also applies when parents try to control and manage the lives of their offspring. In my new logbook, at the beginning of this eventful family summer, I put "Bound for Roque Island."

RJR, Telluride

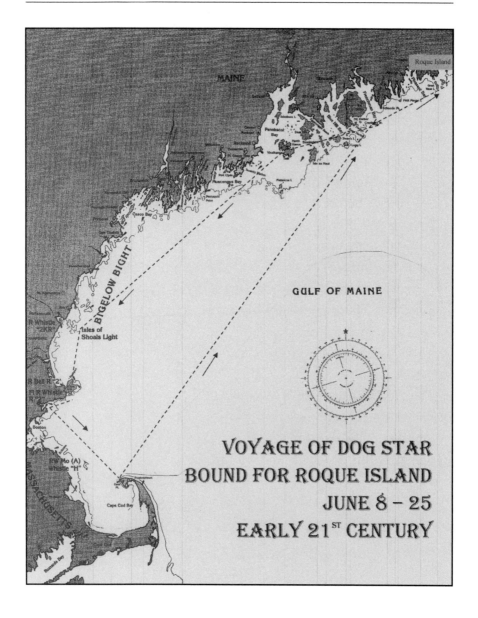

GULF OF MAINE

VOYAGE OF DOG STAR
BOUND FOR ROQUE ISLAND
JUNE 8 – 25
EARLY 21ST CENTURY

ONE

BELFAST

The Belfast Boatyard at the head of Penobscot Bay on the midcoast of Maine is held together by sulfurous red painted pilings with the girth of century old oak trunks and plain Yankee stubbornness. The substance of this rickety wharf and waterfront operation is often more theater than reality. Optimism is the major product of this small enterprise. Tenacity holds the line as the single largest ingredient. The roadstead of the historic town of Belfast is open to wind and waves, the water dangerously skinny alongside the docks twice a day, and the currents boil in the tug of war between freshwater flats up river and the double-digit, salty tidal bores rolling down-east towards Passamaquoddy.

The boatyard crew is made of working class Mainers, trying to piece together a living wage one day at a time, and longhaired young dreamers from the heartlands to the west who wander through from time to time. These odd bedfellows are surprised to discover they share a common addiction to the craft of boats and the joy of being at home on the water. This legacy of the sea is part of their souls and is more about what and who they are, not where they were born. The goal, from sun up to dusk, is to remedy the bad habits of gentlemen boat owners and to be beholden to no one in particular. We amateurs are credited with a common bond of incompetence, and it would take a first-class idiot to walk around this yard looking anything but bewildered. Keep your confidence, earned or not, close to your vest pocket.

Alex Turner owns and runs the operation. The boss is sparse in words and lean in body, with a lame pup named Sam and a blind old dog named Molly. Turner is seldom still. The Popeye forearms seem out of place on his thin frame, and he holds them away from his body when he walks. His gait rolls as if the whole world were the planked deck of a schooner. A tattered black Red Sox ball cap is cemented to his head. Alex went to Bowdoin, down in Brunswick, the *alma mater* of Nathaniel Hawthorne, Henry Wadsworth Longfellow and Franklin Pierce. Alex, originally from someplace else, had settled on the rugged granite and spruce coastline and never left. A born and bred Mainer, if he were feeling kindly, would comment that Alex Turner could almost pass for the real thing.

"Mournin'," Alex says as I catch his attention between jobs.

"Been a good winter?" I ask as he gives my hand a quick and painful squeeze. Denim blue eyes search past me for a lost shoreline.

"Fair to middlin'. Some snow. Cold though."

"Boats all good?"

His look is chastising for such a question. I give ground.

"Things look busy."

"It's a might thick these days."

"Anything I need to know about getting splashed?"

"Can't charge enough," he says.

"For what?" I ask.

"For anything," he says, and winks.

"Charge more."

"Folks wouldn't come," he says.

He was right.

"I'll never be rich or fat, right Sam?" Alex bends and tugs at a ragged ear on the offered head. The dog leans against my leg and moans like a constipated cow.

"Part Gurnsey," the Boss says and moves off to another job.

Alex lives every day with a fragile economy compounded by rot and decay that would try the stoutest of hearts. A few years ago, a piling a couple of hundred yards across the roadstead at the tourists' lobster pound dock collapsed. The stump showed the honeycombed and rotten core, riddled to the point of dust. Inside the pulpwood were teredos. The very worms that haunted Columbus, defeated the Spanish Armada, and plagued eons of plank-on-frame shipwrights throughout maritime history, had found an unlikely home in Penobscot Bay's cold waters. The insidious boring snakes are normally considered a tropical blight. The strange news of their northern migration seemed a death sentence to an already beleaguered boat yard in a town best known as a former world-class chicken slaughterhouse. The discovery made big news in the national boating journals. The worms have staged a comeback in direct proportion to our national commitment to clean up the waters of our coastline. As pollution goes away, the teredos make a new home. No good deed goes unpunished. It is a given truth around boats that doing the right thing is often rewarded with unexpected consequences.

Harvestable old growth timber is presently in short supply in Maine; but wood, the value-added and end-product side, is still a vital part of the state's economic survival. Maine has in the past twenty or so years become the center of a growing movement to preserve the art and craft of wooden boat building. *Wooden Boat Magazine* founder Jon Wilson sounded a knell almost thirty years ago about a vanishing part of America's historic maritime legacy to the world. In a modern publishing miracle his "niche rag" survived the lean years and has become a revered spokes-periodical for the beauty and form of sailing craft and the centuries old skills that they require. The affliction of becoming a wooden boat owner is akin to people choosing between the dirty daily option of shoveling coal into a furnace to keep warm rather than setting a thermostat twice a year. Stepping back in time is often less romantic and more labor intensive than we can possibly imagine.

Maine is the perfect place to attack the pressure of the modern world with iconoclastic thinking. The rugged coastline wiggles and curves like an Etch-a-Sketch gone wild: miles of granite, home site-sized islands, spruce headlands, and deep water coves. Passages with names like Thrumcap, Thread o' Life, Cuckolds, and Devils Head keep the navigation colorful. While the rest of the state verges on being admired to death by the car-hopping travelers from the Boston-New York megalopolis, the hardy flavor of Maine remains secure in the small coastal islands and communities where modern renegades survive in spite of the crush. The only way to find this glimpse of something almost gone from American life is by sea. Luckily I have learned how to "float," and I've passed this skill along to my kids. They are still making up their minds if my gift is a blessing or a curse.

I finish my tentative launch scheduling with Alex, leave the yard office, and take a deep breath in the fog-filled liquid air that smells of rotting seaweed and slimy wood. Spring boat maintenance is a game of chutes and ladders in this part of the northern hemisphere. Some of the yard workers on coffee break, gathered around the wood stove in the carpenter's shop, seem to recognize me from my last visit in October when *Dog Star* was taken out of the water and put in the shed. Others eye me with the justifiable suspicion reserved for unknown boat owners, wondering what kind of mischief I might have in store for them during the next weeks as I make the boat ready for the water. People like me are sometimes called, "the summer complaints." I try not to live up to the moniker.

If there is a universal mold for third world immigration/custom officials and small town politicians, there is certainly one for New England's boat yard minions. I could never picture any of these men or women saying "No" to a good idea to make a boat better. Yet they will look at you as if you have dog shit on your nose while you try to explain something you want done to your boat they haven't done before. But almost any request made in the form of a question, no matter how bizarre, is approached with an "Okay, let's try it" attitude. Ulcers curse lesser folks. I wave self-consciously and don't expect a response.

The first time you see your boat after a long northern winter is a potent mixture of joy and angst. As my eyes adjust to the dim light in the massive wood frame and metal shed three miles from the sea, the bulk of her six tons towers over me and rises up fifteen feet

towards the rafters. I look for signs of age in her planks, sighting along her sheer line. I'm critical and tentative like a forlorn lover after a forced hiatus, looking for wrinkles, warts and sagging skin. I circle her slowly, stepping over the wide bases of the metal jack stands. I touch her red bottom, running my hands along the raised seams where the seam compound stands proud like a varicose vein. It feels right and solid. Love, no matter how long dormant, always does.

My emotions are more than the normal stewpot this year. Usually my veins sing drunken shanties long into the night with the beginning of a new summer's sailing adventures. I anticipate the treasured logbook drawing out the quips about the foolishness of cruising with a full family aboard a vintage wooden boat. But, at this moment, all I hear in my head is a dirge to the tune of the "Volga Boatmen." Something is coming to an end. Time is rolling faster than a tidal flood, and this season marks a major milestone. I will be a grandfather. It sounds so final. My kids are having kids. I try to shake the lethargy and the funk; neither goes away easily.

It isn't the boat's fault that something beyond my control has my imagination tripping into an open grave. I exhale and without embarrassment whisper, "Hello." The tin roof cracks, expanding in the rising temperature of the late day sun. *Dog Star* gives me a response in her unmistakable body language that she is happy as a squirming puppy to see me, too.

My first attempt to converse with a hunk of wood and metal fastenings was in 1969. I slept aboard a sailboat for the first time. She was old and tired; black-pocked mildew had gotten the upper hand with the interior trappings. I ridiculed her for what she wasn't. Regret for those disparaging remarks about a lady in need still haunts me. The thirty-foot Atkins designed wooden schooner was named *The Green Dragon* after the pub that launched Paul Revere's famous midnight-ride. Some unkind denizens of the waterfront spread the rumor that the old girl looked as if she had actually seen the gallop first hand. The boat was at a mooring packed into the inner basin in Manchester Harbor a few miles down the North Shore coast from Gloucester, Massachusetts.

A friend from Vermont, where my winter had been spent on the ski patrol hauling broken and bleeding bodies off the slopes of Sugarbush Mountain, had arranged for the berth. My plan was to wile away the summer months teaching sailing at the Wingaersheek Beach Yacht Club. My friend's older brother owned *The Green Dragon;* and in exchange for some varnishing and nightly bilge pumping, I was allowed to sleep aboard. This would have been a fairly straightforward good deal except I knew nothing about varnishing and even less about sailing. All the good of the deal was on my side of the ledger. I figured how hard could any of it be? I was full of untested potential and the undeserved self-confidence won by surviving my teen-age years with only a few noticeable scars. The world was a plate of oysters.

The Manchester Town Library is a marble edifice in the center of town overlooking the harbor. It had been gifted through the amazing largess of Mr. Andrew Carnegie, a builder of centerpiece libraries in small towns across the country. Outside balustrades and Ionic columns held aloft the vaulted arches and bas-relief roman numerals; inside, the shelves were stocked full. One ten-foot long corridor was filled with books by and about voyaging sailors. Slocum, Chichester, Alcard, Hiscock, Rose, Heyerdahl, Dumas, Robinson, Tillman, Snaith, Smeeton, Plummer, Hayder, Crealock, Tangvald, Petersen, Calder, and the other early legends of sailing followed me home one by one. I rolled through the entire section with the Dewey coordinates of 797.12. In a mildewed bunk in the dank cabin, the mast creaking in the step, while gulls provided a

Greek chorus, I read by the pale glow of a small oil lamp, straining my eyes until I fell asleep.

Nothing can ever shrink an open mind back from the impact of a new idea. True and well, I was a hooked "lunker." A kid from the salt flats of central New York State, who had never navigated anything but a tin canoe on an Adirondack lake, was dreaming of tropics and storms and white sails against azure skies. Add the cobalt seas. It is sage advice to beware the dreams you dream in the light of day. They might come true.

TWO

FIRST YOU HAVE TO ROW

After a hastily downed sandwich, and with barely an hour before a bone-chilling sunset, I secure a ladder to the side of the boat and drag a bucket of water and assorted spray bottles of cleaners up from the truck. I pull back the covering tarp and push open the main hatch to the cabin. It looks like a lumberyard scrap pile stacked by kids who went to school on the short bus. Every cupboard is open, floorboards up, exposing red lead painted bilges, the innards exposed of the sink and engine compartment, hoses askew, cupboards amidships piled on the settees, odds and ends of galley hatches tilted on edge; stacked slats of varnished wood occupying every flat surface. It's a disaster of grand proportions.

I smile and step down the companionway stairs. The interior is just as I left it six months ago. The boat smells sweet, maybe a hint of Murphy's Oil Soap and Marvel Mystery Oil or WD40 from the engine. Air circulation has had its way all winter long; now it's my turn.

After a few trips up and down the ladder, I have a settee berth cleaned, swabbed, and a mattress installed. I put a few floorboards in to save a turned ankle. I pull an oil lamp out of its plastic tub and fill it carefully with oil. The warm glow soon staves off the darkening shadows. I lie down and prop my head against the bulkhead. A part of me I usually don't even know I have finally relaxes. It's been this way between *Dog Star* and me for a long time, and I don't want to do anything about it. I settle into my bunk, on my boat, and sigh.

During that long ago 1969 summer, reality had a tough-love way of interfering with my daydreams. Before attempting to be the youngest sailor to take on the watery world of the high latitudes south of the three great capes single-handed, I first had to learn how to row. The sound of one hand clapping is nothing compared to the cosmic futility of a one oared dinghy. Alan Bezanson, the owner of the *Green Dragon,* had protected his six-foot pram from wharf thieves by placing one of the oars in a secure place. He had forgotten to tell me where the secure place was. My two-hundred-yard sojourn from dock to boat was anything but a straight line. Dignity is hard to come by when you are kneeling in the bow of a wooden shoe paddling with a six-foot oar through a congested mass of moored boats. I felt like a pinball. The defenseless boats were the scoring cushions. Their owners lit up as I ricocheted off. After a few days of apologies, one owner gave me another oar in the spirit of self-preservation. It was two feet shorter than the original. My rhumb line from A to B got marginally better right off the bat.

Rowing is not a simple, natural motion. My golfing friends say the same is true of a golf swing. If you try to equate the movement of oars and a small boat to something else in life, you will get it all wrong. I don't know about hitting little white balls, but I can still recall in minute detail my flat line learning curve in that skittish plywood pram.

I found the first major hurdle in rowing is to convince yourself that proceeding backwards towards your destination is a good idea. Going somewhere off in the distance by staring back at where you've been is a hard sell for most of us. Try walking backwards across a busy street sometime. I would like to think this acquired skill is some profound metaphor for life's unique challenges, but it's probably not. The problem is simple ergo-mechanics. If our elbows bent the other way, we could row facing forward, but it would be hard to hug your sweetie. Life is full of compromises.

Practice your rowing before you are taking someone you want to impress out to get on your boat. Practice often and do it around things that don't need expensive repair work when you collide. Rowing is the first impression you offer to any other boat in an anchorage. It pays big dividends to work on this skill with the same tenacity you work on a controlled jibe in a crowded racing fleet.

My kids believe rowing is a necessary, if arcane, skill. Outboard motors are not on *Dog Star*'s inventory or wish list. I've taught both of my children to take rowing seriously. They do so as long as I am watching, which is about all you can hope for. My training method is stupidly simple and probably should not be a model for best practices. I don't let them row unless they do it exactly how I do it. Nothing is a greater incentive than the pre-adolescent need to be rid of parental supervision for a portion of the day. A sailboat on a family cruise is often viewed by the younger set as a floating Alcatraz. In order to leave the herd pen you must be able to row. It is easy as pie to instruct motivated learners. History illuminates these hard facts:

"Hey, let's get ashore," my ten-year-old daughter Skye says at the top of her lungs.

"Let me get the anchor down first," I groan, letting out the last feet of chain as we drift backwards on the wind. We are in Tarpaulin Cove on the northern side of Naushon Island in Vineyard Sound. It is 1990.

"Mom, Dad says I can't go off the boat."

"I did not."

"Did so."

"Did not."

M. gives me a look from the companionway that lets me know I sound worse than my kids. She also has a come-hither gleam in her green eyes that suggests I might just get lucky if the kids went off somewhere by themselves. She knows the buttons that work.

"How about some rowing practice?"

My daughter gives me a look reserved for day-old road kill.

"I want to go," said Tristan, age six, adding his Elmer Fudd impersonation to the mix.

"Of course you do," I said. It was mock enthusiasm.

"No, you don't." Skye places her now clenched fists on her hipbones.

"I don't?" Tristan's voice rises quickly from confused to belligerent. "I got to 'pwactice' my 'wowing' too."

"I 'vant' to be alone." Skye gives us the Marlene Dietrich line in response to my son's problem with his r's. The back of her hand is at her forehead and I know she means it.

"Get arrested." I give her a scrunched face, knowing my own hoped for outcome of aloneness will only come true if we divide four by two, and factor age groups into the pairings.

"Mom." Her voice is an alto pitched, melodramatic plea that immediately informs the rest of the quiet afternoon anchorage that I am probably holding her small hand over the flame of the alcohol stove.

"Look," my wife says. "Horses."

And sure enough at the far end of the two-mile crescent beach are a brace of riders moving their steeds slowly along the sand in our general direction. Members of the

Forbes Family Trust that owns the bulk of the Elizabeth Islands often ride on the beach in the late afternoon. Less well-heeled visitors, who can only access the island by private boat, are restricted to the white sand that rings the cove. Our children are safe to run the length of their freedom without being for a moment out of our sight. God knew what she was doing when she put this little bit of paradise together for the rest of us who were not born to the Forbes' legacy.

"Let's go," my daughter said with a razor's edged excitement, and we are suddenly all a flurry of activity, pulling *George M*, our 7'11" Dyer dinghy alongside, shipping oars, slathering on sun screen, finding hats, clogs, and Snoopy life preservers. Soon the two of them are off, pulling like starving castaways towards the only land in sight. No technique, but plenty of muscle from my daughter, while Tristan sits in the stern holding on tight and acting the mute bosun. Their upper bodies pump fore and aft in perfect unison.

I frown at the flailing oars. M. notices my judgment, winks at me in spite of my sour puss and disappears below with a suggestive flip of her blonde hair. I lose the frown as my libido comes stampeding out of hibernation. With a last look I watch my progeny beach the boat on the run, bury an anchor in the sand, and beeline for the riders. With a lecherous laugh I disappear below decks. How often in cruising does one thing lead to another and another, and all is suddenly well with the world?

In the cold and shadowed Maine morning, work on *Dog Star* begins. Three solid hours are spent wiping down every locker, bulkhead, overhead, sink, cubby, knee, frame, crook, and shelf with a lemon fresh scent. Seventy-five odd pieces of varnished wood are put back together like a giant jigsaw puzzle. After a quarter-century of this exercise, I seldom have to look at the cryptic hints I have scribbled on the hidden edges as to where the piece fits. The tarp is pulled off the boat over the bow, and I begin to organize my time for the next week. I will strip the boomkin to bare wood and build up with seven coats of varnish; I will sand and paint the cabin top and inboard bulwarks with Miami Tan. I have to get two coats of varnish on the masts before I re-rig the shrouds, running rigging, and stays. I want to lightly sand the teak decks as the black polysulfide filler is standing proud and is liable to be worked loose underfoot. It all seems too much for seven days, but then I remind myself that the Big Kahunna created the universe in a week. One small mystical step at a time, as I live fully in each tedious moment.

Dog Star has a conventional layout below decks—v-berths forward that extend up under the foredeck, with storage under the six-inch foam cushions in three top loading bins. The pointed forepeak itself holds two flaked anchor roads suspended on canvas hammocks and the business end flukes of our hundred-pound Luke Storm anchor. The chain locker is just settled in the crook. The main mast will soon sit solidly just aft the bunks in the V and become a very helpful accessory to pull yourself up and in.

A bulkhead with a draw canvas curtain separates sleeping quarters from the heads, with sink and commode to port and a large hanging locker to starboard. A full bulkhead with a hinged wooden door to isolate the head then opens to the main cabin with two six-foot-two settee berths with six pull down lockers in slatted opulence outboard of each. Further aft is the galley with a deep icebox to port and a two burner Shipmate alcohol stove with oven to starboard. A single deep sink, a huge, bronze hand pump for freshwater, and the companionway ladder are centered along a mahogany counter at the end of the cabin.

The interior is light elm with dark mahogany trim and teak counter tops. The rich mocha brown of unfinished teak floorboards balances the gloss white ceiling and cabin sides and the eight opening ports. These ports give the eye a bright, light filled space to admire the polished bronze of ship's clock and barometer and the four gimbaled oil lamps that help warm cool evenings.

I slide open the small drawer under the port V-berth, and the treasurers within roll and clatter. This is Tristan's drawer. These few remaining bits are artifacts that never leave the boat: a hand sized American flag on a small wooden dowel from a Fourth of July parade in Marion, Mass when he was six; a pair of Fisher-Price binoculars, bright blue and yellow on a sturdy cord that hung around his neck from age two until five; a rubber ball he loved at three; a folding wooden knife, with wooden blade, I made for his fourth birthday; a rookie baseball card in hard plastic of Ken Griffey Jr. that was his prized possession at ten; a picture of the girl he took to the Junior Prom. All are flotsam of a young, still remembered, and evolving life.

Opposite is Skye's drawer. It also contains childhood artifacts: the bookend of the same American flag on a stick; a plastic case for her retainer that made her smile sparkle a sapphire blue when she was twelve (She now puts quarters in it.); a beaded barrette made by the same Eskimo who combed Skye's long brown hair as she grew from toddler to school-age and called her "Arrigaa" (beautiful); a book from the *Babysitters* series she hasn't opened in a decade; tweezers; a map of Oak Bluffs on Martha's Vineyard folded neatly; a high school graduation picture sporting a huge smile of straight white teeth is shuffled in among the detritus.

As I look at the two drawers my mood shifts gears. I try not to think again that this summer will likely be the last time the four of us will ever cruise together as a family unit. These simple little trinkets mock those who imagine time is a slow meandering river. It's all over in an instant. Both of my children weighed less than a sack of sugar when they came aboard for the first time. Now Skye is degreed and married, lives six thousand miles away, and will give us our first grandchild in the fall. Tristan is bound for his freshman year at college in a few short months. I close the drawers. Time is a thief, and denial is the attempt to make it stand still. I remind myself that fretting is for chumps. I have a ledger list of

projects to do before I can afford being weepy and nostalgic.

The hours fly by, and then the days. I stay out of the way of yard workers as they scurry about on various owners' tight timelines, and they appreciate it. Fog and rain shut down my mast work for a few afternoons, and I spend the time rebuilding my head. Sounds New Age, but I mean the manual toilet. In the evenings I see a few movies at the cinema in downtown Belfast, but mostly tumble into bed exhausted. The boat slowly comes together. This kind of work has about as much to do with sailing as roadwork has to do with boxing. Necessary, maybe, but you can't use it to protect yourself from the moment of truth when the boat is in the water. I know this fact from hard-won experience.

The Wingaersheek Beach Yacht Club interview committee of 1969 had trusted me when I said I knew everything there was to know about sailing. My resumé clearly demonstrated that in spite of my tender years I had already held instructor positions for swimming, skiing, tennis, rock climbing; my employers all gave glowing references, and I was deemed competent in putting a broken body back together long enough to get it to the hospital for real medical care. I think the latter is what won them over.

Twenty-seven little sailors lined up the first day to meet the new sailing instructor. Crammed into my brain like hard pressed sardines were all the technical terms of the sails, the boats, the points of the wind, and the maneuvers to make the boats fly. But I had still never actually been sailing. There is a point where sheer audacity ends and karmic retribution begins, but I hadn't arrived there yet.

The morning started off right because I pulled right up to the club on my vintage 1957 650cc BSA that had a deep-throated rumble like a thunderstorm in the Sonoran Desert. The bike, a fourth hand wreck, took just about every dollar I had earned during the last winter. I must be cool to drive a hog like the easy riding Peter Fonda. Everyone crowded around the bike while I tried to figure out what to do next.

Luckily I had two teenage assistants who were just out of prep school, heading to Dartmouth and Harvard respectively, and had come up through the ranks at the club. I asked the two young men who was the better sailor. The Dartmouth frosh grudgingly admitted in a bashful flush of honesty that he had won more races. I gave Harvard the assignment to get the beginners started with the names of the parts of the boat and sails while Dartmouth and I got the motor launch fired up and took the higher level kids out to the floating docks on which the boats were stacked.

Beginners headed for the Turnabouts. The teen boats were Lasers. These little flatbeds are single crewed rockets that have the initial stability of a tippy canoe. Sleek and fast, they looked like fighter jets, and I knew I was in trouble. I wasn't going to get near them until I was beyond embarrassing myself.

"Gear up," I said through the megaphone. "Let's see what you got."

They all responded like a well-oiled machine. In minutes boats were rigged, kids were pushing away from the dock, the loud flutter of sails matching the rhythm of the butterflies humming in my stomach. Then raised voices started to rage against rights-of-way and who was "burdened." Chaos grew like a twister as one close call followed another. The noise of the stalled sails, the screams of indignation, the collisions of plastic on plastic hulls, were more than I could take. I panicked.

"What drills are they used to?" I asked Dartmouth with a dry mouth.

"Tack on the whistle, follow the leader, overlaps around the marks, start scrambles, that sort of thing."

Dartmouth felt my pain and grasped my clueless expression. The kid was smart enough to spot panic born from stupidity.

"You want to drive the boat?" he said.

"Don't mind if I do."

He quickly took the megaphone and restored order. Soon, like a flock of happy, well trained little ducks, the class scurried off towards an orange pillow floating on the water a couple of hundred yards away. I followed along driving the launch over the slight chop. A steering wheel and an internal combustion engine I understood.

"Is it hard to drive your bike?" Dartmouth asked in a conspiratorial aside.

"About like sailing a Laser," I said with a wink. "Easy, once you get the hang of it."

He nodded. The deal had been struck without his calling me an incompetent ninny; it was a tit for tat. I sold Dartmouth the BSA at the end of the summer. His parents have always felt the bike and I were responsible for his flunking out of school the following spring. I didn't accept the blame. Today, he's a doctor just like his father. Well, maybe not just like his father. Ex-Dartmouth is with the international Doctors Without Borders program offering emergency relief in third world countries. We all get to where we need on our own terms and in our own way. We can't push the tide; it rolls along by itself. By the end of the summer my new young friend had taught me how to sail well enough to get by, while I bought the beer and pretended to pass along my own nautical wisdom to the club's next generation. I guess I would call it a case of no harm, no foul.

THREE

PASSAGASSAWAKEAG RIVER

The Brownell hydraulic trailer launches *Dog Star* on a foggy Monday morning. She begins leaking like a sieve straight away. Even though I am used to the sight of water filling the bilges when she takes her first dip of the season, panic is a hair's breadth away. I chat nervously at a non-stop clip with the trailer driver and his accomplice. They eye the saltwater current cascading aft across the keel bolts with calm indifference.

"She's always like this," I say as I pop below decks to check the five through-hulls again. One of those damn things has to be open and contributing its two inch gusher to the flood. She can't possibly be letting this much seep through her seams. The electric bilge pump moans away with sloshing and gurgling sounds that tear six-inch valleys in my heart.

"A-yup," the driver said to his sidekick. "She's opened up a might."

The eager assistant nods assent. I grit my teeth. Commenting on the condition of my boat without being asked is pretty close to telling me my wife is chasing the postman down the street on Tuesdays and Thursdays naked as a white lie.

"She's tight. Give her an hour. You'll be amazed."

They aren't buying it. But duty calls, and watching a boat sink, as entertaining as it is, needed to be postponed. They leave to sling another boat to her fate at the bottom of the ramp. Tides are not to be wasted.

Below decks, sitting on the settee with the water slowly gaining ground on the pump, my hands dangling between my knees, I have a familiar launching day-mare about General Patton.

I was back in Vermont waiting for the snow to fly after a summer learning to sail while teaching sailing, and mentoring the Zen of motorcycle etiquette to a young preppy on his way to perdition. M. had flown the coop and departed for her junior year studying abroad at the University of Vienna in Austria. She claimed it was for German; I knew it was for the Lipizzaner horses of the Spanish Riding School. I was washing dishes for the dinner crowd at the Common Man Restaurant in Waitsfield for room and board and getting in all sorts of mostly innocent trouble with other ski patrol crazies with more time than sense on our hands. A typical night would find us crammed into a decrepit Volkswagon Bug for a moonlit dash two-hundred plus miles to Montreal to see a concert by Taj Mahal, or Ike and Tina Turner, J. Giles, or The Who. Back at dawn, we just made the first lift to the First Aid shacks and our jobs clearing the trails and getting the mountain ready for snow.

A call from the Eastern Point Yacht Club during the dinner rush at the restaurant put my ear to a gruff voice that informed me I had been selected on the basis of my sailing experience to accompany the Colonel and his wife and help deliver a boat from Portsmouth, New Hampshire to Annapolis in the Chesapeake Bay. I was speechless.

"You don't have long hair do you?" the Colonel said.

"Longer than what?" I said.

Silence. I thought the connection had been cut.

"The people at the club recommended you," he finally said. The Colonel made it sound like an accusation of being a blood relative to Benedict Arnold.

"I'm glad they had the nerve," I said.

"Are you trying to be funny, son?"

"No. You'll know when I'm trying to be funny, sir."

Further silence. I regretted throwing in the "sir."

"I expect that you will want to be paid."

"I'm sure we can work it out," I said, dreaming that anywhere as far south as the Chesapeake Bay was sure to have palm trees, coconut oil, and bikinis even though we were almost into November. Geography was not my strong suit. "What's the name of the boat?"

"*General Patton.*" If he had had a riding crop in his hand, he would have used it on his thigh for emphasis.

"Of course it is," I said.

"I'll expect you by oh-six-hundred on Tuesday."

"Pardon? Oh, sex, what?"

This time the click did come, and I was alone with my good fortune. I was going sailing, real sailing in the ocean, and I was going to get paid for it. Giddy would have been the right word to describe the next forty-eight hours as I made my way east. In retrospect, I've learned that gift horses should always be examined right down to their tonsils.

The brutish Nor'easter the *General Patton* had been trying to outrun in a mad dash to catch a vanished weather window continued to drive us further offshore away from the Gulf of Maine and out into the wintery North Atlantic. Unless we got a break the next stop was Georges Bank and the Flemish Cap. We were running before the huge seas without any sails set and still I knew we needed to slow the boat down. All twenty-five tons of the Nova Scotia built, fifty-foot gaff rigged wooden schooner was being tossed along at a dangerous speed by the wind and the water. She careened wildly; losing all steerage from her barn door sized rudder each time a wave would catch her, twist her, and push her ahead like a toy in a tub. Twin telephone poles as masts, with no sails to hold her steady, kept the pendulum in full motion. The wheel would try to spin quickly when the wave passed by, and my arms ached from wrestling with the swirling tons of turbulent water. Each dark threat of a wave appeared suddenly out of the darkness like a rushing mountain, topped with cascading avalanches of white foam. It was as cold as a crevasse.

Broaching is the nautical word used to describe the moment a boat loses her ability to keep momentum going straight ahead and suddenly, turning sideways, is caught by the slower water just beneath the surface of a rushing wave, trips on her own keel, and finally rolls completely over. I cursed at the top of my lungpower the endless succession of twenty-foot waves that sounded like rumbling freight trains above the shriek of the wind. Over my shoulder I knew, with primal certainty, that the one huge wave with our name on it was out there in the black night. I remember thinking that broaching was too nice a word for the watery grave it described.

Through the small crack I'd left in the hatch I watched Gretchen, the Colonel's dachshund, roll across the cabin sole, so seasick and disoriented that she could no longer stop herself from banging from one side to the other each time the boat lurched. The water in the bilges slopped up around the heavy floorboards at the extremity of each roll. We were slowly sinking and the boat was feeling more sluggish each hour. The electric pump, along with the engine and the VHF radio, had given up the ghost at sunrise this morning soon after the storm began. I hoped we could stay afloat until dawn. I couldn't leave the helm for a moment to help either the dog or the boat.

I could see the Colonel, the owner of the *General Patton*, over the bulging canvas lee cloth that held him securely in his bunk against the rough motion that would have launched him across the dimly lit cabin. I hoped he was still breathing. From here, I couldn't tell for sure. I wondered in my exhaustion if I would be more comfortable with a dead body rather than a dying one.

I had done what I could, but a probable heart attack was way beyond my abilities to splint and bandage. He was stable and alive, but the survival time was unknown unless I could get him to a hospital. His wife would recover from her broken clavicle, caused by a sudden lurch that had catapulted her into the forged iron edge of the galley stove early this morning. The morphine had worked wonders and she slept, drugged, in the opposite bunk. She would survive, if any of us did.

I wondered again what more could I do. My arms were tired, my back ached, and I knew I couldn't hold this wheel for much longer. I had been at it without a break for almost fourteen hours, and the storm showed no signs of letting up. I was barely twenty, and the knowledge that I couldn't pull the stamina and strength needed to overcome this problem from some hidden reserve was a startling new discovery. In spite of my misguided belief that immortality was my birthright, for the first time in my life I was truly frightened. It was a totally different fear from scaling a vertical rock face without ropes on a sunny afternoon, or tumbling out of a plane with a hastily packed parachute. It was exposing, demeaning, alone and cold. What to do? The hours passed slowly, and I waited for my cramping arms to finally give out.

I thought of the Colonel and his bold dream of retiring and living aboard this boat, wandering aimlessly through tropical ports of call. He was fifty-seven, career military, Army man, and Vietnam hawk; overweight, gruff in words and manner, given to eating, drinking and arguing with the same reckless disregard for the consequences. It was the Age of Aquarius, and he wasn't happy about it. He was a Nixon man who used the terms "nigger," "draft dodger," and "hippie" often, and with equal vehemence. How could the two of us, so different inside and out, find common ground on the deck of a boat? It was many years before this dichotomy made any sense at all. These days I seek diversity in age and core beliefs for my own good. It isn't wisdom; it's just good common sense.

I still remember many things about this, my maiden voyage: the incredible violence of the North Atlantic, the terrible sounds of the storm; somehow finding a tear-filled strength to continue when you finally give up all hope. But it was the look in the Colonel's eyes as his heart attack began that will always be the most important lesson. It will define for me that startling cliff's edge of mortality each of us will surely face in our own time, in our own way. His eyes were normally hard and sure of themselves, always fixed in an aggressive, confrontational stare designed by years of practice to make whoever might be the focus of his gaze ill at ease, unsure, ready to take orders, obey. At the moment the pain struck, his eyes suddenly opened wide in disbelief, then wider into a vulnerable, confused, and wordless plea for life. Three-plus decades later I can still bring those eyes back in vivid detail.

We finally made landfall, with the help of a series of fishermen who gave us a course to steer, a day and a half after the storm started. I brought the *General Patton* back to where we began at Dion's Yard in Portsmouth, New Hampshire. We all survived. Yes, even Gretchen. The yard kept the dog while my employers were taken off to the local hospital. The Colonel never set foot on the boat again. As far as I know, he found another life better suited to his retirement years. We didn't keep in touch. The yacht was quickly sold to another dreamer. I saw the boat a few years later at a mooring on Nantucket. It was renamed *Dandelion*. I didn't row over to give my part of the boat's history to the new owner. Some things are best kept to oneself.

* * *

Dog Star's masts are finally stepped just before the crew leaves for the day. The water has slowed to a trickle at the stem and we are swinging to our mooring in the inner harbor in the last light of early evening on a change of tide. Gear is stacked everywhere, and I hold in my lap the pile I moved in order to sit down. The long days have caught up with me, and I let my eyes close. The boat chuckles over a small wake coming from a late arrival at the gas dock. My head lolls from side to side. This is the milestone that has kept me going at full tilt for ten days. I enjoy it fully.

I am still fretting on the short, two weeks M. and I will have Skye and Tristan aboard. The summer has never seemed long enough even when we were able to cruise and live aboard all together for a solid two months. No matter how long I am able to stretch our time, it always seems that the very day I have finally finished my endless lists of spring commissioning towards putting *Dog Star* right, I begin to take her apart again for the long winter.

As the light fades in the twilight, I stand at the foot of the companionway leaning against the wooden teak steps up to the cockpit with my chin resting on my arms. I look upriver past the flickering traffic on the Route 1A bridge. The Passagassawakeag River is a small meander by Maine standards, swelling twice a day to a major body of water a quarter mile wide and a few feet deep as the tides fill the mud flats to the distant banks. The Indian name means "Place of Many Ghosts." The locals have stopped trying to get their tongues around the name and refer to it locally as "The Passy." Whatever the name, it still has ghosts, and I try to put out the welcome mat in my mind.

Off the stern the first tendrils of mist are rising off the slow moving surface of the water. Herons and sandpipers wade in the shadows along the shore in the shimmering lights of the few waterfront cabin windows. The dark trees just beyond the range of my vision stand out against the last horizontal red clouds of the sunset. The wild spookiness of the Maine woods of Henry David Thoreau is just a short trip up river in a poled canoe. I notice the hairs on my neck tingle and feel the presence of tiny spectral shipmates closing in around me.

Don't stand in the companionway. Up or down. My eight-year-old daughter Skye says with a stern voice, mocking the grown-up mantra that hounded her young seagoing life.

Go wowing if you got a long face. You can't pwactice enough. Tristan's four-year-old squeal pumps up the volume with another of my daily helpful hints.

Stop mopping around, you scallywags, this is sailing. It's the happiest time of your life. They both give my blanket remedy for everything; quoted back to me in a loud mocking chorus.

I blink to clear my ears and focus my thoughts for a moment on the varnish of the mizzenmast just three feet from my nose. The rich golden color of the layered tung oil flickers in the lamplight coming out from the cabin. I find myself remembering babies, their smell, their gear, the mess of moods. Finally the collage of images focus on Tristan's first trip through the notorious gauntlet of Wood's Hole on Cape Cod.

He was barely six months and strapped into a car seat that was lashed to the mizzen in the deep cockpit. Shaded by a cloth cap with Winnie and Tigger on the dome, he was all eyes and giggles. My son was constantly giving me lessons in enjoying myself. Skye was wedged in next to her mother under the dodger with a *Star Wars* life jacket on. She looked worried because she had done this passage before and knew I would not be normal again until it was over. It was one of the million times I said to myself that I had no right to be putting these innocent children through this danger. A thousand things could happen and I couldn't control any of what fate had in store. Tension sat like a hungry baboon on my shoulder. I tried to smile, but it probably came out scary.

Dog Star has a way of sailing on the current with her full-length keel. She has a mind of her own, unlike the shapely little fiberglass buckets designed to modern racing rules. Her 42 hp Gray Marine engine and two bladed prop is just barely enough power to keep her tonnage moving forward against five knots of swirling foam. We always try to arrive at slack water, the time between a tide rushing east and a tide rushing west, but if you miss it by ten minutes, or the wind is up, or you forget to add daylight savings time back into the *Eldridge Tide Tables*, the place is rocking and rolling. Punctuate the nightmare with five-story-tall car and passenger ferries heading out to disgorge their cargo at Vineyard Haven. Add the normal amount of large powerboats and their fun loving "peddle to the metal" drivers throwing up six-foot wakes. Life can get exciting in a hurry. The goal for surviving the maelstrom is to thread your way through the less than a hundred foot wide gap between sometimes visible rock ledges. This half-mile of angst has all the makings of an "E" ride at Disneyland.

Tristan was holding tight with both tiny little fists around the tail end of the mizzen sheet as it came off the cleat. The boat rocked, the ferries blew their horns, M. and I checked each other checking off the buoys one by one. The normal aids to navigation were often sucked

horizontal, if not completely under, by the volume of ocean trying to make a short cut from Buzzards Bay to Vineyard Sound. After thirty-five years of traipsing to and fro through the thoroughfare, I still have anxiety attacks about the "Hole." Tristan and Skye, on the other hand, have no fear, no soul baggage, and years ago I turned the tiller over to them for the annual runs through the very heart of my untrusting nature. M. and I share chart duty, and I stand like a greyhound, "straining on his starts," ready to trim the main that is always up for the passage. A back-up just in case the engine sputters. I don't usually get my heart rate back to normal until we are half way to West Chop on the Vineyard.

"We missed the oily little sea serpents again," I would finally say. "How about a beer so that we can pour a little into Poseidon's eye." Everyone would smile at the thinly disguised need as an offering to the God of the Sea, and we would each pour a tad over the stern. If it was early morning, M. would pour more than a tad before handing me back the grog.

The mischievous little spirits remain underfoot this night, scuttling about up forward into their bunks, telling each other to keep their "oily little sea serpent" feet to their own side. I let out a little sigh and wonder how the kids of my kids will behave, or not, aboard the boat. Will they laugh at my stale jokes, or will they write me off as a doddering old fool? I decide speculation is a wasted science for a born pessimist.

Skye pregnant? Tristan now an almost uncle and in college? Both of my babies moving on with their own lives without a thought for what it was doing to me? How could that be? It was only yesterday they were just a twinkle in their mother's eye. I smile sadly remembering how much I love that twinkle and those hazel-green eyes, which are probably snug in a bed three-thousand miles to the west in the high Colorado Rockies at this very moment. The lonely oil light draws a mosquito that wings past my ear. I put in the snap-on screens over the companionway and the forward hatch and curl up in my bunk. My eyes blink once and then I'm gone where ungrateful children with questions I can't answer chase me in slow motion along dark cobblestone streets.

FOUR

GRAND BANKS

"Go home, you Canadian Bastards."

"That's what you said?"

"Yes."

"Loudly?"

"They were all the way across the quad."

"And your question to me was…?"

"Why would they be so offended?"

"Let me think," I said into the phone. We were quiet for a second or two.

"They shit everywhere," my daughter said in her own defense at the tone of my silent judgment.

"So you mentioned."

"Running to class you couldn't help but step in it," she says. "So gross."

"But you don't go there anymore. I thought you graduated." My daughter indeed held a sheepskin from the University of Alaska where she was student body president, chancellor's pet, and all around volunteer workhorse for four years.

"I wanted to show off the baby."

"You are only six months pregnant last time I checked," I said.

"Not being a mother, you wouldn't understand."

I give her the point.

"So what did this offended couple from Canada say?" I said.

"They said a whole bunch, jumbled all together. You know how they are."

"No, how are they?" I said while trying to maintain my balance in the topsy-turvy world my daughter calls home.

"Don't be dull," she said. "And they said it all very loudly. I was embarrassed for them. We drew a good sized crowd."

"I expect volume is normal in this kind of cross border exchange." I try to imagine the scene. My daughter always gives a crowd its money's worth and some change to boot.

"Shrill in fact, and they said all the worst things about our whole country, and the president, together, like a screaming duet."

"Did you even try to explain that you were calling to the unwanted, special needs, illegal immigrant, resident geese who feel the Anchorage campus with its heated flat rooftops is plenty far enough south for their winter migration?"

"I couldn't get a word in. I said 'Goose' once, and they called me a silly one. Imagine." She sounds lightly frantic, searching like a drunken lemming for the moral high ground from which to plunge.

"They swore at me in British. They called me 'bloody'. I'm sure they said 'bloody'."

"Poor girl," I said, but she knows I am not sincere.

We are quiet for a half-minute.

"Are we really going to cruise Maine again?"

"Where else? Besides, we haven't been past Schoodic since you were bashful with boys," I said.

"Fog is fog, cold water is cold water. The sun never shines." Her voice is gaining octaves again at an alarming rate. We have broached this subject before.

"Now you're getting it," I said with enthusiasm.

Skye changes course and talks about baby showers. I have to throttle startling images of pink-cheeked cherubs falling from the heavens. She endearingly calls me her "maniac" after a while, and we promise to talk again soon. I am sure of it. Skye does not give up having her way easily.

When I officially documented *Dog Star* as a United States Auxiliary Sailing Vessel a quarter of a century ago I was given the option of choosing a random port in the boat's home waters of New England or the capital of the state I resided in. In retrospect I should have thrown a dart at a map of the colonies of 1776. Although Alaska occupied two decades of my adult life and I consider it still to be my true spiritual home, making Juneau my boat's hailing port was a mistake. Four score and ten times a summer I have to answer the question of how I brought the stout little ship around. My crew always rolls their eyes as I make up one lie after the other depending on how fertile my imagination is running at the moment. Yes, I could change the hailing port with a few hundred dollars and a ream of paperwork, but that would be ignoring my stubborn nature and admitting I had made a mistake.

Age caught me in a hammerlock as I rolled over, on this my first morning of the new season aboard my floating life. My body is giving off alarms as if I were back running Ironman Triathlons for entertainment. Everything inside my skin aches in four-part harmony from the labors of the past ten days. Folding myself vertical off the bunk is a slow painful process. Deferring pain until you least expect it is the sly trait of a body trying to get the mind to bone up on its addition. I live in denial. I always tell my wife to not think of me as an old fart in his mid fifties, but as two hot twenty-eight year olds when we hop in the sack. Age is a state of being. The only good news about feeling ancient and getting older is that the alternative is a lot worse.

I start the galley stove by twisting the black Bakelite knob and counting out the three seconds of alcohol, which I slowly let into the small heating basin under the burner on the antique Shipmate Stove. During the few minutes the fire takes to heat the burner, before I can have a pressurized flame, I pop out the mosquito screen in the hatchway and fill the kettle from the long handled bronze freshwater water pump over the sink. I am consciously trying to move as few parts of my body as possible.

"AHOY, *Dog Star*." A voice helped by an electric-powered loud hailer booms across the water. It sounds like God with a Brooklyn accent.

Under tousled hair that I am sure has spikes and rat's nests galore, I blink into the morning sun through the mass of gear still stacked in the cockpit. A huge floating condo disguised as a plastic trawler twice as long and high as necessary is on a collision course with my stern. The bow wave is a couple of feet high. I swallow my tonsils and hold a hand up like a traffic cop, blink my eyes to make it go away, and wait for the crunch. Gears clank, engines scream, and *Dog Star* rolls to her scuppers in the wash from the reverse thrust of a couple of big diesel engines and their three foot diameter propellers. I am struck speechless with choice epithets in my head. They are screaming to be let loose. I astutely remember I'm naked and it is very hard to get seriously behind a four-letter rant in public without clothes on. I bite my tongue.

"You from Alaska?" The loud hailer has yet to show me a face. His windows are tinted dark.

I am still "starkers" and lean my head an inch out of the companionway that hides my manhood from my shoulders on down.

"Alaska? Juneau? Right?"

I nod and clench my teeth vowing to immediately change the offensive lettering on my stern to Jones Beach.

"I've been there." Now the whole world within a half-mile knows this startling fact.

A woman in bright yellow shorts and a blue and white polka dot halter-top tied in a crisp square knot above a deeply tanned, flat belly comes out a side door on the second of the three floors and waves. She wears a pallid half smile outlined in pink lipstick and appears nervous as she notices how close the two boats are getting as we bob up and down, the motor yacht drifting on the current in my direction.

"What a place, beautiful, glaciers, bears, the whole shooting match." The faceless voice is now a raspy, bigger than life whisper that still reaches across the harbor with disquieting ease. I nod again.

"Lots of whores." The voice suddenly exclaims with emphasis. I swear I can hear the whole town of Belfast gasp for breath over their second cup of coffee.

The polka dotted lady blanches. She turns without a wave good-bye and slams herself back into the main cabin. The engines crank over and the boat backs up and then pulls away. A high-pitched, electrically amplified woman's voice is reaming a new hole in the morning.

"Really, honey, lots of them." The subdued male voice still amplified for effect is barely audible above a continued litany of high octave abuse. The loud hailer finally squelches off. The boat departs in haste with complete disregard for the no wake signs. The name on the transom is *Seeme*, and under it in gold leaf, *City Island, New York*. I sit down on the settee and try to calm my still thumping heart. My first smile of the day gradually takes hold. I haven't even had my coffee and already I'm armed with a full morning of entertainment value from my infamous hailing port. Juneau will stay a by-line for a while longer.

Halloween in 1969 had left my head hurting in a way I don't think I have ever suffered from since. I had been busy celebrating my new lease with this life on the day chosen to honor all the dead things that frighten and terrify us. Surviving the Nor'easter in the *General Patton* the week before should have made more of an impression on me. It was late into the morning of All Saints Day before I stumbled out of bed. I was staying with Jeff French in Rockport on Cape Ann. Jeff and I had waited tables at an upscale fish restaurant during the busy summer season. I couldn't survive on what the yacht club paid sailing instructors so I moonlighted at night. He was trying to save enough money to start veterinary school in January way out in Minnesota. Jeff has now been the vet of choice for Gloucester and the North Shore communities from Ipswich to Manchester to Rockport for almost three decades.

"Rough night?" Jeff said.

"I hate it when they pin my arms and pour that stuff down my throat," I said, trying to keep in my stomach a trio of dueling aspirin.

"Georgio called."

"They did this to him too?"

"You're going fishing." Jeff laughed at the thought. Super Dog, Jeff's fifty-seven-variety mutt, barked. My head almost imploded.

"Not a chance."

"Noon, at the boat. The Grand Banks for a week. Lucky guy."

"I'll die first," I said and knew it to be true.

"Probably," Jeff said.

Georgio Fortunato was the venerable captain of the *Edna and James*, a sixty-foot trawler, one of the rusting remnants of the once proud Gloucester fishing fleet. We had met Georgio when a local Rockport artist, Jeff's neighbor, begged him to let his crusty Portuguese features be oiled on canvas wearing a small blue beret. Georgio spoke little English between smiles and looked like a rougher and tumbler Spencer Tracy in *Captains Courageous*, the movie. His blue eyes sparked like iron on flint. Somehow he had taken a liking to the two of us college sissies and would stop in for a drink when Jeff and I would finish our shift. He would then take us to his two favorite bars: The Portuguese Seaman's Association and the Knights of Columbus. He laughed like a fog horn and drank like a big fish. I would always beg him to take me out on his boat so I could write an article for the *Atlantic Fisherman*, make the big bucks on the freelance, and see what the ocean was like from a real seaman's point of view. He always put me off with a wink and a shake of his head. Last night, I must have convinced him I was worthy. I barely remember arriving at the Knights of Columbus let alone leaving. It was all a bit unsettling.

"He said not to be late."

"For my own funeral," I said, holding the top of my head on with both hands.

Forty-five minutes later the *Edna and James* and I were passing Ten Pound Island in Gloucester Harbor outbound for the distant fishing grounds, and I was already down to stomach lining in my attempts to get the poison from the night before out of my guts and over the side. The other four crew, each older, stouter, and rougher looking than the captain, had already given their opinion of me with sad black eyes and derogatory Portuguese one liners that brought shrugging shoulders and sniggers from everyone but me. Georgio chose to ignore me in order to hide his own hangover and his embarrassment at being responsible for bringing me aboard. Even in the still waters of the inner harbor I thought the boat had the motion of a tumble-drum clothes dryer.

In the first twenty-four hours as we steamed steadily towards the Grand Banks, about a hundred and eighty miles just south of east, I learned all I needed to know. Enough to understand that this was another gift horse I should have sent off to the glue factory without getting aboard. My four crewmates were each captains of their own vessels; and while this should have been comforting, Georgio confided that each of them was already bankrupt from a series of poor seasons and aging boats with debts too high to ever repay. This was a last ditch effort to get some money for Christmas and each had pooled enough to buy the gas and risk a November passage. But that's another story.

As we left Norman's Woe far behind, I could almost hear the verse of Henry Wadsworth Longfellow wrecking the *Hesperus* on its granite teeth. Gloucester, fishing, and death have been bunkmates since the beginnings of the European occupation of this continent. It is speculated that Leif Erickson sailed into this harbor over a thousand years ago and set up the first fish weirs on Stage Fort Rocks. Fishing was a thriving business here before the Pilgrims ever set foot at Plymouth. During the sixty-five years following 1830, more than 700 schooners and almost four thousand sailors took their final leave from this harbor never to be seen again. The gulls swirled and squawked, hoping for lunch in our wake of poorly-combusted diesel fumes. If each held the soul of a departed seaman, as legend has it, our ghosts were legion, and they were egging us on our way to whatever fate waited on the Banks.

My immediate concern was for warmth and creature comforts once my stomach had settled down. I asked about dinner. One of the smiling quartet of unshaven, dwarf sized, muscle bound sexagenarians showed me the larder. One cardboard case each of pilot bread crackers and tinned sardines packed in virgin olive oil were the solitary staples of our diet until we caught fresh fish.

Georgio sat in the deckhouse in his ratty admiral's chair on a huge macramé pillow embroidered with the word "Grandpa," his head bobbing in cat naps while watching the radar screen and the self steering compass for the whole first day. The out-of-tune engines in the *Edna and James* rumbled the loose fitting rivets of the hull and decks like a continuous 6.4 earthquake. The rest of the crew sat below decks in the crew quarters, smoked cigarettes from tip to butt like an assembly line, conversing in shouts that would make a pro quarterback envious, and got drunk on huge blue bottles bound in wicker containing a wine that looked like thin cranberry juice and stank like kerosene. I thought I would stick to water until the spigot I spotted in the galley shot some swirling rust into a dirty glass. I drank wine with the rest.

I awoke some time the second day to a grunting ugly fight in the bunk across from mine and a filleting knife found a rib and a forearm before we peeled them apart. I stopped the blood with a dirty sheet, found some superglue in the tool chest to seal the lips of skin together, and medicated the victim with a shirt full of ice from the fish hold. Minutes later the two combatants were back at the table with arms entwined, crying with flooded open eyes and daring each other to drink to the health of the Blessed Virgin Mary.

Then we started to fish, and it started to snow.

Snow on a calm ocean two hundred miles from land under a leaden sky the color of the sea is a surreal experience. Imagine a hundred thousand tons of goose down so thick that you can't see the end of your extended arm, yet not a single feather seems to land on the smooth molten surface of the blacker-than-black water. You could already be upside down and not know it. It is like being trapped inside one of those shake up table ornaments with a red Vermont barn and a spindly legged cow. This signature event is not to be fully appreciated unless you are dead-dog hung over with a horrible wine buzz going. My anxiety level was already running at full tilt paranoia expecting the banging bilge pumps to stop their thousand gallons an hour gusher over the side and the boat to sink away beneath our feet in a matter of seconds. Did I mention the black water temperature was about forty-five degrees?

We set an otter trawl and dragged for days and nights without stop. Each recovery netted a disappointing but slithering deck of flopping fish that we sorted and washed in stainless steel tubs and threw on ice. The hours melted away and I thought I would die from the endless noise, the stink of the diesel, the back breaking work, and the lack of anything on board that would stay in my stomach. I was praying I wouldn't prolong the suffering and survive, so I worked to exhaustion alongside the rest, sleeping in the cold cords of line under the silently falling snow until I was needed again to shovel the decks clear, haul the weighted net guides onto the drum, and flake the running gear into waist high coils. When Georgio appeared on deck with a worried look and spat a rush of Portuguese into the dark night on our fifth day of fishing, I felt the slowly blossoming camaraderie with the rest of the crew at the news that we were finally heading home. I then was treated as an Anglo surprise: a tried and true shipmate risen from the ashes of a liability. We quickly hauled in the last set and clapped each other on the shoulders. What a guy has to do to overcome the handicap of not being born Portuguese.

The never-empty wine jugs were back on the table. The smoking lamp was lit and we ate the last tin of the sardines communally with swollen and puckered fingers in celebration. Cooking fresh fish required a cook and no one was willing to take the job. An air of celebration lasted until dawn a few hours later. We slept sitting up at the table, our cheeks splatted on the rough boards, the wood spittled with drool. The wind began to blow with the setting of the sun and from the same direction. The snow never stopped. Neptune was showing himself to be reluctant to let us get away with a hold full of fish.

By midnight we were locked into it. Twenty-foot swells marched past us on a reciprocal course. The wind blew the tops of the cascading hillocks clean off, scattered the freezing snot over the boat. Ping-pong sized hail that must have been formed by the surface combination of wind, water, and cold rattled against the boat from stem to stern sounding like ball peen hammers. The endless snow grew thicker in the troughs of the waves, which for seconds at a time shielded us from the howling wind. Sheets of ice started to build on everything above the waterline with a vengeance. The *Edna and James* struggled up one watery hill after the other, wallowing like a drunken fat lady with the radio antennas, radar dome, and wind instruments looking like a frozen Carmen Miranda hat on her head.

We took shovels and two-inch thick metal pipes and tried to break the ice that was forming in heavy thick slabs on the superstructure. The weight of the ice sheath was threatening to turn the boat turtle and dump us all into the cold North Atlantic. We slid around the deck like pin balls on a scoring frenzy. None of us wore safety harnesses attached to jack lines or life jackets. These frills to protect sailors from a mistake had not been invented for Portuguese fishermen; they probably never will be. After a few close calls, arrested at the last minute by the stranglehold of a shipmate, I wondered if any of us would survive. The building wind, the endless horizon of chaos, and the slow drunken wallow of the boat quickly put us all on notice that we weren't winning this battle. The faces around me began to grow long and worried under the floppy sou'westers. And then Georgio gave us the bad news.

We were almost out of fuel.

My short life flashed before my eyes, again. Not surprisingly, nothing much had changed since the premier of the short feature on the *General Patton*.

Pedro, one of the other captains, gave me a big wink and a wide nicotine stained grin. He clapped the back of the person next to him and got the same wink and a grin back. This was good? One sixty-year-old shipmate, looking like Gimley the dwarf in black oilskins, even danced a short jig. I was aboard a sinking insane asylum, and the inmates were all captains.

We were back at the wicker wine bottles in a few hours after the Coast Guard Cutter *Newport News* radioed that they had us on their seventy-two mile radar. In broken English the crew explained to me over the roar of the wind and engine that they had only pooled enough money to buy fuel for the way out, the fishing, and half the way back to Gloucester. The tow was all part of the plan. And the stalwart young crew on the federal cutter would be swarming all over the boat in a little while doing their heroic duty by helping to keep us afloat, so why waste any more Portuguese energy. They made me practice making a pathetic helpless mug like a refugee from a POW camp, rough and calloused hands pushing my cheeks around until I got it right. One of the captains put his good arm in the bloody sling from the knife fight. They wanted the "coasties" to feel good about themselves. We drank to their heroism.

It had been a reasonably successful voyage and they would each come out a few hundred dollars ahead once the fish in the hold was sold. It would put Barbies and G. I. Joes under the tinseled trees for their grandchildren. "Merry Christmas," they saluted each other with eyes that sparkled with glee while the *Edna and James* careened with the last of its diesel fumes over mountainous seas and hummed a defiant moan in the banshee wind.

I never wrote that article for the fishing trade journals. Why close a loophole for real heroes? Even here, the names have been changed to protect the long dead. Commercial fishing in New England is not for the faint of heart. Georgio "lost his grip on the bar" at the Knights of Columbus shortly after he turned ninety-three. Although my friend had never been anything but a poor struggling fisherman all his life, the entire town flew their flags at half-mast. His funeral had over four hundred cars in procession from downtown to the graveyard. I flew six thousand miles from Nome, Alaska, to be sure my rented Escort was one.

FIVE

FINDING THE WIND

After my early morning visitor with the bullhorn, I spend hours stowing away all the gear needed to make a boat a home for the summer. Half a ton of "stuff" that is divided by purpose, weight, and size fits like a tight shoe into the thirty-seven different nooks and lockers, crannies and drawers I list on my stowage sheet. The detailed stowage plan is over two decades old and has curled yellow edges when I open to its place in the Operations Book's three ring binder. I am a creature of habit and like to know where I can find things in a hurry. My wife is overly fond of saying that the memory is the second thing to go as we age. Life is unfair, so I keep my memory in a book stowed in a locker over my bunk. Engine spares forward to port under the V berth, center locker; spare flashlight and radio batteries in Tupperware on centerline under the sink, lower shelf; small paper bags of charcoal for the Luke stove behind the head outboard of the towels, etc, etc, etc.

I finally row ashore for brunch at Dudley's Café. I tie off the dinghy with a long painter at the boatyard's dock and shake my head at the row of wide-rumped, half sunken, sagging inflatables that are chained and locked up for weeks on end like trophy SUVs against a curb in front of the latest Tribeca food experiment. Each of these squared off rubber sausages is jammed up tight against the scant few yards of wood slats allocated by the marina or boatyard for the transient cockles sailors use to get to and from their boats. Ten dinghies on seven-foot long lines would comfortably occupy the same five feet of dock space that one of these tightly bound, bloated dock hogs takes up with its two inch long wire tether and massive, bullet-proof Stanley lock.

I repeat under my breath an often voiced observation that short painters on dinghies at public docks usually indicates that their owners either have small IQs or a variety of unmentionable social problems, which they must compensate for by becoming the center of my derisive attention. Often, being especially vitriolic when I get a wet foot from having to step through one of these floating bathtubs in order to get into my own small hard shell dinghy because I can't wedge it in close enough to the dock for a leap, I conclude the culprit is both. This pet peeve is bound to have me put a large wire-cutting utensil in my dinghy toolbox in the near future. I will become the "Scarlet Pimpernel" of dinghy docks. Be forewarned you of the short painter and heavy lock syndrome, I may well teach you common courtesy even if I have to be discourteous to do it.

And, while we are at it, for god's sake leave your outboard engines down in the water at a crowded dock. Leaning them forward exposes the lethally sharp blades of your propeller to your neighbors who have as much a right to be there as you do. Each ripple puts your sharp metal weapon against the hulls of other dinghies. When you gouge and abrade everything within a dozen square feet because of your incompetent seamanship, you can and should be held accountable. What are you people thinking?

Dudley's Café is vinyl checkered tablecloths and opens for breakfast and lunch. Dinner service would be too pretentious. You are always greeted with a warm "Sit where you like, honey," and a "What'll it be, sweetie?" as a steaming mug of black coffee is thrust under your nose. The menu is a single six by eight inch card encased in plastic with breakfast on the front and lunch on the back. Asparagus spears or Muesli, crepes and truffles with wild rice are not on the docket and never will be. A toasted American cheese sandwich on white Wonder Bread is. The burgers are shaped by hand, the home fries cut from potatoes in the kitchen, huge onion slices and a less than delicate dill pickle is a side with everything except homemade pie.

"Hear you got a lot of whores in your parts," said Bess as she pours the obligatory coffee into the white porcelain mug that would survive a drop from a two-story building on to concrete.

"Word gets around," I said with a shy smile, squirming uncomfortably in my Naugahyde seat. The truth was I had never seen a member of the oldest profession practicing her trade along the rain-slicked corners of Alaska's capital. Shameless lobbyists, special interest hoodlums, and other self-aggrandizing egomaniacs abound, but a working girl wasn't part of the pay for service underworld of Juneau I worked in.

"Tip me big and you might get lucky," Bess said with a stage wink, snaps her gum, and wiggles her ample, grandmotherly behind in my direction as she leaves me to make up my mind on lunch or breakfast. The dozen or so other customers understand fully the subject of my ill content and smile among themselves. There are no secrets in a small harbor town. The Belfast village telegraph is quicker than Bell's theorem of simultaneous communication regardless of distance. The laws of physics don't always apply in Maine. A good story travels infinitely faster than the speed of light; especially if it is a joke with a "rusticator" in it.

"Mushrooms in an all white blanket and a side of fake pig toes." I call my order across the room. "Dry wheat shingles."

Bess nods and puckers me a kiss through the air.

"That one's free," she said. "I'm chummin' the waters."

Back aboard I take one last tour through the cabin to be sure nothing is going to go airborne when the boat begins to heel. It is time to go sailing. *Dog Star* seems to shiver under my bare feet. I flip on the VHF radio and hit the weather channel. The computer animated female voice is in the middle of the report for the Hague Line and I go about my business of putting down the toilet seat in the head and securing the forward cabin door open with its handy bungee cord around the knob. In two shakes I am up the companionway and looking out across the field of boats towards the Bay. The sun is bright with a few puffy cumulus clouds off to the south. It is a beautiful day on the coast of Maine. The computer voice drones on about this and that. I wish I had turned it off. NOAA weather radio is likely to be wrong about the current state of the weather, let alone speaking with some credibility about their prognostications of what to expect a few hours from now. I let my eyes and skin feel the day.

The normal onshore wind from the sou'southwest is just beginning to fill in as the ship's clock strikes noon. Small puffs and eddies riffle the calm. The moving cobblestone patterns show football field sized pockets of disturbed water coming up Penobscot Bay and into the harbor. The wind speed is struggling in the single digits, but likely as not within the next few hours it will probably find fifteen knots or more before dying away with the sunset. My first decision is an easy one.

I open the gas line under the port cockpit hatch and face the moment of truth. I switch the key to on and press the ignition button to crank the engine. The hunk of iron starts, after a number of ghostly groans from the starter motor, with a cough of black soot and a surge of water from the hydro lift muffler spitting a healthy gob out the stern tube. The alternator kicks in and the amp meter jumps to indicate a charge flowing to the batteries. The old Gray Marine sounds like a purring Harley after a few minutes of obligatory hiccups from the fuel line, and the glaze of winter shellac on the piston heads causes the exhaust to tinge blue before settling down.

I once had an artist friend who remarked after a perfect day sail from Bristol to Newport in Rhode Island that *Dog Star* was a sculpture that did things and went somewhere. How true it is. With the engine settled into its low ticking cadence, I leave the cockpit and on my walk forward strip the sail cover from the main boom and shove it down through the forward hatch. Casting off the hawser from the mooring ball I stand still for a few seconds to see how the current is carrying the boat. The mooring drifts away, and I engage the engine in forward and we begin to move slowly out into the channel. The tiller comes alive in my hand as the large, three-bladed prop tends to walk the boat to port. I stand in the cockpit and let the tiller rest against my thigh to nudge against the boat's drift on the current. We straighten out towards the entrance buoy a mile or more off in the distance. The engine ticks along at high idle. People on the municipal pier point, and a little girl in a wide straw hat clutched in her mother's arms waves. I wave back. She waves again. How many anonymous waves in history were from strangers to sailors bound out from port?

Moving slowly is a prerequisite to being a competent seaman. I have come through hard-won experience to admire those sailors who have found the wisdom in proceeding just fast enough to accomplish the task at hand. At times I embarrass my crew because I move the boat like a glacier during an ice age. If everyone aboard is not bored to death, you are going too fast. My logic revolves around the simple fact that boats have no brakes. To watch ten tons of plastic and shiny topsides roar towards a dock, or through a mooring field at hull speed, is for me a supreme test of faith in the feckless nature of the gods. These particular misunderstood deities who protect fools and sailors just might be taking a nap. It is an illogical trust in technology that when you ram the engine into reverse and hit the throttle to stop going forward everything is going to function perfectly and those fragile things in your way will all be safe.

Marine engines are notoriously ill-mannered. Your foul smelling hunk of metal whose sole purpose is to control thousands of small explosions each minute will surely let you down when you least expect it. This truism should be a warning label affixed to every starter key. Those who wheel their boats around anchorages at full throttle probably believe they are demonstrating their verve, panache, and skill as true "boat jockeys." The exact opposite is true. Professionals with a few sea miles under their belts know that these lead-footed landlubbers with their hands on the wheel of their recently purchased half million dollar floating condos just haven't taken out a dock, or an anchored neighbor, or plowed under a helpless slow moving rowboat, yet.

When sailing alone, you must think things through twice before taking action the first time. Things can go wrong in a hurry, and the result is always soul numbing embarrassment, even if no one else is around. Very often a simple mistake means broken gear or bleeding body parts that can ruin a perfectly good day. The transition from motor vessel to sail is an obstacle course of decisions, and it is why I prefer sailing right off the mooring if possible. Best to start off on the right foot, just like a tango; one wrong step at the beginning and you'll never catch up.

With the current against us, and the cat's-paws of light and variable wind in the inner harbor offering no reliable means of propulsion, using the engine on this day is the prudent thing to do. Even though I have raised sail on this very boat ten thousand times, I still go down a mental safety checklist before I leave the cockpit.

First, find the wind. This is often not as easy as it sounds. Moving forward, even at a sedate three and a half knots may fool you into believing the wind on your face is the true wind. With three hundred and sixty degrees of options for the wind to arrive at your ground zero, it is a sucker's bet to believe you have laid a course out the harbor on the single degree of your compass card that the wind has chosen to blow on this particular afternoon. A look at the boats on their moorings, lined up and pointing all in the same direction like spotted cows in a field, can also be misleading because of the current rolling by their keels below the surface has more power than the fickle wind to orient the boat. If the wind is light, as it is today, finding the true angle is like an old-fashioned murder mystery. Be like Sam Spade and check the clues, observe the obvious, keep an open mind, and don't forget to watch your back.

Dog Star is the opposite of high tech. My tendency, overruling most of the suggestions of family and sailing friends, is to keep her as close to a 1930's state-of-the-art cruising auxiliary as possible. Would you put a spoiler or a Hemi air-scoop on a seventy-year-old Jaguar? Today, most yachtsmen would simply check their instrument panels and read the apparent wind direction as it is transferred from an array of electrical instruments at their masthead down to a gauge that looks like a missile targeting scope mounted in front of their pedestal steering station. Instead, I glance up at a foot long strip of audio cassette tape floating snakelike on the breeze, secured around the mizzen shrouds with tape both port and starboard with a snip of a plastic straw acting as a sleeve. Simple, effective, and I have an unlimited replacement supply from an old Jackson Brown favorite that broke a couple of years back.

Taking my almost limp cassette tape wind direction finder into account and knowing my forward motion is skewing the data, I try to pick out flags and pennants on the moored boats to give me a second opinion. Watching the exhaust smoke from the circling lobster boats out in the Bay gives me yet another clue, and with some certainty I decide the true wind is off our starboard bow about eighty degrees, so I put the boat into neutral and slow her down. I nudge her off to starboard with enough forward momentum to carry her a hundred yards or so in the direction from where the wind is building. My hand lets go the main sheet, making sure that plenty of tangle free line is ready to go through the blocks so the sail will safely luff without pressure until I am ready to move again.

Taking up the winch handle, I move forward. I pull free the sail ties and let the main sag down onto the coach roof. I free the wire and rope halyard, toggle it to the head of the main and pull down, hand over hand, watching the sail track clips slide up the mast. The beeswax I put on the track before stepping and launching eases the ascent, and I feel only a few minor catches as the sail shoots up from the deck. When I reach the wire splice, I wind the halyard four times around the winch, insert the handle and snug her home until the cunningham, or downhaul, under the boom comes up taught.

Back in the cockpit the main is fluttering lightly, the boom rattling back and forth, and I push the tiller over to bring the bow to port and back on our course out the channel past Steels Ledge. I trim the main to where I think the wind will like it, and she bellies out to port. I free the jib roller furling line, taking time to loosen out the coil and insure it will run clean. Then the port sheet is looped to the winch and pulled by hand until the 120% genoa is all the way out. Trim to give a few feet of slack. The sail bangs about a bit and seems to be looking for something not there, but I know that the mystery of how much to trim will soon resolve itself as the boat loses way and finds the true wind. Although the water is still glassy calm and seaweed stands in clumps along our side, the boat begins to draw, tilting slightly from dead level. I shut down the engine and throw open the locker to twist the gasoline tank valve shut. We are sailing.

My boat speed measures a single knot, a barely discernable puff and she adds a half. The heavily varnished tiller presses against my hand like a golden retriever demanding a pet: I move the oak handle and its barn door sized rudder slowly to put the bow a few more points up on the wind and the speed shoots up another half knot. We are "climbing the wind" now and everything in the universe changes. From this moment on, as we sail, no two boats will experience the exact same wind direction, velocity, strength, or feel. Everything is relative only to you, your momentum, and the air foil of your particular boat. A thousand different variables colliding in one Gestalt moment that drives a boat forward. Galileo was right. Until the boat stops moving, creating its own set of rules, you are at the very center of it all, and no one has a universal truth in their pocket that can change that. This was a hard lesson to learn. I am still learning. It is why each and every time you go out for a sail is a breathtaking new experience that can never be cloned, only experienced and learned from.

Once past the outer bell buoy I strip the canvas cover from the mizzen and hoist more sail. By now the boat is purposeful in its movement, sliding down a compass bearing as though a set of steel rails has been laid on the water. Wind, lift, friction, pressure against the sails, all combine to match a silent symphony of observations in my head. I take a deep breath and feel *terra cognita* and its boring stability slip away in our wake.

My second spring sojourn from Warren, Vermont to Gloucester found me bunking in with Steve Smyth, his wife Carol, and baby Eric while I search for a place of my own. Steve was a woodworking bartender who created remarkable sculptured pieces of furniture that nourished his soul, but he poured drinks to pay the bills. It was the end of April, and Cape Ann was still in tourist hibernation. We had time on our hands, so we scoured the local papers for both the obituaries and the want ads.

The obituaries led us to treasure troves of ancient woodworking tools and odd bits and pieces of sailing gear from the days when Gloucester was the heartbeat of the New England fishing fleet. Waiting a discreet time after the passing of a local Italian or Portuguese patriarch, Steve and I would stop by to offer our sympathies to the family and ask if we could make an offer on any of the junk that had been stored for decades in dirt floor basements and the rafters of off-kilter garages. We would leave behind tip money and carry away bits of Cape Ann's maritime history.

"What's this?" Steve said. He holds up a varnished piece of *lignum vitae* a foot long, shaped like a sausage, with a hole bored through the middle out of which a finger sized braided lanyard of tarred hemp hanging a full eighteen inches finally ended in a baseball sized monkey's fist knot.

"A thing," I said. All young men (and older ones) are notoriously reluctant to admit their ignorance.

"A thing, you say." Other young men are often there to point out your ignorance at the drop of a hat.

"A two handed pulling thing," I said. Snatching the club from his hand I demonstrate.

"For pulling what?" he said.

"Things."

"What things?"

"Things you never heard of."

"You kidding me?"

"Trip trawls, dados, and gurry buckets. Sometimes a reluctant belaying pin. Okay?"

I had spent the better part of my winter reading anything that had to do with sailing and continually boring my friends to exhaustion with lengthy explanations of sheer lines, derivations of uncommon nautical terms, and the method of calculating vectors for drift. It helped that none of my fellow ski patrolmen had the slightest idea of what I was talking about. Being the sailing expert in a shack on the top of a ski mountain in Vermont was a no-fault victory. I was not used to questions, only vacant stares.

"Bullshit," Steve said and he was right.

I paid three bucks for my thing. It is still up forward above the spare anchor rode tucked in tight between a varnished knee and a deck frame. I move it aboard each spring and take it off each fall. I've varnished it a few times down through my nearly forty years of ownership, and it glistens while awaiting the day when its use will become apparent and having it aboard will mean the difference between life and a watery grave.

SIX

CASTINE

Dog Star is now rolling to the first of the short afternoon waves in a steady twelve-knot breeze as we make our way across the western shipping channel in upper Penobscot Bay. Searsport is off our port beam. The tip of Islesboro Island, called Turtle Head, is directly on our bow, and four miles beyond is the green mound of Dice Head and the abandoned lighthouse that marks the entrance to Castine. Looking south down the long half-mile wide channel to starboard are the blue hills of Camden fifteen miles away under a canopy of puffy white clouds. A three masted schooner is working her way down channel tight up against the land over near Lincolnville Beach. She is looking for a reprieve from the incoming tide. There is enough history within eyeshot to choke a cable channel network for a month.

The Penobscot River rises near Mount Katahdin in the heart of north woods Maine and drains much of the state that lies south of the Canadian border. The watery course we are galloping across today has been a war zone since Samuel de Champlain stopped here in 1604. The French, English, and Dutch traded propriety and battlements until a French Baron married the daughter of the local Tarrantine Tribe sagamore, Madockawando. The bride's name was Mathilde. With the help of his Native American in-laws, Jean-Vincent d'Abbadie de Saint-Castine established a fort named Pantagoet on the bluff in 1674.

Nearly a century later the British began work on another fort at the same site named for Good King George. It was during the first years of the Revolutionary War when the upstart colonists further south knew the danger in letting the British gain such a strategic toehold on the continent by fortifying the mouth of this major river. The Penobscot Expedition was launched from the Massachusetts colony to stop the threat. The result was the worst naval defeat in American history before Pearl Harbor. A Colonel by the name of Paul Revere commanded the artillery and was accused of "unsoldierlike behavior and cowardice" by General Lovell who blamed everyone but himself for the defeat. It took Revere two years to clear his name through a court-martial inquiry. The American Republic lost seventeen armed vessels, twenty-four transports, and 474 men to a much smaller and worse equipped British force. Those who escaped fled into the woods for the long walk back to Boston. Fort George was the last British post to surrender at the end of the war.

As we pass Turtle Head on Islesboro, the wind is blanketed by the hills of Islesboro and our progress slows to a knot and a half. Because of her seven tons *Dog Star* maintains her momentum in the light, almost non-existent air. I tie off the helm with shock cord and duck below for a beer. The wind should build back as soon as we work our way out from under the lee of the land. I could wait. Turning around or starting the engine were options, but something about the day and the voices out of our country's early history makes me want to push on under sail and leave our fates open for a while longer. I put a cushion behind my back, drape my leg over the tiller, sip my beer, and let the boat ride both the wisps of wind and the flooding tide. Patience is a hard won lesson in my life. Practice in this virtue is important. I let my mind wander while I practice. A ghost from a seashore shanty shows up on cue.

* * *

The inner harbor of Gloucester is a tightly packed anchorage called Smith Cove. This basin is formed by the mainland and a thin peninsula called Rocky Neck. In order to pay for our morbid daytime occupation of visiting the junk of dead people, Steve had found a job at the Rockaway Hotel, a 1920's white elephant of a structure on the highest point of land along the tightly packed Rocky Neck waterfront. I was waiting tables at the Rockaway and moonlighting after ten p.m. bartending at the notorious and historic Rudder Restaurant just down the hill right on Smith Cove.

The Rudder was a narrow, derelict, wharf building of questionable lineage whose only door swept the buckled sidewalk as it opened. The service area of the enterprise extended out over the water for a precarious thirty feet. Canted wooden pilings covered in green slime and mussels held the main floor and rickety porch twenty feet above the high tidal line. With a strong wind rolling up the harbor, you could get seasick with the movement of the building while enjoying the finest fish chowder and freshest little neck clams on the eastern seaboard. The Rudder's notorious reputation for raucous good times was due to its owner.

Born before the turn of the century, Evi was the daughter of a Gloucester sea captain. A faded black and white picture on the wall behind the bar shows her at the huge spoked wheel of the fishing schooner *Gertrude L. Thebaud*. She was four. Her flaming red hair formed a halo around the toothy grin of a sea sprite. Her father, standing with thumbs in his vest pockets behind her, wore a coat and bowtie under his Greek styled cap, as all professional seamen at the turn of the century were required to do. The *Gertrude L. Thebaud* was a working boat from the Grand Banks that won fame and glory against the Canadian schooner *Bluenose* in the premier sail-racing event of its day. As an aging veteran of this historic sailing legacy, Evi greeted three generations of yachtsmen and sailors at the door of her establishment with her stock greeting of a firm handshake and a salutation delivered in a voice that was tempered to reach to the yardarms: "You're glad to have met me!"

Evi had a mouth on her. Her nicotine hoarse voice, coupled with an irreverent style of banter, was a major part of her charm. I gained an education in the oaths sworn by sailors. As a bartender and hostess, once the evening wore on past her first couple of drinks, she was a show unto herself. In the speed rack alongside the bottles of Scotch and Vodka was a ten-inch dildo that she brought out to stir the cocktails of her more liberated guests.

"I've been looking for the man who modeled for this my whole life," she would snort. "He better show up soon or he'll never know what he missed."

She called me her "cabin boy," with a knowing wink at her patrons. She split tips, which was for a poor cabin boy a financial blessing the likes of which I never saw again. Evi would also talk up my sailing abilities in the same sentence she advertised her chowder. One of the appreciative yachtsmen who caught the floor show that early spring was Walt Gubelmann from Oyster Bay, New York, and Annapolis, Maryland. Walt owned the 73' Hinckley built, Sparkman & Stephens designed yawl *Windigo* and while under Evi's spell he invited me along on his upcoming race to Bermuda. I think it was the only time Evi talked herself right out of something. When I stopped by the next day to say goodbye and to thank her for getting me the berth, she flat out refused to let me go. When she died a decade later a big part of the true nautical soul imbedded in the legendary Gloucester waterfront died along with her.

The wind is back and *Dog Star* is pressed hard over on her beam ends. Water pushes along the port gunnel, leaps over the teak cap rail and slides out the scuppers in a trail of white foam. I ease her weather helm by letting out the mizzen sheet a foot and letting the main traveler slide to leeward. She appreciates it and stands up a little more to the wind. The knot log pops up over six knots. My empty beer bottle is stuck into an open winch handle holder on the mizzen mast and it moans softly with the wind passing over its mouth. Price Head grows in size off the bow and I try to imagine the Baron Castine with his arm around Mathilde staring out over his domain. If the Quakers, Shakers, and Pilgrims had married more brown skins, and taken advantage of the original landowners less, our country in its formative years would have been a lot happier place. The Indian tribes along this coast got a bad name in the Old World simply by sticking up for themselves.

One of my children's favorite historical stories gleaned from the stacks of cruising guides in our permanent shipboard library is as gruesome a saga as any Brothers' Grimm fairy tale. Matinicus is the outermost Maine island inhabited year around and is situated just south of us at the mouth of Penobscot Bay. The first European settler of record was Ebenezer Hall in 1751. The very same Tarrantine Indians who had helped Castine build his fort resented the fact that Hall, in order to increase the yield of hay for his stock, set about burning the brush on their traditional eider harvesting lands on the outlying islands. Hall wouldn't listen to their objections; after all, he had a piece of paper signed by an English lord that waived all claims to the land but his own. In 1757 the slow to anger Tarrantines had suffered enough.

They launched their canoes and laid siege to his house. Hall was finally relieved of his scalp and his wife and four daughters were taken in bondage off the island. Mrs. Hall was eventually ransomed in Quebec, but the daughters were never heard from again. Legend has it, on the full moon in a thick of fog a bloody headed Hall is seen wandering the shore line of the remote island calling after each of his daughters by name.

I shake myself away from the gory stuff I pumped into the minds of my defenseless children and begin to think about the entrance to Castine. Hitting something hard named Otter Rock Shoal that hides two feet under water and protects the fringes of the sheltered harbor is not on my agenda for today. Easing sheets in the chop under the headland I make for the bell buoy that marks the deepest channel to the inner harbor. The large red navigational aide bobs in the swells with its clanging rhythm sounding like a discordant horn section against the violins and woodwinds of the wind and hull. My adolescent nature forces me to cut the bell close, passing the sharp edges and steel girders by mere feet as we scurry past. Cutting buoys is not my usual style, but I feel the adrenaline rush of a successful near miss and imagine the wide eyed stares from the specters of my absent crew. It is satisfaction enough to know that I still have the unsound judgment and luck-infused skill it takes to measure stupid risks with an inch ruler in my hand.

Racing sail boats is an affliction. A reporter once asked Ted Heath, England's Prime Minister, what competing for tin cups in large sailboats was like. In his normal, irascible style Heath told the reporter that the only way a non-sailor could truly know what it was like to be in his deck shoes was to get fully dressed and stand in a cold shower for days on end while ripping up hundred pound notes until your eyes can't stay open and your fingers won't work anymore.

Add smelly crewmates in tight quarters, a jack hammer motion under your feet, deafening sounds marking the end of the world, ultra light gear stretched beyond design limits, pressure forces of sail and rope which can kill, maim, and render you unconscious on a storm tossed sea, then mix into the chaos slippery food that won't stay on a plate or in your stomach, and you have the glamorous world of offshore ocean racing. The difference between yacht club sponsored around-the-buoys racing and doing the world's ocean circuit is just like a breakfast of ham and eggs. The inshore folks are like the chicken, deeply involved in the menu, but the offshore racer and the poor pig are committed to the success of the meal in a whole different way.

Newport has been at the center of the philandering nature of our country's upper class for a century or more. "Cottages" for the Vanderbilts, Whitneys, Cabots, and other scions of the Industrial Revolution are still perched like castles in all their splendor on the shores and highlands that surround this bustling Rhode Island town. To cater to the ultra rich and their magnificent yachts, a haphazard series of ocean races were brought to the waters off the mouth of Narragansett Bay with the finish/start line marked by the Brenton Reef Lightship. In the 1930s the start of both the Bermuda Race and the America's Cup series were brought to Newport. For me, the journey from Gloucester to Newport was a spiritual pilgrimage from Mecca to Medina. I was agog.

Windigo was built in 1956 by the Hinckley Yard in Southwest Harbor on Mount Desert in Maine. Henry R. Hinckley, founder and owner, called her "the best wooden boat ever built." In spite of his obvious prejudice, he was darn near right. She was launched as *Venturer,* and in her first year of racing broke the Bermuda Race record that had been around since 1932. In 1960 she was first to finish, a feat she repeated two years later under new ownership and named *Northern Light.* After six years of racing and cruising on the west coast including winning the Transpac in 1967, she was purchased by Walt Gubelmann who was looking to replace his twenty year old boat named *Windigo* that he had campaigned hard and successfully across the oceans of the world.

On June 1st I stumbled down the dock at Goat Island with a duffle bag over my shoulder and my heart in my throat. At seventy-three feet *Windigo* was massive and imposing. Winches were as big as fifty-five gallon drums. Lines to the dock were the size of my wrists. A three spreader mast towered over the waterfront and made my neck ache when I looked aloft.

This vehicle of my race-laden dreams also had a professional captain who didn't know I was coming along. The owner himself had only a vague recollection of his invitation on that wine tossed night a full week before. I was later to learn these early morning offers from drunken sailors were more courtesy than commitment. But here I was, and I wanted to go to Bermuda in a bad way. I lied and told him Evi would be terribly disappointed if I didn't make the trip. Walt was a successful capitalist and a seasoned realist with a full knowledge of what Evi would be like if she was somehow disappointed in you.

A bunk in the forepeak containing a full inventory of bagged sails was finally identified for my gear and I was put to work making sandwiches for the half-dozen crew laboring in the last frantic stages of putting a boat together for an offshore race. I applied myself to the making of the baloney with cheese and lettuce, cutting up apple slices, peeling oranges and arranging the pickles just so, finally piling on the potato chips in a stalwart mound that allowed for easy access to the whole smorgasbord. I set the paper plates in wicker holders, put out napkins and gallons of red kool-aid in plastic glasses on the eight-foot long gimbaled table below decks and banged a pot with a spoon. Heads peered in apprehensively looking down the companionway expecting a major catastrophe. Slowly it dawned on them that lunch was served.

Smiles followed awkward introductions. The crew was accustomed to making their own. In a hummingbird's heartbeat I became nigh close to being indispensable. This was the humble beginnings of the role that was to lead to a series of boats during the next few years. In the racing world of the day only two positions on a Class A ocean racer were paid: captain and cook. And those barnacled owners who were successful campaigners knew that you couldn't swing a dead cat in a waterfront bar in Newport without hitting a half-dozen captains looking for a ride. Cooks on the other hand were traded like military secrets. I had created the expectation aboard *Windigo* that a major problem for the race had been solved with a baloney sandwich feast. But filling the space between two slices of bread and a baked tuna noodle casserole were the extent of my expertise in the galley. I figured, just like the summer before with my lack of knowledge about instructing sailing, how hard could it be? Learning my inaugural lessons in the culinary arts would take the stomachs of the crew of *Windigo* on a wild ride.

Castine Harbor is the open mouth of the Bagaduce River. It is deep, and the current runs strong past the tightly packed mooring balls. I let *Dog Star* race along the narrow channel past Dennet's Wharf and Eaton's Boatyard until the peaked roof of the Castine Yacht Club is off our beam and then, timing a lull in the up and down wind, I bring us about in a flurry of released and winched jib sheets and head back out the way we had come in. The long pier where the *State of Maine,* a huge freighter that serves as a floating classroom of the Maine Maritime Academy, is empty, and a solitary fisherman is dangling a line in hopes of dinner. He waves as we scuttle past. I envy him his perspective on our quick full sail tour of the harbor.

Harriet Beecher Stowe and her son, The Reverend Charles, passed a handful of summers here. It is rumored that the ladies of the town felt that Mrs. Stowe wore her hair in "a rather frowzy style and that there was a slatternly air in the way she put on her clothes." The story has it that the petty judgment of the woman's club would have ceased immediately if the author of *Uncle Tom's Cabin* had but chosen Castine as a setting for one of her novels.

I give the channel buoy a little wider berth on the way out and set us on course for Turtle Head. As I tie off the helm to keep us on track for a minute or two, I duck below for another beer to celebrate a successful first half of our round trip. The chirping of the cell phone intrudes on my impending date with a bottle of Heineken.

"Dad?"

"Skye Marie." I smile, pleased that someone wants to talk with me. "How goes the baby factory?"

"I feel like a stuffed sausage."

"Don't fret. It can only get worse."

"Thanks a lot. Whatch'a doing?"

"Dancing naked on the foredeck with my bagpipes in Bar Harbor." Skye knows this couldn't be true because I usually don't tolerate Bar Harbor and its tourist infested waterfront.

"Fine," she said and gets down to the reason she called. "Mom says you won't listen to reason and we are still going to stay up there in Maine when we come to the boat."

"Dirty, filthy liar, the woman can't be trusted," I said, "but she's right."

"But we can't swim in Maine, and I want this cruise to be so perfect."

"You can swim in Maine. I see it done all the time."

"By morons," she said.

"I've even done it."

"In a full body wet suit," she said.

"The boat was sinking."

"Duh, I hope not to have that motivation."

"C'mon I've seen you do the flying fish dip off the boat when you were younger. I think only your belly button ever got damp.

You just can't swim for very long in Maine." I correct her choice of words.

"But the baby," she said.

"Listen, 'Fiona Darling' needs to know what she is in for. She's been born to the sea...the cold, cruel, heartless sea, just like her mother."

The proud parents have already decided on a name for their soon to be born daughter and it isn't Fiona. The little joke I won't let go of will probably taint my relationship with my first grandchild. I can imagine her asking her mom in tears: "Why doesn't Grandpa know my real name?"

"How about Buzzard's Bay? The Cape and Islands?" my daughter said. "Block Island even?"

"We're bound for Roque," I said.

"Plans can change," she said. It is a thinly veiled threat that involves talking to her mother again. "I just want it to be perfect."

"You like Maine," I said with a passion. "The lobster, the quiet anchorages, the outlet stores in Freeport..."

"I don't like all that isolation, fog as thick as pea soup, endless rain, and cold water," she said quietly.

"Yet," she said after the pause.

This from my daughter who thinks Anchorage, Alaska, is heavenly.

I bite my lip to stop a quick, snide rejoinder.

Don't you hate it when those rules you make as a parent come back and bite you in the butt? With our children M. and I fixed a rule about new food, experiences, books, etc. If you tried something first, you then had the right to say that you didn't care for it as long as you added the word "yet." Broccoli, Shakespeare, the opera, bagpipe music were all things you might grow to be fond of some far off day, but committing to "hating" them without condition or chance of parole seemed a little short-sighted to me. We all grow into things. Now, my magical open option "yet" was being thrown back in my face.

"Today is a beautiful day. The sun is baking. The sky is clear as a bell. It sparkles," I said.

"Sure," my daughter said, knowing I am not above telling a fabulous fib to make a point.

"Really," I said, swearing the affirmation with the over the top sincerity of a television evangelist. I look around at the banner day as *Dog Star* charges out into the funnel of the wind with a bone in her teeth. I hold the phone at arms length wishing it took pictures to support my assertions. The roar of the weather, the crush of the bow wave is loud. It must sound a full gale.

"I'll talk to mom, again," Skye said with the certainty of a guillotine. "Got to go. Get some clothes on or you'll catch cold. Love you, Dad."

"Love you too, you traitor to all that's good and holy in the state of Maine." We finally hang up knowing this is only act two in a three-act play with a working title of "Changing Father's Mind."

Castine was the very first body of water the noted mystery writer Stuart Woods, who wrote the classic non-fiction sailing memoir, *Blue Water, Green Skipper*, ever navigated in a sailing boat. His story is as blind a leap of faith into the sailing world as you could possibly imagine. After feeling the heady rush of the wind on sails pushing an open skiff around the Maine harbor, he was well hooked. He would drive from his job in New York City each weekend during the short sailing season to get a flying fix. He sounds like a guy I would like to meet.

Although it took a few years after settling by the sea in Ireland, he found a leaky old Mirror dinghy to learn the basics. The water was as cold as Maine's, and he made very few wet mistakes. Here was a man who set his sights high, and during the next few months bought a Ron Holland designed racer, learned to sail, navigate, and cook, entered the 1976 Observer Single Handed Trans Atlantic

Race, and survived. Actually he finished 63rd, and his words are a rich stew of pith, pluck, and verve. I think of his story each time I sail on these beautiful waters of upper Penobscot Bay. Like the country-western song, I thank God for unanswered prayers. I know I would have leapt at the chance to test my luck without a trace of skill against the Atlantic if I could have all those years ago. It was wise that God in all her infinite wisdom spared me the challenge until I was ready. It gives me the willies just thinking about it.

Dog Star and I round Turtle Head and line up on the granite monument on Steel's Ledge at the entrance to Belfast. My second beer has evaporated, and I can't leave the tiller to replenish it as we push along on a close reach showing our red bottom paint to the gulls who ride the growing swells as the late afternoon wind reaches its zenith. The great thing about a sailboat in twenty knots of wind is that the illusion of control can make your heart sing with joy. The simple fact that things can go south in a big hurry is held at bay by the predictable bucking of the tiller and the steady rhythmic glide towards home. In reality, all control is an illusion. There is nothing like your kids getting older and starting their own lives to bring that point home like a switchblade at your throat.

By the time we reach our mooring the wind has begun to huff and puff itself out. The inner harbor in the long twilight of this late spring night is growing shadowy tendrils across the surface water in the last ripples of the afternoon breeze. Lights come on along the shore in the century old brick buildings as I put the sail covers back on. My face and hands burn pleasantly with the remnants of sun and salt.

I grapple with my daughter's need for swimmable water on our final cruise as a nuclear family, and her desire that the time we will spend together this summer should be perfect. But, I remember, in hindsight all cruises are perfect. Doesn't she know that? Suddenly

I think of my eighteen-year-old son Tristan and the cold waters of the North Atlantic he is probably plowing his way through on this waning day. Perhaps he is at the helm watching the same sunset from the deck of the aging schooner making its way towards Boston with a full crew of scalawags. Every voyage changes you in some profound way. I wonder what five thousand miles will have taught

him about life and about himself. Would I be able to handle the answers that he has found without me around?

Going below, I light the oil lamps one by one. Soon the cabin is aglow with the butterscotch color of varnished elm and the white gloss of enamel paint. I put on the kettle for tea and pull out the logbook. The first page of a new summer stares back at me, blank as a softly whispered promise. I take up the pen and put "Bound For Roque" inside the cover. Then, in short words and simple sentences, I begin to draw boxes around the endless possibilities of an afternoon under sail on the coast of Maine.

SEVEN

BERMUDA RACE

The day of my first Bermuda Race began with an event being seared into my brain like the first forbidden peek at a Playboy centerfold when puberty arrives like a cavalry charge. The sound track for the epiphany was a John Philips Sousa marching band playing "Dixie." This unlikely drive-by sighting of my future would eventually mold and change my whole life. Do random earthly circumstances dictate our fate, or is each step simply a part of a well-planned destiny set in stone before we are born?

With a full complement of eleven souls, *Windigo* cast off her mooring lines from Goat Island in Newport Harbor at 0800 hours. Walt steamed across the crowded harbor to Brenton Cove on the far eastern shore, past the America's Cup Defender *Intrepid* at the Williams and Manchester Shipyard, and on to the chock full and rafted guest moorings of the Ida Lewis Yacht Club. We slowly motored through the fleet and spoke with the crews and captains of the New York Yacht Club entries, offering unflattering commentaries on the readiness of their boats and the manhood of their crews. *Windward Passage, Stormvogel, Ondine, Kialoa,* Ted Hood's *Robin,* and Dan Stroehmeir aboard the thirty-nine foot Concordia yawl *Malay* (the pair who shocked the yachting world and won the Bermuda race in 1954) were crowded in among scores of others. They were all making last minute adjustments to stowage and putting ashore the groupies and hangers-on reluctant to turn the racing crews loose for a charge through the moody Gulf Stream.

Since 1936 the Ida Lewis Yacht Club had been the gathering place for the biennial sojourn to Bermuda organized by the Cruising Club of America. Ida Lewis had been a lighthouse keeper at the important harbor beacon called Lime Rock Light rising above the same granite pile where the yacht club now stands. She must have been one remarkable lady. Ida is credited with single handedly saving eighteen seamen between 1857 and 1906, the last rescue documented when she was sixty-three years of age. Many of the rocks around Newport Harbor bear her name; the very ones who caused the demise of the boats and nearly claimed her famous posse of human salvage. Her heroics are celebrated with the eighteen gold stars on the yacht club's burgee.

Ida became so famous that during one summer over nine thousand people made the pilgrimage to the Rhode Island coast in order to stare at the heroine and the rowboat she used in her work. One of these was President Ulysses S. Grant who stepped out of the rowboat at the lighthouse and got his feet wet. He was said to remark, "I have come to see Ida Lewis, and, to see her, I'd get wet up to my armpits if necessary."

The Ida Lewis Yacht Club constructed a three hundred foot wooden pier from the light to the shore when it organized in 1928. The elegant white structure built around the remnants of the old light speaks of the golden age of yachting with women in elbow length white gloves sipping tea on the shaded porches and men with massive Cuban cigars standing at the bar arguing about the latest Herreshoff or Starling Burgess designs.

I must have been lost in a reverie of times past and tired of the banter among old friends and foes girding themselves to do battle with the six hundred mile course. As I returned reluctantly to the present, I caught a glimpse of a single boat moored in near the floats of the club. My heart stopped. Just as quickly, she was gone, hidden behind an intruding yacht as *Windigo* spun around again to make another run of the verbal gauntlet among the almost solid field of boats. I scrambled to the cabin top straining for another look. Had I imagined it?

No, wait, there she was. A double ender, with a sheer that leapt towards her bow like a gull's chest, a varnished bowsprit, cabin sides, boomkin, and dark green, nearly black topsides that glistened between the sparkles on the water and the river stone gray of her solid teak decks. She was a ketch with two tall varnished spars that spoke to confidence and seaworthiness. She was  without a doubt the most beautiful boat I had ever seen in my young maritime life. The design represented all the science and art that man could possibly put into a small, but comfortable, seagoing yacht. My eyes followed her for close to an hour until she was just a speck on the water lost against the backdrop of Newport Harbor. For months afterwards I saw her every time I closed my eyes.

Two years later, the soft decaying wood of her hull and decks, full of blemishes and terminal problems hidden under the gloss of paint and patient care, were drenched in gasoline and burned to ashes, putting an end to forty years of useful life. The two workmen in dusty coveralls and the volunteer firefighters who stood by to make sure the fire didn't spread to the wooden buildings at the fringes of the yard were said to have shed a tear. When the final glowing ember was doused, the two, way past middle-aged, workers went back to their shed and the newly hewn keel of a brand new boat that would occupy their working days for the next three years. Scattered around the old barn were the bronze fittings, opening ports, gear and lead ballast from the burned hulk. Each of these pieces, along with ten pounds of the mahogany coach roof corner post that carried the soul of the pile of charred timbers outside, would be placed with love and careful determination into the new boat. The blueprints of hull and interior plans from the desk of Philip Rhodes bearing the year 1931 were tacked above the work benches that held the tools of the boat builder's trade.

As *Windigo* rounded Fort Adams to the outer harbor and made her way towards Castle Hill and the starting line along with the 151 other entries, my world had been profoundly changed. I remember feeling the sureness of a young man in love with this new chapter in my adventures on the water and knew that no matter what happened in this life I would someday own my own boat, like the beautiful little ketch I had just seen, and cruise off into the sunset with the love of my life at my side. I had yet to learn that one should be careful and very certain of what one wishes for because it just might come true. I was lucky to have my dream work just like I imagined it. Except, of course, for the sailing off part; once kids came along, time aboard was limited to a few summer months each year. I have learned that those fabulous sunsets we are always writing into our dreams of long range voyaging are actually just the same ones we find closer to home. The best sunset anywhere is the one you get to see and experience with your loved ones on your own boat no matter where it is anchored.

The next morning in Belfast dawns with a heavy wet mist that Mainers describe as "liquid sunshine." *Dog Star* is slicked and varnished from a rain squall blowing through before dawn. Clad in oilies and sea boots, I row ashore and spend two hours shopping for food and grog for a week and replenishing the paper goods and household equipment and cleaners I will need for a summer of travel. By noon I am at the fuel dock taking aboard the last sips to fill the thirty-five gallon gas tank and loading fifty pounds of block ice into the ice chest. Eighty gallons of fresh water are hosed into the two tanks below the settee berths in the main cabin. The day has yet to improve weather-wise when once again I am underway pointing towards Steel's Ledge at the harbor's edge and the upper reaches of Penobscot Bay.

Getting such a late start, I pull out the charts and tide tables to see what the old girl and I can do before it gets dark. The wind is virtually nonexistent. I put the engine in neutral once I am well outside the last buoy, take one final look around for other boats in the vicinity and go below. The charts are spread on the counter above the icebox with the tools of the navigator's trade ready at hand inside a pull down cupboard to port. Taking the bronze calipers, I lay it along the left hand margin of the chart of the bay and open it to five minutes of latitude. At eleven hundred rpm the engine will push our hull at about five knots, so each hour is measured in the distance I can travel. Unlike a road in Nebraska, we can seldom travel in a straight line along the coast of Maine. The boat has obstacles in our way including twenty miles of Islesboro Island, the rocks of Seven Hundred Acre Island, and the shoals off Great Spruce Head. By walking the handheld spreaders along the weaving path of safe water I count off the hours. This exercise narrows my options for the afternoon to the half dozen anchorages in Gilkey Harbor on Islesboro or the home of the schooner fleet in historic Camden. I weigh the mood and choose the seclusion and security of the mud bottom off of Thrumcap, a rock on Islesboro, and write in the log "Bound for Dark Harbor." Somehow the name sounded just right.

Back at the tiller I put the boat in gear and nudge the gas lever until the sound and the vibration under my butt tells me I am right at the edge of Maximum prop rotation and minimum engine mount vibration. I look down at the gauges and check engine water temperature, amp meter charging, and rpm. I smile when the gauge reads exactly eleven hundred. *Dog Star* slowly accelerates until the knot log mounted on the port aft cabin side facing the cockpit reads five and a half knots. It is sixteen miles to our destination and I settle in for a three-hour tour down the Bay. Engines are marvelous things when they do what they are asked. Experience has taught me to appreciate motors when all is well and to curse them to hell and back when they cause trouble. Today my engine sounds wonderful, and I relax from internal combustion paranoia all the way down to guarded optimism. My foul weather gear keeps me warm in the drizzle and my sou'wester hat, with its long rubberized bill protecting the back of my neck from errant trickles, keeps me happy. It hasn't always been this easy to stay dry at the helm of a boat.

Tacking seventy-foot vessels in a tightly confined space around a windy starting line as if they are Optimist Dinghies is not for the faint of heart. It is only an owner with a will to win and a deep pocket who can put fifty tons of boat on a collision course with something equally as big and expensive and calmly sing out "starboard" as the rock and a hard place brace for impact. Crews scramble and grunt in flapping sheets, corralling dangerous loads of force, and rush from low to high side as if their lives depended on it. Sometimes it does.

Windigo got off to a good start, slightly trailing *Ondine* who opted for the other end of the line. A race that usually lasts three to four days is seldom won or lost by a matter of seconds at the gun, and the show of a full competitive duel at the line is more bluster than strategy. This start was a spectacle and all the Class A racers were off in a bunch dodging through the spectator fleet like a herd of runaway horses. *Kialoa II* hounded our windward rail in the steady fifteen knots of breeze, and our respective crews had a good chance to get to know each other while we sailed together within meters as the boats plowed out towards the Brenton Reef Tower and the swells of the North Atlantic. It was heady work for a young man who was experiencing this all for the first time. My main goal was to look aware and competent and stay out of the way of those people who actually knew what they were doing.

My visual memories of that first hour are of the spectacular power of these huge boats surging along under full canvas at the very edge of their design limits. I marvel at the calm control of the cockpit tacticians and helmsmen who seem to be constantly tweaking things to gain every inch of advantage. The speed is breathtaking, rivaling the thrill of plunging head first from an airplane, yet the reality is that the boats are traveling at barely ten to fifteen miles an hour. The sun, the spray, the spectacle of a hundred and fifty colorful racing machines pounding their way to windward will stay with me as a treasured memory. I have had many starts to ocean races in my life, but none approached the mass and scale of these first experiences as an outsider with an insider's seat on a perfect day off Newport.

The race itself was marked by a front of incredible thunderstorms that hit the fleet just at dark the second night out. The wind was hurricane force; our wind speed indicator bit the dust in a gust at fifty-seven knots. I quickly learned that anything that flapped on the boat was powerful enough to kill me. Wind was very strong throughout the race. The Gulf Stream and its three to four knot current meandered in unpredictable ways and divided the fleet quickly. *Windward Passage* guessed right on where to enter and exit the stream and was first across the line in eighty-seven hours for an average speed of 7.8 knots for the 635 mile course. This is the same boat that the very next year covered the 811 miles of the Miami-Montego Bay Race in seventy-five hours to set a race record that held for twenty-five years.

This particular Bermuda race, the 27th running of the classic, was unique in that it was the first and the last time a turning mark was added to the course. The change was to provide the fleet with a closer hauled ride, perhaps even a beat at the final stages down the southern side of Bermuda Island, if the prevailing winds blew their normal stink. The mark to make was Argus Tower Light located twenty-five miles south-southwest of the finish line.

Larry Glenn, the navigator on *Windigo*, in John Rousmaniere's beautiful book *A Berth To Bermuda* is quoted as saying, "We just

couldn't find the tower. There was some kind of anomaly that drowned out the radio beacon with one from San Juan, Puerto Rico. We sailed on and on and finally decided we'd sailed too far, so we turned around and set a spinnaker. That was when Dick Sykes came on deck and spotted the tower, so we sailed for it and *Ondine* passed us. They'd been looking for it too, so they followed us in." The hundred watt light bulb in the Argus Tower was torn down the next year and never spoken of again in future races to "the Onion Patch."

The lovely *Carina* saved her time on *Ondine* and won the race. *Windigo* finished a few hours back, beating many of our rivals and earning us all a "huzzah" from the crews of the already finished yachts when we skirted around Kitchen Shoals and pulled in sight of St. David's Head for the final drift to the line. I confess that I had loads of help in the galley from the veteran crew, so stomachs were kept happy and no one died from food poisoning. I even managed to stand a few turns at the helm with the port side watch. I still have friends made during my first foray into the clash and dash world of deep water ocean races. From our berth at the Royal Bermuda Yacht Club, I stepped ashore on my first almost tropical island. I had found a paradise with pink houses under palm trees. I was learning an art from the best of the best aboard the high tech rocket ships of their time. This poor mongrel was a long way from upstate New York, and I had found a new way of accessing this dream of sailing—a decision that would guide my way from then on.

EIGHT

DARK HARBOR

Dog Star and I round the channel buoy that marks the entrance to Gilkey Harbor. The cut between the lighthouse on Grindel Point and Seven Hundred Acre Island opens up in the drizzle, mist, overcast, and fading light. This protected southern coast of Islesboro has a long history dating back to the Indian fish camps that eventually became early white settlers' homesteads. The F. S. Pendleton Fleet once sailed to all parts of the world from the decaying wharfs off to port. Beginning in the 1890's wealthy Boston and New York socialites came to the island and laid their claim. As in many places where the very rich choose to live the quiet, unhurried way of life away from their cities, the charm and peace of the place is a welcome remembrance of our prim social past. Such scenes, like Jekyll Island in South Carolina and Fischer's Island in Long Island Sound, are a private heartwarming salve to any cruising sailor.

We leave Spruce Island well to starboard to avoid its shoaling nature and see off along the far shore the distinguished white porch of the Islesboro Inn where lights are already flickering across the dark water. I steer 145 degrees magnetic. Shifting to neutral, I let her slow to a crawl before I go below and flip on the running and steaming lights. On my way back to the cockpit, I grab the handheld VHF and turn it on; making sure the hailing channel 16 is up. I give the chart one more extensive look, noting the rocks off of Thrumcap Island and the shallow beach to the east. An old Maine sailor once said to me that when approaching a strange harbor the trick to being "right smart" is not knowing where every rock in the harbor is; the essential key is to know where every rock in the harbor isn't. After another ten minutes of steaming into the dusk, I throttle back to idle and we coast slowly towards the small gathering of boats between us and the Inn.

My normal routine for anchoring begins with one eye on the depth sounder and one eye on the boats as I do a slow but thorough tour through all those anchored and moored obstacles to a good night's sleep. When idle is too fast, shifting to neutral lets me slow down to a stately crawl. I check each anchored boat, noting if they are on chain or rope and how they are lining up with each other in the current. The fickle wind is not giving me any clues tonight. From past experience I try to identify the underwater configurations of the boats. Are they full-length keels or dainty little spade wings that will not turn as readily to the current when it changes direction. If the wind pipes up, the same knowledge will tell me who will lay docile behind their anchor lines and who will charge around like a hungry wolf on a chain. I then try to find an open zone where *Dog Star* will have a good wide radius to swing without getting into anyone's space. Tonight it is easier to choose the outer fringes because I don't plan on going ashore.

After I complete my grand tour and decide where I want to set the hook, I let the boat slow and drift out of the anchorage while I leave the helm and go forward to ready the anchor. I set it over the bow and let it trail just in the water with a safety line secured to a cleat so that it and its chain will not drop to the bottom in a lump until I want it to. When all is ready, and about sixty feet of chain lifted from the locker and flaked on deck, I once again power up and slowly approach my chosen spot. If the wind had been blowing I would naturally head upwind to the target area. I sedately leave the cockpit, having timed the moment our forward motion ends and the rolling current begins to move *Dog Star* backwards. Tonight it is a little trickier without the wind, and I will have to use the engine to back us down. Slowly walking forward, I release the safety line and gently hand out the anchor until I feel it hits bottom and rolls over, then I reattach the restraining line to the chain and return to the cockpit to engage the idling engine into a slow reverse. Back at the bow as the boat begins to move astern under power, I again pay out the chain hand over hand until I have let out about four times the depth of the water I am anchoring in. I again secure the restraining line with its chain-snubber taking the load and wait to see if the anchor will catch.

The chain comes taut and the bow dips a curtsey to the strain. I amble back to the cockpit and put the boat again in neutral. Back forward I let out an additional length of chain more or less equal to the depth and proceed to the final check with the engine in reverse to be sure we are well and truly dug in. Revving the engine in reverse to put a solid load on the anchor for a second time is my own tried and true security system. I then pick two or three lights or boats that will be visible as darkness falls and take a crude bearing on them from the cockpit compass. I go below and write these points and bearings into the log. I then switch off the engine, heave a sigh of arrival, and begin to relax. On a calm evening like this with a full larder, ice cold beer, and the soon to be warm and toasty cabin I can imagine pulling a Captain Nemo and never setting foot on terra firma again.

"Yo dad." The voice on the cell phone is crackling.

"Tristan, you slimy sea serpent, how are you? Where are you?" I said over the static.

"Just off Cape May, New Jersey."

"And I thought you were smart enough to stay south until the weather got warmer."

"Gotta go where the boat goes. It's too cold to swim for shore."

"At least I taught you something useful."

"Skye says you won't listen to reason about where to go on our cruise this summer."

"Who is this 'Reason' character you all keep talking about, and why should I listen to him?"

"I told her I'd call you."

"So you called. I'll take the attention any way I get it."

"There is a lot to be said for sailing in warm sunshine."

"Is any of it useful in real life?"

'You're born, you suffer, you die, right?"

"That's the bloody Irish in you, by golly."

"You going to change your mind?"

"You know me, always ready to compromise."

"So we stay fog bound in Maine unless it's declared a nuclear waste dump." Tristan understands me completely.

"Bingo," I said.

"I told her that already."

"Who said boys were the dumber sex?"

We talk for another few minutes as he answers all my questions about the trip from Puerto Rico with brief diplomatic statements overheard by the on-watch crew sharing a cell phone break before they get too far off shore. Tristan is experiencing his final high school semester at sea with Oceans Classroom aboard the schooner *Harvey Gamage*. Four months with eighteen other students, four teachers, and a trio of professional crew working the 131' sparred length wooden schooner down to South America and back to Boston. This is a rare chance for a new eighteen-year-old to log five thousand sea miles without subtracting from his school career. Tristan sounds great, full of life and comfortable with his shipmates' easedropping in spite of the poor reception. We are cut off abruptly when the signal fades. I yell that I miss him loud enough to disturb the entire quiet anchorage, but the phone is already dead.

I light the oil lamps, start the stove, and pour a can of clam chowder into a pan. I slurp a nice merlot from a stemmed wineglass as I stir the white glop so that it won't burn black. When not dining alone I insist on china crockery and real glass goblets for dinner in a quiet port. Paper plates and plastic cups can work for other meals but something about candle sticks and a decent table setting always makes the evening dishes I turn out with the two burner alcohol stove taste much better. On the flip side, I also carry a stack of wide based heavy stainless dog dishes for those hot meals when everything aboard *Dog Star* is on a bouncing slant. Broadening the gear you carry to handle the extreme ends of any spectrum is all part of a learning curve that progresses each day you are out moving a boat.

I imagine the *Harvey Gamage* working her way north with a heaving swell and full gaffed sails pulling her along in the dark. I am glad my son seems to find the same comfort I do at sea. Tonight I envy his shipmates who enjoy his company as I eat from the pan with a serving spoon while feeling sorry for myself, and, after hanging an anchor light in the rigging, with a final look around, I crawl into bed with a book pulled from the shelves above my bunk that is sure to take my mind from my melancholy.

During my second summer in Gloucester, 1971, when the student sailing season at the yacht club was taking all my weekdays, nighttimes found me back working with my partner Steve Smyth exploring the odd hobby of hunting down the spoils of the departed while pouring expensive gin at the Rockaway Hotel. On the weekends I tried to earn a few bucks offering sailing lessons during the day aboard the two Turnabout sailing dinghies at the hotel dock down past the gazebo just below Ten Pound Island. M. was back finishing up her senior year at St. Lawrence University in the boonies of upstate New York. I was lonely, out of sorts, mostly broke, and wasn't gushing enthusiastic about another long winter mending ski-twisted bones up in Sugarbush, Vermont. I answered an ad in the Boston Globe that was placed by a family who was taking their brand new sailboat to the Caribbean and wanted an experienced person to go along. On reflection I was short on pleasant cruising experiences, but I figured I could learn how to kick-back and enjoy myself aboard a boat heading for paradise if given the right opportunity.

I met John and Arlene Buckey at their home in Concord, Massachusetts the next day. I must have said something right (besides the fact I would work for fifty dollars a week plus bunk and board) because on the following weekend they brought their three children up to sail the Turnabouts and talk about the trip.

A short week later I was in Mamaroneck, New York, south of Scarsdale and north of Hell's Gate, moving my single duffel aboard a spanking new LeCompte Northeast 38. The smell of fresh resin and fresh satin varnish was a full step up from the mildew and rot of the wooden hulks I had lived aboard before. I tried to stay out of the way of the yard workers as they put the finishing touches to the boat that had arrived from the builder in Holland only a week before. She was as flawless and shiny as a glass eye.

Brewer's yard is a local pride handed down since the first settlers landed here in 1650. The workers are proud Yankees and talkative to a fault. I found out that James Fennimore Cooper married a Mamaroneck girl and lived in her family's house for a while as he dreamt up *Last of the Mohicans*. The yard minions also pointed me in the direction for the best burger, the best breakfast, and the best place to sit under a tree when the sun got too hot. I wasn't all too sure what my role was. Watching, learning, soaking it all in was about the only thing I could do with any authority. So I did.

What I learned during the next weeks is that most boats are very complicated combinations of systems that try to duplicate all of the conveniences of modern living folks have ashore. Electricity, propane gas, running hot and cold water, communications, refrigeration compressors, forced air heat, etc, etc. are all crammed into micro-compressed areas that only contortionists can reach. Keeping it all going, without the services of a cadre of public utility offices and their crews on twenty-four hour standby, is what makes boatyards the heroes and villains in this futile exercise of taking it with you out on the water. You would think a new boat would be easier to manage for a while because it is under warranty and the engineers have drawn it out so perfectly. This is not the case. How often can we pinpoint in the rearview mirror exactly when an acute paranoiac phobia begins to occupy our life? It was here, watching the gyrations and frustrations of getting every single thing to function just right on a boat called *Indiscretion,* that I vowed to keep it a lot simpler if I ever had a boat of my own.

One night, as the yard shut down, I couldn't stand it any longer. I was a sailor, by god. This was a sailboat, by god. I stood at the wheel and tried to convince myself that I could certainly get this boat off the dock and out onto the water without causing any damage. The boat was owed this dignity. I looked at the road map I had brought along in my duffle and aside from the imposing names of Execution Rocks, Sea Cliff, and Scotch Cap Shoals it looked pretty straight forward and plenty deep enough. Keep the red ones to the left going out and reverse it on the way back. What could be simpler?

So without permission or a "by your leave," I cranked up the diesel, let go the lines, and made my way out through the tight highway of buoys to the waters of Long Island Sound. All went well as I shut down the engine raised the brand new sails, sorted out a few glitches in the running rigging and ran down wind towards the Northeast.

My soul sang as the bow wave rippled back along the waterline. She was tender and feisty without the tons of cruising gear still waiting to come aboard. The wheel jumped in my hands as she got a bone in her teeth and rode downhill like a gull. The wind whistled at my back, white caps tried to keep pace but lost the sprint. I was in idiot's heaven.

The coming sunset should have sent shivers down my spine, but I was too full of myself and this first solo on a new boat to notice. We were bonding. Lights began to come on along the shore. Pockets of brilliance marked the large cities that feed the work force of The Big Apple. Suddenly, almost without warning, it was totally dark. I had lost my bearings. The wind was pushing me along, away from where I needed to go at a breathtaking rate. I didn't have a chart. Was that Stratford or Stamford off to port? Car taillights and the port running lights from fast moving barges and tugs looked about the same. I'm not the brightest bulb on the circuit, but it didn't take me long to understand I was in big trouble. God sometimes takes care of brain-dead young fools and sailors. That night, she had her hands full of questionable decisions from both categories at the same time. I'll tell the rest of the story when my palms stop sweating.

NINE

CAMDEN

The choices I had on that dark night when I was lost and alone off the coast of Connecticut with *Indiscretion* were few. I eventually found one of the channel buoys, a green flashing light on the top of a fifteen-foot tall metal erector set and figured that I had to stay in sight of this safety marker and out of the way of big boat traffic until dawn.

It is distressingly easy to read the understated words from a pioneering solo circumnavigator's account of their epic voyage: "I was forced to remain at the helm for the last thirty-six hours as we closed with the coast, fearing that my position was uncertain." I imagined the rocks and breakers were just ahead, lost out there in the dark, snapping like jackals in the driving wind and solid sheets of rain.

When a long dark night stretches out in front of you, it really doesn't help that I had all the lights of the free world barely a mile away on the most populated coastline in our country. I watched cars braking for stoplights. In fact the electric glare was so bright against the low clouds on this moonless night I could see the compass rose without its light on. It was still damn scary, and staying awake and in control of the situation becomes a gnawing test of manhood that you know, in that uncertain corner of your mind, you will probably barely manage a D-plus. I would have taken the breathless certainty of a charging bear anytime.

The wind died at midnight. Bouncing in the slop left over from the sea breeze, I crawled forward and let go the sails. I was struggling with a gut wrenching premonition that something bad was going to happen because I had done the wrong thing. I had put a boat in jeopardy because I was full of myself and didn't have the experience to know any better. If you want to get on your own case, a dark night alone in a boat's cockpit, plunk in the middle of a danger zone, is the place to do it.

The adage is one hand for the ship and one for yourself. Tying down the hanked-on jib on a pitching bow and furling the main against the boom is tough to do one handed. But, my head kept playing over and over a snippet of advice from a seasoned offshore veteran on the Bermuda race. He laughed a Vincent Price laugh when I stumbled on the foredeck during a sail change and said, "You know the only difference between falling off the wing of an airplane at twenty-thousand feet and falling off a boat in the ocean is that in the water you die a bunch slower." Paranoia is an unwelcome, but often useful watch mate.

Indiscretion and I watched a parade of tugs towing barges and large cargo ships move to and fro in the shipping channel as we idled within a hundred yards of the buoy. The water had become oily calm and was as dark as printer's ink. For the first few early morning hours adrenaline kept my eyes open. Each time a wake from a ship rolled the boat my stomach leapt and my sphincter tightened. Fear would keep me awake forever. Then my eyes suddenly felt like ten-pound window sashes were tied to my eyelashes.

I drank coffee. I splashed cold water on my face. I chewed gum. I kept my bladder full to the bursting point. I slapped myself, hard; no joke. I stood up, refusing to get comfortable. I told myself gruesome and chilling stories. I put a rubber band around my wrist and snapped it until I was black and blue. I still couldn't keep my eyes from slamming shut.

The deep baritone horn came rolling over me like boiling oil from a castle wall. I was standing at the wheel, both hands griped to the spokes, but must have dozed off. My eyes saw the bow wave in white froth and a huge black wall of steel forty feet off the port beam, a tangle of white woven rope seemed at mast height, blocking out the clouds. I threw the helm to starboard and put the engine in gear cranking the throttle wide open. The roar was painful to hear. I expected the crash of impact at any second.

Slowly, *Indiscretion* gained momentum; just as I thought we would never make it, the stern lifted, the bow spun away and she rolled down to almost dip her mast in the drink. The water rushed down the deck and into the cockpit in a steady dark flow. The wheel was wrenched from my arms as she jerked back up and rolled the other way letting the six-foot wave slam against her beam and deposit another hundred gallons into the cockpit. Twice more she rocked from beam to beam and then started to settle down as I gathered the courage to scream epithets into the dark night. Another blast of the horn that was probably heard ten miles away told me to shut up. I did.

My heart was a runaway train. I throttled back the screaming diesel as I watched the stern of the huge ship pull away. I was all right. I tried to calm myself down. Shaking, watching what could have been a watery grave pull away into the night, I heaved air into my lungs. It was during my first nervous smile that celebrated dodging a bullet that I saw something leap out of the water a few yards from my bow. What the hell?

The horn blasted. I looked again at the receding stern light and yelled, "Okay, okay, I screwed up. Give me a break." The water parted again twenty-five feet off my bow, throwing a phosphorescent line towards the night sky.

"Oh, shit!"

The steel towing cable was probably five inches thick. My still groggy brain finally registered the danger, and I looked away from the departing tug and saw the wall of water pushing against the flat bow of the barge. It was coming out of the night like a giant tsunami. I gave the diesel full power again, and spun the bow up towards the backside of the departing tug and began to angle away from the white wave that was gaining ground behind me. I wasn't going to make it. The water was lapping at our heels as I finally spun myself beam-to for a final chance to grab the extra few feet we needed. The tug missed us by inches, not yards. The horn screamed again. We rocked and rolled in the wake; the mast arcing through a hundred degrees or more. I held on with all the strength drained from my body. Knees wobbled. I sat down. A lone figure on the barge's stern gave me the finger and yelled something about my lack of a named father and my competence as a seaman.

After washing my face with my hands, my skin felt like a cold frog's belly. I looked for my safety buoy. It was right where it was supposed to be, and I was well out of the lanes. I learned that night that shipping channels on Long Island Sound are more a suggestion than a rule. I hoped in my thumping heart that all my lessons would not be so hard won.

I have never, in the last thirty-five years of sailing, fallen asleep on watch again.

Purists will say that voyaging is a simple matter of two factors: keep the sticks up, and keep the liquid out. Having experienced the absence of one or both of these factors on occasion over the years, I can attest to the fact, they are indeed prime ingredients to a happy sail. I would add a third factor, and that is a clean, uncluttered bunk for the person in charge. Morale of the crew is very often dependent on the vagaries of the captain's foul mood. But a foul mood is hard to come by when you are dry and warm and everything else outside of your private domain isn't.

On this particular Islesboro morning, the screen in the companionway is laden with a full load of water drops from the thick fog that swirls away to the ends of the visible world five feet from the deck of the boat. *Dog Star* is as wet as a slippery seal from the mist. Her varnish is beaded in lumps of honey colored drizzle; the cockpit teak dark as a plain doughnut.

Describing the wonderful world of a small cruising boat, E. B. White wrote: "It is without question the most compact and ingenious arrangement for living ever devised by the restless mind of man – a home that is stable without being stationary, shaped less like a box than a fish or a girl,… "

Amen, brother.

"…and in which a homeowner can remove his daily affairs as far from shore as he has the nerve to. Close-hauled or running free – parlor, bedroom, and bath, suspended and alive. It is not only beautiful; it is seductive and full of strange promise and a hint of trouble."

It is the "hint of trouble" that nails this description clear on the head. The edge of the sea is a feckless place. Dangers to boats are legion. But the coasts of oceans are where the truly afflicted spend their time aboard the craft they irrationally support with affection and money. It is here cruising sailors make a home for a short while each year. Every nook and cranny anchorage, day sail or overnight passage is only one small incident from a catastrophe. In Maine with its sheer number of obstacles, dimensions of fog, and swift tidal currents, any prudent navigator is unlikely to forget how close a partner trouble is in every decision. These are my coasts of summers' past.

A true sailor, involved in a love affair with his boat, has constantly stood in awe within his surroundings below decks. Marveling in the total rightness of his cozy dry cabin while tugging at a mooring, he dodges the rain, waiting to pull the sticks on another season. It is the ancient cave dwelling instinct to find a haven, comfortable and safe, away from the terrors of the world. Ghosts of past dreams are always screaming for attention. These are the recurring times you mortgage your soul by citing the adult excuses why you shouldn't "go." Why you can't sail the damn boat south. We are all brothers-in-arms against the sad, redundant torture of "berth lounging," drowning in self-pity, wishing away a chilly late-fall afternoon.

I pump the alcohol stove pressure pump, open the spigot, and let a small pool of fuel into the burner cup. A flick of the long handled lighter, and a blue flame begins to lick the bottom of the large tea kettle with just enough water so that the preheat will probably give me the liquid part of a full mug up of tea, and no need to actually run the stove. A passive cooking convenience from old school technology is making my morning rosier.

I put my elbows on the companionway, rest my chin on my crossed arms and try to gently blow free a window through the waterlogged screen. Every boat owner has found a few ergometric places aboard their boat that fits him or her to a "T". This was one of mine. My hips meet the teak counter top in front of the sink just so, my feet brace against the ice box elm paneling outboard and the companionway stairs in total security, a slight leaning aft puts the weight against my arms and makes a bomb proof perch to watch the waves roll past when we are hove to in a bit of wind. And I can assure you that standing below watching the scene through my Plexiglas wash boards is a hundred times preferable than sitting at the tiller trying to crash and bash into heavy seas to make a knot or two to the good. *Dog Star* and I prefer to stay-put when the wind on our nose gets above twenty-five knots. To me heaving to is like stopping to smell the wildflowers when you are on an all-day hike in the Rockies. The fear factor goes down and appreciation factor goes way up. Besides, it is something everyone should practice often for that special day or dark stormy night when the need is safety, not only comfort.

I give a full body shake as I try to get my mind away from imaginary bad weather and focus on this dead calm, socked-in, sheltered cove in Maine. I don't want to worry a hex on Tristan and the crew of the *Harvey Gamage* as they work their way northeast, offshore in the often-treacherous North Atlantic. I smile as I think of that little squid grown up enough to be off doing fun things on his own. It isn't fair. I changed his diapers. Now he's having seagoing adventures? Without me?

M. says this special brand of regressive, self-centered, delusionary framing of the reality of things is a straightforward case of arrested development; mine. It is a selfish, old-man kind of thinking, and I hate knowing I am marching to that drummer. I glance down at my still naked body for reassurance on the old man line of thinking. Alas, no rebuttal to the facts down there. I don some clothes to hide the evidence.

The kettle is hot and I put the cup into the drain-hole at the bottom of the sink to pour the hot water so that it won't spill on me. This is an offshore technique, a kind of overly careful way of doing a simple task, out of context in the millpond we float in this morning. I sit back on a settee and let my mind wander.

Indiscretion and I found our way home to the yard as soon as the first glow of feral light tipped the skyline of Manhattan. I had her all tied secure and safe by the time the first of the workers clomped down the dock. That fitful night during my prolonged adolescence proved that PDL (Poor Dumb Luck) beats skill every time.

During the next few months the entire ship's company of six, aboard a thirty-eight foot boat, traveled as a family from Long Island to Nantucket and up to Marblehead. We had our moments of pride in our emerging skills, and frequent squalls of acute embarrassment, as we handled the bright new boat in crowded New England harbors. Mystic, Stonington, Fisher's Island, Sag Harbor, Falmouth, Hyannis, Nantucket, and Martha's Vineyard, were all delightfully added to my logbook. Each entry was full of single syllable declarations of eye-opening exuberance. I try to keep this ghost of me in a state of euphoria very close to hand when I need advice. This is my "Go For It" advisor.

Weathering a very strong Nor'easter aboard *Indiscretion* in the Great Salt Pond of Block Island helped to mark a milestone in modern history. The wind, with little warning from the weather gurus, caught a weekend flotilla in this virtually un-buffered wide expanse of shallow water and gave them a three star licking. Sustained winds of fifty knots and dragging anchors gave us much to do as our tenuous hold on the soft mud bottom stayed put. At one point I had to go hand-over-hand down our anchor rode up to my chest to cut free a motorboat's torn loose anchor that was tangled with our rode and holding his tall slab sides against *Indiscretion*'s rubrail. At the height of the storm I remember remarking on a twin-engine plane bucking and twisting over the pond, scrambling for altitude. It was crazy enough weather to make it notable in the log. In the morning we heard that the FBI had apprehended and transported Father Daniel Berrigan, the Vietnam War activist and liberator of the Pentagon Papers, from the town. He was one of my '60s heroes. I still feel like Forrest Gump for having been that close to an icon.

The Buckey's finally decided that a full year on the smallish boat with three young children, and a full-of-himself deckhand, was not the vehicle to take them towards the utopia they had in mind. It was fall again when we put the boat away for the season in Manchester and the mountains called me back. On a whim I joined a friend for a quick drive out west to see if the grass was greener. After a hurried return to collect my gear, I traveled to Steamboat Springs to work again in mountain rescue for the winter. During the long drive to Colorado, I took a brooding assessment of where I was in my life and wound up making myself a little crazy. In a few short months it would be 1972. That is a big number, huge, and I hadn't done squat with my life yet. Richard Nixon was still our president. Inner city riots by the poor getting poorer were normal summer events. Vietnam raged. It would have been easy to go crazy. I did find something near close to crazy perfect in Colorado. After years of working to turn boards at ski areas in the east, chattering across boilerplate, thinking it was almost fun in a suicidal vein, I found powder, waist deep and feather light, and the troubles of the world faded away for a few long, sunny winter months above treeline.

The anchor is finally up and secured after my bout with lethargy on this damp Maine morning. Fog has given way to a knee high mist that hugs the water like a down comforter. The mainsail catches the light air, and we ghost out of the anchorage heading down the cut towards Job Island and the blue hills of Camden beyond. The fog condenses on the rigging, dropping huge balls of water that splat on the teak decks and the top of my head. Once clear of the lee of Seven Hundred Acre Island I lay a course for the small lighthouse on Curtis Island to keep us off of the spiny rocks of The Graves. The fog is beginning to scale up quickly with the mid-morning sun and, although we can't see the coast ahead, above the dissipating mist the peaks of Bald and Mount Battie stand proud against a flag blue sky.

The wind, forward of the beam, is light and barely keeps the main and genoa full as we hover around the three-knot barrier. The water slides aft in a small slick of white puffballs from the island weeds. Lobster pot buoys are thick off Little Bermuda Island and *Dog Star* tip-toes her way through the maze. The boat's heeling angle is barely a dozen degrees and the tiller hangs on its own weight. This is the type of sailing that teaches you patience and sail trim.

My girl likes to be sailed loose in light airs. The sheets are fairly slack. A flitter of a luff at the head of the sail is expected. The mizzen is not a help with the wind pinching her nose and is usually not set. Her advantage is momentum. A purposeful gait keeps the apparent wind steady and flattens out the small waves in her path. For a lady with five-thousand pounds of lead in her keel, she ghosts along just fine. Her turn of speed in even a zephyr surprises most other boats who might mistake her for her slower classmates.

It is still early in the season and not much traffic is churning up the West Passage. It is Tuesday, so the schooner fleet is out and away on charter even this early in the season with a week's worth of trouble between their gunnels. I look forward to the dozens of times this summer when I will see these magnificent sailboats from another age earning a living and gracing the panoramic views with their presence. *Dog Star* and I have shared anchorages with the likes of *Mary Day, Stephen Tabor, Harvey Gamage, Appledore*, and a score more. The crews have made my boat feel right at home with random drive by compliments and friendly smiles and waves of encouragement when we meet each other out sailing. It is a fraternity of the afflicted. Admittance is automatic for anyone who strives with the patience of Job to slow the gradual decay of a beautiful wooden boat.

We are soon off the sheer face of Curtis Island and are making our way under sail through the outer harbor. Wayfarer Marine comes abreast on the starboard, and we lose wind as we start down the small channel that leads to the inner harbor. The roundabout of a single lane for navigation runs around the Camden Docks. The harbormaster packs in the middle of the loop a stack of four deep moorings, and many floating docks tethered both for and aft, to allow two boats to raft up securely with no swing room needed. Our sails hang limp. I kick over the engine, putting it in gear under slow idle.

I look for old boats I know and admire, but many of the moorings are still vacant this early in the season. The dockside restaurants are not thronged with the tourists of summer. A cold morning wind, in spite of the sun, comes down the green hillside above town. There is no reason to stop. *Dog Star* has fuel, water, ice, food, grog, so I make my way back towards the harbor entrance. The noontime chime in the bell tower begins its cadence countdown.

TEN

FOX ISLANDS THOROFARE

Once working clear of Camden's outer defenses, I set a course for the Red Whistle "8" and plan to leave Robinson Rock, just off Mark Island, to port. We are bound for the Fox Islands Thorofare between North Haven and Vinalhaven Islands. Our destination is SSE and about twenty miles away. The wind speed is up to fifteen knots out of the southwest; high fleecy cumulus clouds parade across the blue sky. Small corduroy waves slide up the Bay at an angle to our bow. I set the mizzen and the knot log edges over six knots in brief spikes. Tying off the tiller, I duck below to put on some water to heat. The day is crystal and bright, but the wind across the water is chilly on this early June morning. *Dog Star* will steer herself for brief periods when the wind is on the beam. I pop up and down the companionway adjusting her course until I can sit back down in the cockpit with a hot cup of tea in my hand.

Wind forward of the beam, *Dog Star* is slicing the three-foot rollers with a clean, rocking horse gait. Her rail is over, but nowhere near the water, a trace of lee helm to hold against. She keeps her head up, loping along, and powers aside the water in a soft rustle below decks. The green hills of the north shore of Vinalhaven give no clue to where the entry to the Fox Islands Thorofare is located. I steer for the two mounds of Hurricane and White Islands knowing the cut will open only during the last half-mile. I pull my wool watch cap over my ears. The wind still whistles. My cheeks are tight as drums and cold. It is heaven's gate.

Local history screams for some special attention in this natural cut between the two hard granite islands named for the indigenous foxes found in 1603 by Martin Pring of the *Speedwell*. Most famous perhaps was Charles Lindberg's visits during  the wooing of Ann Morrow. He would fly from NYC to land his bi-winged seaplane on the calm waters of the channel. The Morrows had a gentlemen's salt-water farm and wood shingled house along the water on Deacon Brown's Point on North Haven. Dahlias were planted by gardeners and harvested by ladies in long white gloves. Could anything in real life have been more Hollywood? The dashing aviator and the beautiful, sensitive debutant and poet were finding love in the skies above the wild coast of Maine. North Haven was the summer world of the Cabots and Saltonstalls, Lamonts and Watsons, Jays, Gardners, and Rockefellers.

Vinalhaven on the opposite shore was, and still is, working real estate where the names are Dyer and Carver, Calderwood and Coombs, and they wrench their living from the sea and the "rusticator" tourists. Between these two islands the tidal currents are strong. The cut contains ferries from Rockland that provide access to both communities, and a lighthouse that was built during Andrew Jackson's presidency. It has been nearly a century since shots were fired across the moat.

"Dad?" A small voice beckons from my cell phone.

"Skye." I answer in a shout. "How's Fiona?"

Silence.

Why is it, when I am in a hole, I never stop digging?

"Boo-ful day here," I said above the whistle of wind. "W'really special." My lips are numb. I flap like a penguin and hide behind the dodger.

"I have my flights," my daughter said. It sounds like bad news. Getting away with a little funk is part of my penance for liking Maine.

"Anchorage-Seattle-Boston?"

"Yeah, in fourteen hours."

She gives me the specifics. I write it in the log.

"Enjoy it," I said. "Next year you'll be carrying a human boom-box without a volume control."

"Cute."

"Did I tell you how hard it is to change a poopy diaper in a plane's rest room? Oh, the stink, the humanity, the apologies, the lines."

"Can we talk about something else?"

"Coming from politics, I'm expertly capable of small talk."

"Aren't you always telling me to be flexible and adaptable?" she said in a first grade teacher's voice.

"Where are you going with this?" Alarms go off each time my daughter quotes my own words of wisdom back at me.

"Aren't you always saying," she said again, "that compromise is the highest form of intellectual achievement, except for Jeopardy when you know the answer?"

"Sounds right, as long as the results allow me to do exactly what I want to do."

"And that is to make your only daughter totally happy."

"Absolutely," I said, "as long as it doesn't violate rule one."

A sigh. A deep exhale.

"A man of my years is expected to have his enthusiasms."

"Enthusiasms?"

"Emerson: 'Nothing great happens without enthusiasm.' I got a posse of the devils."

"How about delusional obsessions?"

"Tell me you don't believe there was a second gunman on the grassy knoll?"

I feel the reluctant smile.

"Still Maine?"

"Why would you ask?"

"Have you talked to mom yet?"

I experience a chill. A conspiracy crawls up my spine. What was my family cooking up? Treachery, mutiny, and skullduggery no doubt.

"Well, ta-ta," she said, "gotta run, talk to you later."

"Wait, what?" I try but she is gone.

The ice is getting thinner.

The first mark I pick up as we come up under Vinalhaven Island is the granite four-cornered spired monument on Fiddler Ledge. Further on is the red day-beacon for Drunkard Ledge. I notice the current wake on a lobsterpot buoy as we go by. It is directly on the starboard beam and I now know we are being set right-smartly to port. Brown's Head Shoal should now be somewhere off our starboard bow in the shore haze. A lot of ledges, and a lot of leeway, call for a right-smart decision. I harden us up to give a safety zone of ten degrees for the next mark, adjust the sheets. We begin to move like a happy horse cantering upwind, lunging over the steady swells in an easy rocking motion. These are the times you can feel the boat being what she is, pushing the sterile pencil lines of the architect into a moving, powerful presence. A boat on the blustery edge of a breeze comes alive for the whole world to see. *Dog Star* sparkles against the froth parting in her path. I let out a deep breath of appreciation.

As the Fox Islands Thorofare opens up in front of us, my daughter's unexpected presence jars me from euphoria. A specter of her sits across from me, arms folded in a determined manner. She has a puss on her face that lets me know I am in trouble. Why was I being so obstinate? Why Roque Island? What is it about Maine and my peculiar, long held belief that it is the only real cruising left on the U. S. east coast? Are the brief moments of comfort and beauty, so vividly framed by the fog bound misery that surrounds it, actually worth the rest of it? Would voyaging Down East still hold its cachet if three hundred sunny days a year broiled its granite shores? Would a few yacht centers located east of Schoodic be so bad?

The coast of Maine is a candy store for a member of Peter Pan's Lost Boys gang. Every new anchorage is an adventure on the edge. The weather is part of the scene and jacks up the scale on the prime challenge of not hitting anything solid. The howling afternoon sou'wester charging up Penobscot Bay; the deadly calm in a-thick-of-it; the roaring freight train of a nor'easter as it bullies through a quiet anchorage at two in the morning are all players on the endless stage of rock and pine. Past Schoodic the best of Maine hides behind heavy fog, Fundy tides, even colder water, vicious currents, and a lack of marinas, moorings, and hot, or even warm, spots.

I truly believe that one of the highest endeavors of mankind is to seek adventure. Not foolhardy stunts, but healthy, challenging endeavors spiced with a hint of danger that expands who you are as a person. As you age there are lots of things you can't do anymore, even for the first time. But sailing a well-found cruising boat in a way that is safe and seaworthy is within the reach of us all. Using what skills you have to take the boat to new places is what keeps the learning curve migrating for altitude. Maine's nooks and crannies have more places to get in trouble than I could do in this lifetime. It took four hundred million years to shape the feldspar, gabbro, porphyry, and pyroxene into the jagged cliffs and granite coves. Shouldn't a significant amount of time in a true sailor's life be spent paying homage to the tremendous effort Mother Nature has thrown at us?

I will be nothing short of persuasive the next time Skye and I talk, and I will win her over to the idea of Roque Island before she gets her mother to weigh in. I shoo Skye's ghost away and get back to the task at hand.

Sailing past the Sugar Loaves, the black cormorants stand tall on moss covered rocks and flap their swimming wings in the air as if clapping for *Dog Star*'s romp clear of the center channel rocks. Marking the location of can "17" that covers a big shoal stretching out into the otherwise straight natural channel, I steer for the cluster of buildings far down on the distant shoreline that is North Haven. In a matter of yards we are out of the wind under the lee of Brown's Head and the landmass of Vinalhaven Island. The sails fall limp and stumble in weak weaving shimmies, like a drunk on the street. We search for huffing zephyrs coming through the ragged tree line to windward. Slowly we gain traction. I continue to steer to place us dead center channel and try to will the momentum to keep us on track. A necessity in this exercise is keeping the rudder adjustments down to the barest minimum.

It is two-hundred-yards before the old girl comes to a stop and I can leave the helm to roller furl the genoa and drop the main into its lazy jacks. I let the mizzen stay sheeted tight amidships in case the wind filters through the trees along the way. The Gray Marine engine rumbles to life with a throaty roar, and I engage the gears into forward. The current is pushing us along at a sedate amble as I admire the houses, their wide expansive porches, and the polished boats moored in front of them. We soon come abreast of the town dock. A lobster boat with an un-muffled engine spins around in its own length at high throttle and kisses gently up against the fuel dock to take on gas. My cheeks are a bit numb, but warm to the sun as it breaks through the big nimbus clouds. The smell is the iodine fragrance of dried and blown seaweed, kelp above water, and dead bait fish. Pleasant enough though, as it mixes with pine and salt air, wood smoke, and hot tar roofs.

J.O. Brown and Son Boat Yard has stood its ground just east of the ferry landing since 1899. A house front that looks like the behind of a monstrous Spanish Galleon seems right at home nestled part way up the rise where the couple of dozen town buildings disappear into the trees. I keep the speed at around 3 knots and take in the closed down beauty of the channel. In times past I have seen seals, dolphin, and even a lost whale using this shortcut across the bay. I keep my eyes sharp for sign.

The land to the right backs away across a shallow cove. I round the corner to the right, sighting Hopkins Point, and bear south. Soon a small wooded islet marks the entrance to Perry Creek. It is almost dead low water, and I carefully gauge the length of the underwater ledge that makes out from the shore. Once inside, the depth sounder shows a steady 12 feet. I make my way past the moored boats at the entrance to the fork in the stream a couple of hundred yards away. Only a green and white boathouse set amidst a manicured lawn is clearly visible among the dense wall of pine. The illusion is a private space. My favorite anchoring spot is vacant and only two other yachts are anchored above me further up the creek. We have beaten the crowds that will be normal later in the season.

I check the tide tables again and note that low tide is still a half-hour away. I smile knowing the timing couldn't be better. The hunter/gatherer in me howls a blood cry. I conjure up a hunt for the illusive and succulent mussel.

Lobsters, clams, and oysters are the industry of Maine's independent water men and women. I support them by buying and eating as much of this wonderful healthy food as I can force on my friends and family. I would not rustle a lobster or illegally rake a clam, but when it comes to mussels I help myself and no one seems to mind. I have built chowders in Perry Creek from the far upstream beds that lie just below the surface at low tide.

Soon *George* is ready to go with the tools of the trade nestled around her centerboard. I sit in the center seat and row. Six and half foot oars make the Dyer 7' 11" fiberglass dinghy move right along. One of the great things about rowing is being able to leave your boat and admire her as you pull away. I soon pass a double ended production yacht in the forty foot range, very well decked out, with a friendly couple reading in the cockpit. We applaud ourselves for being so wise as to catch a day in Maine like this one. Geniuses we are.

I row upstream against an outgoing current for about twenty minutes, gliding over shallow bars until the bow scrapes along the gravel riverbed. The large rock boulders that form the edge of the stream and direct the currents into relatively deep pools are standing out of the water thirty feet above my head. I grab on to a handful of well-attached mussels to keep us from losing ground. Rolling up my sleeves, on my stomach, with my chest over the bow, I visually supervise the harvest. After donning a pair of kitchen rubber gloves

I reach down into the cold clear water as far as I can and start dislodging the beautiful black shells from their thin seaweed tethers. Some come away singly, others in clumps of four or more on a long tendril. I drop them happily into the

plastic bucket. I let the current take me down the rock face by simply letting go and then grabbing on a few yards along. In ten minutes I have half a bucket full and force myself to stop.

Slowly drifting back towards the anchorage, I fill the bucket with saltwater. A small handle scrubbing brush comes in handy as I brush the connecting vegetation away from the lips of the shell. A few are Trojan horses filled with dark sand and mud. These are discarded with proper vehemence. When the job is done, I dip and rinse the bucket, stirring with my hand, dipping again until the water cradling the shiny bright black petals is clear and stays that way. With one oar I keep us in the stream and stir the bucket with the other hand, shifting often as the skin turns pink and the muscles go numb in the chilling water. The mussels perk, rinsing away gritty matter one swish at a time.

I offer the friendly couple on the double ender a bit of the bounty and they are glad to accept, and I give them a gallon sized Ziploc that holds a good three-dozen. We chat as I sit in the dinghy and fend off so our boats don't bump.

"What's the best way to steam them?" the double-ended wife asks. I can see in the aggressive body language she has her own opinion, so I am quickly on my guard. She has the voice of a drill sergeant.

"Everybody has their own favorite for sure," I offer, "different folks, different strokes." My middle name is Switzerland.

"Chicken?"

"I thought we were talking mussels?"

No humor greets my wit. "Ashamed to tell me how YOU do it?"

"It's all in my head. Don't know if I can remember it all."

"Can't or won't," she says, giving me a steely eye.

I give up, mentally snapping to attention and spout: "An inch or two of water in a pressure cooker or deep pot. A big dollop of sweet white wine, a couple of slices of Bermuda onion, a half lemon squeezed hard and then dropped in, a goodly pinch of oregano, same with basil. Add a gurgle of Balsamic Vinegar, bring to a boil. Drop in a steam colander that rises above the liquids, put handfuls of mussels on top almost filling the pan and put on a lid." It came out like a forced confession in a '30s gangster movie.

"Melt butter," I add like a forgotten punch line.

"Just like mine," she says, "except for the wine, onion, vinegar, basil and oregano."

I smile and let go of the boat, drifting away.

"But, what's a dollop?"

"A big mouthful," I say.

"What's a goodly pinch?"

"What you can squeeze between a thumb and two fingers."

"What's a gurgle?"

"A fluid bottoms-up dip from a bottle."

I was forced into raising my voice. The deep "V" between her eyebrows never changes as she scribbles on a pad.

"You know they were banned?" she yells.

"What?" My perfectly planned dinner contaminated by a red tide alert I hadn't heard about?

"By the Pope, way back in the dark ages," she is twenty yards away. I put my hand to my ear indicating the lack of understanding and smile, waving goodbye.

"They look just like a vagina and clitoris when they swell and open up," she yells so the folks in North Haven two miles away could hear. Her husband coughs loudly and disappears below decks.

I row a little faster as I pass the other two boats and the now fully embarrassed cockpits, making a beeline for *Dog Star*. The hellos are polite, but not beckoning. No one waves or smiles. Funny how any mention of sex, or even the word of a titillating private part, puts people a bubble off center. By the by, the lady is right both historically and aesthetically.

Back at the boat I rinse the mussels again and let them stand on deck in the bucket of water. A successful hunt concluded. Let's review the necessary kit. A bucket, a pair of rubber kitchen gloves, a small handled bristle brush, and a few Ziploc bags to share the bounty with straightforward cruising folks who often call a spade a spade at the top of their lungs.

I set aside two-dozen for steamed hors d'oeuvres, fill a pan with water and light the alcohol stove. Pulling out three good sized potatoes I dice them into half inch squares, peels on, and plop them into the heating water. I pull out a deep pan and rumble through the icebox for the bacon. The sizzle, smell, and sound of the crackling fat begins the process of building a chowder. Chowders are built, not made. Each step in line is part of the tasty structure of the beast.

Still smiling at the way my recipes and portions must sound to other people, I won't offer my chowder instructions in fear of offending some Mainer who thinks I stole his or hers. One fog bound afternoon in The Mud Hole at Great Wass Island I built a dinner chowder with mussels whose simple memory still makes my mouth water. Three grown men ate on it for three hours and we all were sorry to see the last of it spooned out of the bowl. I wrote a simple poem in the log that day about the experience of putting a traditional chowder together.

A stomach full of food, I sit in the cockpit, a wool sweater plus a tumbler of brandy, and watch the time-warping sight of three Hurricane Island pulling boats rowing their way past the entrance to Perry Creek and up towards the white fringe beach in Seal Cove. The Outward Bound crew is looking for rest after a long day. Four sets of oars pull the drooping spritsails with a single dark silhouetted figure standing on the bow holding the forestay on the lookout for shoaling. The slow rhythmic cadence animates the fresco, lit from over my shoulder with the sunset red sky of a sailor's delight. The cicadas are clacking the exact temperature, miniature bongos, as the warmth leaves the pine shadows. I wish I could bottle the moment and send a six-pack of the timeless brew to my backdoor-scheming, Maine-hating daughter.

ELEVEN

PERRY CREEK

I received a call in the fall of 1972 from an addicted "deck ape" friend I had met during the Bermuda race. For reasons that will soon be painfully clear we will call him "Andy Mac" to protect his professional reputation. Let's call the boat *Chutzpah*. Her owner will be "Bogart"; her skipper "Ahab." Andy Mac was helping Bogart and Ahab put together a crew for a winter campaign in Florida and the Bahamas. Colorado looked real fine for another winter of skiing and harvesting broken bodies, but the chance to do the Southern Ocean Racing Conference (SORC) aboard a new Sparkman & Stevens designed fifty-six-footer was even better. This was a sister ship to the very successful *Yankee Girl,* and great things were expected from her. Once again I should have been careful for the berth I wished for.

Not much is said in the sailing press or literary tomes about personality disorders among crewmembers. Let's face it; getting aboard a boat, where living space is basically the size of the average living room, with a bunch of relative strangers, and taking off for a three week or longer stint of living in each other's armpits is ripe with the possibility of bloodshed. Mix in marginal food, bad weather, air below decks that is breathed a minimum of four times before someone cracks a hatch and wets their neighbor's bunk, and it is a major miracle that the last great book concerning a mutiny was written about a bloke named Bligh. Even the kindest of hearts and warmest of dispositions are likely to turn rank when out of sight of land, especially when you think you are the only one pulling your weight while trying to be Pollyanna to your watch mates. The reality is you are hearing the screeching violins of the movie *Psycho* each time one of them opens his yap. When you add the strong musk of testosterone, which permeates the high octane juice of offshore yacht racing, it is a wonder more crews aren't a few problem children lighter when they finish a two-week sail across an ocean.

"Bogart" was a wily little chain smoker of unfiltered cigarettes who clawed his way out of his father's garment business and into being a wealthy slumlord in Hackensack. A goal on his ladder to success was the New York Yacht Club. By beating them at their own game, he thought he would get noticed and be let in. If that didn't work, he would buy the selection committee's outstanding debts and foreclose. He was paranoid, manic, a misanthropic hater of his fellow man, and thought that the world was divided into two groups: those who had tried to cheat him, and those still waiting their turn. When we met on *Chutzpah,* he squinted out through the acrid blue smoke curling from his ever present lip-locked fag and let my offered hand hang out there between us like a leper's stump.

"Get a haircut," he said.

Captain Ahab was a Boris Karloff look alike. A huge, powerful, genetic mistake of a man with hands the size of catcher's mitts and canine teeth that looked mill-filed purposefully into sharp points. His ears stood out like Dumbo's and rattled loudly like heavy canvas in a stiff breeze. Halitosis was his calling card from twelve feet. He was from New Bedford, as rumor had it, but couldn't go back because of a dead man and the victim's nine surviving brothers. In six months he said three words, but he said them often. His vocabulary was a minute-by-minute barometer of his mood. "Damn" was jolly. "Shit" meant run for cover. "Fuck" was followed by a shove down the companionway or towards the rail. He and Bogart got along like

Latino lovers. It was either flowers and sweet asides, or nuclear explosions. Never a dull moment.

I joined the boat in mid-October at City Island. Two weeks later I was knee deep in cold salt water above the floorboards just off of Cape Hatteras in what was later called simply the "November Storm." Bogart was yelling Mayday into the radio, and Ahab was in his bunk refusing to get up for such a minor nuisance as a sinking. Everyone else on the crew blamed me for making them surely dead. I, obviously, known by all to be truly guilty, tried to blame the Toblerone Company for making such dark sweet chocolate.

Chutzpah should have pulled into Norfolk at the mouth of Chesapeake Bay to wait out the cold front that was roaring its way southeastward from Lake Michigan. We had just made a forced march under sail and diesel from New York in light winds and greasy seas with the remnants of a large, west-setting swell being generated from a mini gale out beyond the Gulf Stream. We were eight souls aboard under the command of "Bogart" and "Ahab." The vessel was bound for Fort Lauderdale and then on to the staging port in Tampa for the first of the S.O.R.C. races to begin in January. The weather that squawked out of the VHF was calling for thirty to forty knots of wind and line squalls. Ahab called it weather for sissies. Bogart smoked at the swivel seat in the navigation station, listening to the report over and over again, and said nothing. The course remained due south. Things were about to break wide open on *Chutzpah*, so let me bring you up to date.

My job in the pecking order was basically to keep quiet and stay out of the way. I was assigned to Andy Mac's port side watch but, as I was sleeping on the sail bags in the farthest reaches of the forepeak, it was hit or miss whether anyone would stumble past other sleeping bodies in the fold down pipe berths to wake me up. Except when the weather got bad, or it was night. So I wandered pretty much on my own and took it all in. This was a "veteran" crew. All had stories to tell, ports to describe, and boat names to drop that impressed the hell out of me. If these guys hadn't seen it, it hadn't happened yet.

The two-ton fly in the ointment was made apparent during the first watch as we waved to a lobsterman off of Montauk Point at the northern edge of Long Island. He held up a mouthwatering red-backed crustacean and shook it under our noses as we glided by. Taunting was just the beginning of our trouble. Coincidently, the trouble was a lot about food. As Thomas Flemming Day, editor of *Yachting Magazine* once surmised: "Bad cooking is responsible for more trouble at sea than all the other things put together." It reinforces the offshore racing sailor's gut-certain understanding of the old saw that those who go to sea for fun would go to hell for a picnic.

"What's to eat?" A watch-mate asked the obvious question from so many rumbling stomachs.

"I loaded the cans under the sink," Bogart said, "go lightly boys, it's got to last."

"Damn shit," said Ahab.

The off-watch went below and found that the larder held a case each of Dinty Moore Beef Stew and Campbell's Chicken with Rice Soup. They were number 10 cans. There was nothing else (I mean nothing else) in the galley except a large screw top jar of Nescafe instant coffee, a single ten-quart aluminum pan, and a perking coffee pot with a broken glass top. The stove was non-pressurized, non-gimbaled alcohol (imagine a can of sterno under a chafing dish at a wedding). Ten plastic dog bowls, all red, an equal number of light tin spoons, and styrofoam white cups, two stacks. Both watches were stunned. Bogart and Ahab grinned.

"You'll go faster to get to port," Bogart said. "You can buy all the jerk-pork and Bar-B-Q you want when we get to paradise."

"Damn shit," Ahab said.

Morale started a slow tumble off a steep cliff at that very moment and didn't stop any time soon. You see, racing crews got paid *nada*, zip, zero. The Young Turks who powered and nurtured the classic racing yachts of this era did so for room and board and the experience. The "room" was usually a slim bunk or pipe berth crammed in the forepeak, and, as in the case of *Chutzpah*, the experiences were often full of unhappy surprises. Board, as in "vittles", was usually the one bright, shining constant. A racing boat galley was full of the five major food groups: salt, fat, starch, sugar, and meat. And stuff to put in your mouth was always available in massive quantities, because at sea you want at least one someone to be awake and eating twenty-four hours a day. This is called keeping a watch.

During our second breakfast of cabin temperature Campbell soup, we were off Cape May, New Jersey. Bogart had left a smoking fag in the full ashtray on the chart table and it had tumbled out onto the chart. I picked it up and snubbed it out. His bunk was empty so I figured he was doing his constitutional in the head. I sat down to look at the burned hole in the chart. It was then I saw the dangling shiny tag of a gold wrapper leaking out from under the lift up top of the chart station. I opened it up. Five, count 'em, five, foot-long skinny bars of Toblerone chocolate were tucked under the folded charts. You know the kind: juicy little pyramids of dark perfection. I shut the tabletop quickly, I felt like young Jack Hawkins seeing Ben Gunn's cave on Treasure Island.

That night I offered to enter the log at the top of each hour. With Bogart snoring barely a few feet away I stole a forbidden pyramid and plopped it in my mouth like a pickpocket at each entry. Nothing is as sweet as stolen fruit. It was so good in fact that, feeling guilty as I licked my teeth between log entries, I finally offered to share my bounty with the rest of my gang just before we turned the watch. They fell on it like starving dogs on a bone. No one asked the question about where it came from.

The next day, under a sky that looked like the bottom of an ashtray we continued our slow push down the low sandy scrub beaches along the coast of Maryland. We were down to a smidgeon of sail but the boat still moved like a freight train. Each of us wrestled with the huge wheel for an hour before crying "Uncle!" All went well until the weather reports were updated and started to raise the anxiety factor even further. Major storm warnings were in effect for the whole listening area. Boats were advised to seek safe shelter. People were cautioned to stay indoors. Downed power lines were expected. It sounded like the end of the world.

After a dinner of tepid stew, we changed the watch. It was just full dark when Bogart, followed by Ahab, came up into the cockpit like a bull terrier with a ferret.

"Who's the asshole what took my chocolate," he said. His voice hissed like a bow wave.

"Damn, shit," said Ahab, adding for a fine point, "Fuck."

He wasn't practicing to be a lawyer, yet, but the first words out of Andy Mac's mouth were, "You got chocolate?"

The look Bogart gave the watch captain underscored the age old reason why sailor's knives at sea had the points broken off so that it became awful hard to successfully put a blunt blade through someone's ribs. Bogart's beagle-brown eyes bore into each of us in turn. No one spoke. I'd be damned if I was going to jump in there. We had all eaten the stuff. The man's glare turned up a notch.

"All HANDS!" Bogart yelled the order in a fish market bellow, and the sleeping half of the crew scrambled out of the companionway to answer the emergency. The owner proceeded to regale us with the litany of abuse that would fall on the thief's head when he got to the bottom of this crime. I think he used the word "heinous", or was it "dastardly"? Anyway, we understood he was not a happy camper.

"I trusted you," he said.

I was afraid he would break down. I had never before seen any crying in ocean racing.

"And I'm not letting anyone off this boat until we get this thing settled," he had to raise his voice to be heard over the gale warnings blaring out incessantly from the VHF.

"There will be a reward for honesty," he said before herding Ahab out of his way with a backhanded dismissal. He trundled below.

"Shit, damn," said Ahab, adding a funereal "Fuck," as he slammed shut the sliding hatch behind him, leaving the off-watch huddled under the dodger in their skivvies. The wind began to moan in the rigging. It wasn't long before the first shivering giggle was heard above the wind. Soon the six of us were heaving with quiet spasms of laughter. A bolt of lightening and a rumble of thunder added to the hysterical guffaws. The scene was "a two-reel, grade-B horror film from the vaults" meets "special effects disaster movie" stuff. We laughed louder. Nuts.

Huddled in the cockpit of *Chutzpah* with the rain slashing a tattoo on the sails, the shivering crew silently rated the benefits of turning me in to the boss for the great chocolate heist. The problem they had was that I had compounded the crime by sharing the loot. No one's mouth was innocent. Besides, Bogart had been more than a bit of a prick, and he had laid down the gauntlet with the total lack of adequate foodstuffs our crew could expect to live on for the next few months.

"Shit, damn, fuck." The chorus of soggy veterans responded to the current situation in different octaves of shivering and creative rants of vitriolic hyperbole. The weather was getting worse by the minute. The boat pounded into some fairly substantial pyramids of cold green water.

"What's the punishment for mutiny these days?" I asked.

A dozen wide eyes cut the blackness and focused on my absurd remark. The fact that none of these big mouths spouted out something derogatory spoke to two things. One, they didn't know the answer, and two, they had already thought about the possibility. The wind was slowly backing around the compass from south through east.

When it lined up with the front rapidly moving down from the north, we were in for it. Norfolk would be back upwind a hundred miles and the Cape Hatteras ship's graveyard downwind to the south, straight into the ugly washing machine of huge Gulf Stream generated waves. The boat lifted off a short steep hillock and crashed into the trough beyond with a teeth-shattering ka-boom. Green water ran along the deck a foot deep hissing all the way back from the bow.

"We got to slow her down," said Andy Mac pushing himself towards the wheel. It sounded like a death sentence.

Spring mornings in Maine come softly, creeping into the closed up cabin, exhibiting a slow, healthy persistence. With nothing to the east except three thousand miles of flat horizon, dawn begins an hour or more before the sun makes a not-so-surprising entrance. I open a slit of my left eye and talk myself out of a snooze-laden roll over. Bravely a foot is placed outside the warm cotton cover to test the wisdom of a morning scouting expedition. I shiver once like a wet spaniel and bounce out of the bunk just seconds before I second-guess a good idea. I swear I am going to prove my daughter Skye wrong, and pretend this is the tropics. Fleece pants, thermal top and the wool sweater from the night before stop my teeth from chattering in just under the three minutes it takes to preheat the stove and light an oil lamp.

A lonely screech made by a tree topping hungry fish hawk is answered by the muted grunt of a gull that floats on the ebb by the open port. Nothing else is heard above the hiss of the pressurized alcohol as I make up the bunk. I pull the snaps of the mosquito netting out of the companionway, fold it carefully and put it in the locker under the radio to starboard.

Armed with a travel mug of caffeine laced hot chocolate, I pull *George* alongside and gingerly lower my butt to the damp seat. The gold letters stand out at eye level in the growing light against *Dog*

Star's dark green hull. Up close, the imperfections in my lettering are obvious. It argues for the truism that wooden boats are best appreciated when observed from a dozen or more yards away.

I look over my shoulder towards the entrance to Perry Creek and begin to move away from the bulk of *Dog Star*, her masts growing taller in my vision as I pull on the oars. There is something arcane and settling about the ketch rig with its two masts and spider-web of stays running to the mastheads. It is purposeful, rugged, and, of course, full of the redundant but necessary wire and gear aloft, adding weight, windage, the liability of tangs, cotter pins, and stressed metal, when compared to a modern sloop. There are no buoyant optimists who sail a ketch rig. I watch my boat fade into the dark background of trees, rock ledges and water as I row east towards the huge boulder outcroppings at the mouth of the creek that will catch the first light.

I find a bit of a gravel bar between the rocks and beach the dinghy. Mug and seat cushion in hand I find a perch and hold my knees in my arms. I love these transition places between land and saltwater. They are never still. The illusions of permanence fade away. It is here you understand the aboriginal certainty that consciousness is a part of everything we can see, feel, touch. The world is a chorus of personal, "I'm here" songs just outside our audible or sympathetic range. A morning like this wallows in wonder. The sun finally comes up in a rush that leaves me asking for more and the tall islands of Merchants Row cast dark shadows across my route, stretching off to the north and east. It is a humbled and happy man who rows back into the creek.

The cell phone jangles while I am busy cleaning up the mess that post-sunrise French Toast makes in a small single sink galley.

"How hard would it be to get the "puppy" down to the Vineyard?" M. said, using the endearment for our boat, and that tone of voice melts my heart into an attention starved, squirming pile of six-week-old kittens.

"Let me think," I said. "Imagine birthing a full grown orangutan without drugs, or, how about, explaining a fart in church during the moments of silence. Make it an Episcopalian church."

M. plays her silent card.

"How about, it would be as hard as me enjoying Rush Limbaugh's wit and honesty?" I noticed my voice is up an octave. I am losing this argument without her saying a word.

"Your daughter would love you."

"She already loves me. I paid for the wedding."

We wait on each other's next silent assault. I am not holding any trump.

"I could come for the weekend."

I get the same goofy grin I've had since first hearing that wonderful sentence in 1967. I am tumbling down a steep slope that ends up in Massachusetts. Ghosts of exciting weekend trysts past with my forever honey are hooting from the cheap seats.

"I'll be in Boston on Friday night," she said and signs off.

I think I managed a hasty goodbye before I turn on the weather radio.

NOAA is an acronym for a computerized voice that spouts weather prognostications twenty-four hours a day, seven days a week. Any boat with a working VHF radio has access to a series of channels that overlap the local weather up and down the coasts of the United States. The anti-human voice that drones on about wind speeds, percentages of rain, and dire warnings of flooding and wind damage is as annoying as a preacher on a soap box and seems just as certain of divine guidance. Like a broken clock that is right twice a day, this federal government service to mariners sometimes gets the current weather more or less close to being on the money once in a while. The forecasts are another matter. I have technique of boiling this verbal avalanche of statistics and advice on a meteorological future down to two simple wide-open categories. The jet stream coming from the Midwest, that eventually makes all the weather on the east coast, is either changing or staying the same for the next twenty-four hours.

After listening to the radio for a few minutes, I conclude that the jet stream is probably stable as the four-day forecast sounds like a skipping record. I pull out the full size chart of the Gulf of Maine that is rolled and stored in with a dozen others above the V berths forward. I must admit I have modern chart books for the entire eastern seaboard lying in flat security under the cushions of the forward bunks. This fact, it has been pointed out, is incongruous with my old school thinking on everything else I do aboard a boat. The spiral bound, tabloid sized, logically formatted books have small reproduced segments of the ocean and land that, if ripped out and laid end to end, would show you how to get from here to there. Let's face it: they are cheaper and easier to use on a cruising boat whose navigation table is either the flat counter over the icebox or my lap in the cockpit.

But this chart, absurdly full sized (almost three foot by four foot) is an old friend I now hold down with my elbows against the two rolling curls. It is Einstein's bending of time, and my heart thumps as I look back into the past. It shows both the coast of Maine to the Canadian Border and the big hook of Cape Cod out to Provincetown. Pencil marks of fixes, times, and course changes are scattered across the blue-green water from a decade or more of trips between these two destinations. A few whale sightings are also logged on the chart, exciting cryptography marking a Right Whale encounter when Skye was six, the pencil etchings mostly off Cape Ann and Stellwagon Bank. They are scribbles of shared shipmate memories that remind me all over again: the most important things in life are not even things.

It is a hundred and forty miles, more or less, and the wind, what there is of it, will be on the nose. At times I will be fifty or more miles out into the North Atlantic and have to treat this overnighter as if it were a blue water voyage. I pull out my spiral bound *Dog Star* Operations Book and flip it open past the maintenance manuals and equipment lists of every piece of equipment on board and find my checklist for going offshore. It always amazes me that I have taken the past trouble to be this anally organized about one small cubbyhole in my life. It gives me hope. I really don't want my stubborn stupidity and growing forgetfulness to be the major cause of my demise.

There are fifty-three items requiring checks. Many are fairly simple like fill water tanks, store food, check spare batteries, rig jack lines, lash dinghy, tie down fenders, stuff anchor chock with a towel and seal with duct tape, etc., etc. Others require outside assistance like filing a float plan with someone who will check up if they don't hear from me in a reasonable length of time. I spend the rest of the morning getting the boat ready for the trip. My stomach tingles. It is a healthy dose of my skeptical nature finding a home for the passage. I have seen enough strangeness over the course of my sailing life to know that any time you sail farther from shore than you can swim things can get complicated in a hurry.

TWELVE

GULF OF MAINE

"You're doing it? Heading south?" Skye said, excitement bubbling in every succulent syllable.

"You're my little pumpkin," I say in my best grouchy voice, "and I live to make you happy."

"Such crock," she said. She snorts when she laughs, sometimes at my expense. "Mom made you do it, right?"

"We don't make each other do things. We're adults," I said and then add, before she gets around to it, "or at least one of us is."

"I'm sorry that all that pressure had to be applied, Dad." Why is it, I wonder, that others sound so gracelessly smug when they get their way and I don't get mine?

"Oh sure, you're so damn smart, Miss-I-Didn't-Know-the-Gun-Was-Loaded." I give her my best W. C. Fields impersonation.

We laugh. We both snort to seal the deal.

"Drive careful," Skye said, "'Fiona' needs her Grandpa who can't remember her real name."

Dog Star and I are ten miles out, almost to Monhegan Island, and the cell phone is about to give up the ghost. The sun will be a fading factor in the visibility arena for another hour. It is clear, cold, the wind out of the east-south-east at a steady fifteen knots. We power along

114

up wind under a single reefed main and full 110% genoa into the building four-foot seas, sending occasional spray splatting against the dodger. The boat seems eager, happy to be finally let out of the barn. The stout oak tiller in my hand tugs with a will of its own as tons of heaving water pass under the keel. I have a feeling the wind will ease when the sun sets so I carry on, more than a bit over-canvassed.

My first log entry is a simple latitude and longitude fix in degrees and whole minutes. Under "remarks" I put: "Departed Tenants Harbor, Bound for Cape Ann; 1740 hours; course 223 degrees Magnetic; no traffic. Monhegan to weather."

A formal ship's log is handled differently by each sailor. I use the leather bound log as a backup running fix, just in case the GPS heads south just when I need to report my position to a boat bearing down on me in the fog. Remarks entered in long hand are usually cursory, sticking to the weather, wind and sea state, or a sighting of another vessel or landmark. I keep it short and sweet, probably because I also write up the day's events each night in a separate journal. I do this journaling in spiral notebooks as a matter of life whether I am sailing or not. It is a lifetime of dribble; scribbles of life's gifts.

The log, however, is a mariner's legal document and is required to be kept up to date aboard each vessel while underway. I am sure it would make some maritime lawyer happy that I am diligent about the practice, but I doubt it will ever be needed. The dozens of logs of years past take up a lot of shelf space in my study. I don't begrudge them the room. Sometimes I thumb through them for tidbits of passages, courses traveled, or timetables for future reference. Occasionally I stumble across a gem of history. Things like: "Woods Hole on the bow. Tristan lashed to car seat/lashed to mizzen mast, lost pacifier down cockpit drain, crying a jag..." A few short words scribbled quickly on the unlined page to bring back that heart-stopping moment of crisis.

Other times the words are more cryptic and spare. "Sunset a floating crimson barge of layer cake." I am not sure why this peculiar, embarrassing, and badly structured word ensemble should ever be remembered, but there it is in its repugnant permanence, set to trigger a gaudy memory should I ever need an over-the-top description of a setting sun. My log books are not great art, only a collage of memories. Terse words and figures are entombed for a downstream heir to decipher.

Darkness begins to erase the horizon. I lash the helm and sneak below to turn on the navigation lights and the red illumination bulb over the chart table. I feel that unmistakable tingle of apprehension as the long night stretches out ahead. It is a bitter tasting deep-rooted joy, this simple act of putting yourself in a situation where anything can and might just happen; this hoping you will have all the right answers at the right time if things start to go wrong. The act of trying to not focus exclusively on the thousand things that could get the boat and you into serious trouble is a sheer force of will. It is the exact opposite state of existence that slouching into an overstuffed couch to watch a rerun of "Friends" invites. Every nerve is on full alert status, knowing from past experience what can, and often does happen. I roll my hips with the tilting floorboards as we mount another big Atlantic roller.

At midnight, the crew of *Chutzpah* was still in a quandary about how to proceed. The off-watch had suffered some tepid verbal abuse from Bogart and Ahab as they crawled into their bunks a few hours before. The boat was barely forereaching in the steep seas and the building wind that continued to clock around the compass towards our date with a real nor'easter. My watch had debated pulling an all out retreat towards the entrance to Newport News at the mouth of Chesapeake Bay and demanding to be put ashore, but the simple fact was that we liked the boat, if not the captain and owner, and the chance of landing another gig on a competitive campaign for the SORC series this year were not great. We began to challenge ourselves about how bad the weather could get. As young men full of starch and vinegar, we had not yet learned the perils of calling Neptune's bluff. As old watermen from the Chesapeake Bay skipjacks would say, "The wind began astirrin' and a sighin' until it woke itself up, and then Cap'n, it began to blow!"

At about 0200 hours on November 16, the world turned upside down. I was fast asleep on a lumpy sail bag in the forepeak, managing to get ten minutes at a time before I was launched airborne by a particularly large wave rolling us to the gunnels, when I felt the boat roll past the horizontal and keep on going. It was pitch dark as my eyes slammed open. Voices were gunshot loud as everyone woke and asked the same question simultaneously in a chorus of groans and shouts. "What the hell is happening?" The boat lay on her side, a wave exploded against the exposed waterline of the hull and it sounded like a canon shot. Water was pouring in a waterfall down the hatch from the cockpit.

Slowly, slower than you can imagine possible, the boat began to struggle back towards an upright position. It didn't pop up as expected with a lead keel of over ten tons applying leverage. The journey back to vertical was a full marathon of effort against wind and water trying to keep the boat flat on her side. Bogart was half out of his quarter-berth and on the radio trying to raise the Coast Guard as I waded past him in the ankle deep water to check the on-deck watch. I was the lucky one who still had my foul weather gear and boots still on, being too lazy to undress for sleeping sometimes works to an advantage.

The scene was worse than I expected. Tumbling white frothing water was everywhere; much of it appeared to tower above the spreaders of the mast that luckily was now out of the water and still standing upright. The three huddled shapes on deck were wide-eyed and sopping wet with their tethers attached in a spaghetti tangle to the binnacle that held the wheel and compass. The mainsail was flogging like thunder, jerking the main sheet like a bucking bronco, and the lazy jib sheet was flying off to leeward like a writhing snake. All six fists of the on-watch were gripping the wheel to keep themselves from being thrown about the cockpit. They were trying to get the boat moving again and run off downwind to gain some measure of control.

In a moment a couple more bodies were pushing me out into the maelstrom. We took the screamed directions from the on-watch captain and inched our way forward along the gunnels on our hands and knees to get down the jib and mainsail. At one point I remember sitting with the better part of the jib in my lap on the foredeck when we plunged down two flights into a solid wave, and when the un-welcomed wet visitor came aboard I was completely underwater. It was thirty minutes of heart in your throat effort, but soon the boat was stripped of canvas and running off like a drunk downwind with the swells dancing like pyramids and the curling storm-driven waves licking over our starboard quarter. The world calmed down from terminal chaos to white knuckle, and we all huddled in the cockpit like marines who had just stormed an enemy outpost.

As lights came on below decks, I looked back down into the shambles of the cabin. Everything from the port side was piled in the upper and lower berths off to starboard: bodies, rain gear, books, spare clothes, and shredded soggy charts. Water sloshed above the floorboards in curling waves as the boat lurched. I caught Andy Mac's eyes, gave him a thumbs up. He flashed a weak-kneed grin at all the guys in the cockpit, and we couldn't help but crack up in a howl of adrenalin-spawned laughter. The giggles would not go away as the boat began to wobble again, and she settled headfirst into a wave that stopped us dead and lurched everything back the way it had come. We laughed louder as Ahab, still prone in the settee, began his litany of four letter words while protecting his head from flying debris. Bogart was "maydaying" his head off into a microphone that wouldn't squawk back. The owner mistook our laughter for insult, gazed up and gave me a look that could best be described as deadly. We laughed louder. The maydays finally stopped when his voice was nothing more than a croak, and he lit a Camel.

We bailed. We stowed. We ran out to sea for thirty-six hours under a storm stay'sil. We finally pulled into Beaufort, North Carolina three days later. Aside from two bent stanchions, a new radio antenna, and a torn genoa, we came away from the knockdown with only our confidence permanently broken. It wasn't paradise, but those cheeseburgers tasted great. When we left port again the crew had stowed enough food in our private lockers to keep us happy. Ahab and Bogart were the only ones to eat the chicken noodle and the stew from here on out. The crime of the missing Toblerone was never solved. I wonder if the statute of limitations in international waters has run its course?

Tonight, *Dog Star* is giving me a similar but less pressing message as the sun fades behind the hazy tips of the White Mountains in New Hampshire, a hundred miles inland. Shaking myself from the past, I pause to run through the possible options and procedures before letting go of the tiller. Sailing at night and sailing offshore by yourself are two situations that put you outside the box of a normal summer cruise in your home waters. Each of these factors increases the risk to both you and your boat by a pretty sizeable margin. You move slowly and engage the brain before becoming ambulatory. The attributes of patience, forethought, vigilance, and caution are in greater demand then ever. One wrong move and you're dining with Davy Jones, sub-letting in his locker for all eternity.

The crystal clear night sky and the lack of west in the wind is a pretty good indicator that the weather pattern is fairly stable. It appears to be a rare gift for the westbound sailor in Maine. The rarity is called a "clear, dry 'easter." Two days after a northerly has passed overhead anything can happen. No rain in the first thirty-six hours usually means that a slow developing low will gradually work its way up from the southwest and bring back the humidity and warm air slowly over the next few days. Tonight, I might just get lucky and have the true south wind hold in the double digits until dawn when the sun will crank up the easterly sea breezes again. With this in mind I decide to roll-up about half of the genoa and come off the wind another ten degrees to starboard and close the coast. If all goes well I will be just a few miles off the Isles of Shoals near Portsmouth by dawn and can lay a good course with the building onshore breeze for Cape Ann and the twin towers of Thatcher's Light.

The coast of Maine from Penobscot Bay to Portland is a transition zone of changing weather patterns. The land mass forms a sharp dogleg, called the Bigelow Bight, which turns from north-south to east-west. Although I have made this trip dozens of times, I never take it for granted; tonight is no exception as I weigh all the observed data and factor in my own healthy dose of paranoia. The Gulf of Maine can be vexing in the extreme. Just when you think you have it all figured out, the wind will shift, build to an uncomfortable shriek, the clouds and fog will lower the boom, and solid, cold rain will wash away any feeling of security. Make no doubt that this is a passage not to be taken lightly.

With a belly full of macaroni and cheese and a stainless mug of java in my hand, I settle in for the duration. On this point of sail I can lash the tiller with a few rubber restraints of surgical tubing to keep her from rounding up into the wind like a wind vane, ease the jib sheet to let the bow fall off a bit, and she will sail herself until a wave smacks her around and upsets the equilibrium. We are making four and a half knots, the wind stays steady. I exhale and enjoy the moment of harmony.

The bright loom of Portland is almost abeam to starboard. Besides that ball of wasted energy, the land is dark below the horizon and no ship lights are visible from the deck. I think of Captain John Smith and his *The Description of New England* that brought the entire population of the British Isles along in his passion for the New World. I have a framed copy of his magnificent chart drawn in 1614 where "The most remarkable parts thus named by the high and mighty Prince

Charles, Prince of Great Britain" on the wall above my desk. He was Governor of Virginia when he sailed up the coast and coincidentally right along my route tonight from the Isle of Shoals to Monhegan. By 1497, when John Cabot discovered Newfoundland, the British had squandered a big start in settling the New World and fallen far behind France, Portugal, and Spain in exploiting the rich fishing banks off this rugged coast. It was Smith's lyric and effusive descriptions and remarkable drawings of the coast from Cape James (Cape Cod) to Pembrock's (Penobscot) Bay that finally got the English off their duffs and *en route* to New England.

Smith must have been a heck of a guy. An adventurer and soldier from his early teens, he was once wounded during a battle in Transylvania and captured by a Turk who gave him as a slave to his sweetheart in Istanbul. She fell in love with Smith and sent him to her brother in the royal court for training in the affairs of the country in order to keep Smith happy and her fiancé in the dark. I don't think court life appealed to the young adventurer. Smith murdered the brother and escaped to England by an epic overland journey through Poland and Russia in the early 1600s to rejoin his regiment. After he grew tired of fighting everyone in Europe, he hooked up with the Virginia Colony expedition and, while fighting off the Indians at Jamestown, he was again captured and narrowly saved by the love of the chief's daughter, Pocahontas. Whatever this swashbuckler had going for him, if you could bottle, it you'd be rich as Midas.

THIRTEEN

ISLES OF SHOALS

Stay dry. Stay warm. Stay awake. These are the three legs of the
stool to support good watch keeping aboard a sailboat at sea. The
first two directives have gotten a whole lot better since the days of
rubberized canvas overcoats, those heavy, stiff rubber suits sporting
the big double "H" logo on the twenty-dollar price tag that I first used
to venture offshore. Any activity over the aerobic level of sleeping
created as much liquid condensation inside the foul weather gear
as ever tried to enter from the outside. It was much like wearing a
steam room. The rain coats came in two colors: Johnny Cash Black
and sissy-bright Tweety Bird yellow. You can probably guess which
choice I made.

Today the miracle of breathable watertight fabrics has indeed
changed the comfort level of sailors. The best of the lot are cocoons
of stylish comfort and will keep out everything but a determined
kamikaze flying fish. The high-end models come with a guarantee
that you will be a competent offshore sailor just by wearing them.
The price tag for these European imports is just short of a college
education, but yes, at certain milestone moments of midnight
shivering I do think they might be worth it. I'll let you know if I ever
hit the lottery.

On *Dog Star* I carry two complete sets of raincoats and pants.
The primary criterion is that each piece costs fewer than three figures

and that they are not Tweety Bird yellow. The more reflective tape on the shoulders, front and back, and soft pile lining around the collar the better. Velcro at the cuffs is dandy and a fold-away-hood a must. I buy them a size bigger than I normally wear, extra large, because what goes underneath is every bit as important. Layering is a hard-won lesson from sitting in slow moving chairlifts during blizzards and hibernating in cold patrol shacks much of my young life. Each piece is a part of the whole, and the sum of the parts, woven with purpose, is a toasty heaven.

Tonight, I sit in the cockpit at the helm with a brand new set of expedition weight long underwear, two pairs of socks (one wicking, one wool), my pant bibs, high rubber boots, a pile vest, a rain jacket, and a warm wool headband. I am comfy. The sky is clear. The ambient temperature is in the high forties. The apparent wind is a steady fifteen and straight off the port beam from the south-southeast. Wind driven waves ride the normal Atlantic swell that runs unobstructed from the coast of Portugal. *Dog Star* rolls heavily, burying her gunnels from time to time, and the water gurgles out the limber holes. The dark night is alive with sounds and motion.

I begin the rituals of a long night watch. The very first exercise is to run through every terror filled close call from my past, so I know in blood curdling three-dimensional panoramic detail what can happen if I let down my guard. I've had more than a few self-inflicted close calls, so this takes the better part of an hour. I beat myself up a little for every mistake that ever happened when I was in charge of a boat at night. A bruised ego is the banked fire of the mental games it will take to keep my eyes open for the next twelve hours. By the time I am done with my self-flagellation I am hungry.

I try to get the boat balanced with the cat-o-nine-tails surgical tubing and rope lead contraption I use to hold the tiller slightly to weather. The trick is to keep the rudder slightly off kilter, tugging against the natural tendency of the boat to seek the path of least resistance and pivot like a wind vane. With patience I can find just the right amount of tension, three of the skinny tubes or four, sometimes five, for the wind and wave conditions that will keep the old girl from rounding up. I loose the jib sheet until a nice billowing bulge is evident along the luff of the sail. I ease the main sheet a couple of feet and let the traveler run to its stops down to leeward. The boat slows a half a knot, but her tendency to weathervane is lessened somewhat. I duck below to light the stove. Of course, all hell breaks loose before I can get back on deck with the bow slowly pointing directly into the wind and waves; everything shakes, rattles and cracks like a hurricane. I think of Henry David Thoreau's words: "The sail, the play of its pulse so like our own lives: so thin and yet so full of life, so noiseless when it labors hardest, so noisy and impatient when least effective." I haul the stalled ketch back down onto the wind and she leaps ahead.

I admonish myself once again for being such a pig-headed purist and not fitting a proper electronic self-steering arrangement. I experiment patiently with the "Rube Goldberg" rig. Wind and waves on the beam are the hardest for this exercise. Finally, I give up and come up into the wind 20 degrees and she settles into a groove, slicing through the rollers rather than being rolled on her beam ends by them. We will move a bit offshore, but I should be able to heat up a bowl of soup.

From the companionway, with a spoon in hand, I watch the night thicken off the stern. Stars twinkle, even along the horizon; the visibility is stellar. I try to stifle a smile and behave like the curmudgeon I sound like half the time. It doesn't work. I am looking forward to seeing M. and doing exactly what my daughter wants, in spite of myself. Tristan crosses my mind as my knees flex to a slopping sea. Knowing he is out here somewhere in the North Atlantic on his own crossing makes me sappy happy. I think of Sally Field's teary debacle at the Academy Awards: "You like me, you really like me!" Isn't it a wonder how far we will go to justify our life's obsessions by attributing others' actions to our own influence? My son probably just wanted to get out of the house and a chance to flex his young-adult wings for the last half of his senior year and this was the only option that was offered. It is likely he is a reluctant sailor at best, trained against his will. Is that possible? What is the truth?

I promised I would tell you the secret of staying awake on long night watches, and there it is. To ward off the sleepies, carry on stupid, inane, pointless debates with yourself over issues that no one else could possibly care about and that the answer, if you ever found it, would not be worth a farthing anyway. Sprinkle this discourse with self-deprecating humor whenever an opening presents itself. If all else fails, spend some time making up a speech for receiving the highest award you aspire to in this life; to be given to you by all those beautiful people that you know in your heart hate your guts and think you are the world's biggest underachieving loser.

At false dawn, the trickle of light through a stratum of low clouds reveals the gray whaleback rocks of the Isles of Shoals a mile or so off our port bow. My eyes are scratchy and sore, my mind deflated by too much point, counterpoint. The wind has lightened with the sun, and we are ghosting along under full sail at about three knots. I rub my eyes for the tenth time, deciding a quick nap would not be out of order. From past experience I know that although anchoring

in Gosport harbor is deep and tentative over a grass strewn bottom, a few mooring balls are usually empty either in the lee of Appledore, or off the man-made breakwater between Smuttynose and Cedar Islands. Although this is a common port of call for the yachting fraternity of Kittery and Portsmouth, only six miles offshore, I think we will be lucky enough to find room, especially this early in the season. Hanging to one of these public moorings for a few hours of shut-eye makes an enormous amount of sense.

Avoiding the low-lying rocks off Duck Island, I lay a course for red nun "2" marking the northeastern point of Appledore. Nudging the tiller with my thigh to keep on line, I strike the mizzen halyard and drop the sail into the cockpit. A quick roll along the boom, a few loosely knotted sail ties and the mess is somewhat organized. I clear the buoy by a few yards and begin to see emerging from the shadows of the dark western shore the white buildings of the Shoals Marine Laboratory, a joint educational facility of Cornell and the University of New Hampshire. There appears to be no one in residence on the four available moorings they offer to visitors, and I begin preparations to pick one up, under sail. It seems such a violation of the long silent night to disturb the morning peace with a growl from the engine.

As we close with the shore I leave the jib and main up and drawing full. Even on these low lying islands the possibility of a drop in the wind when you put an island in the way mandates keeping the tools for forward momentum in place until stopping is what you want. *Dog Star* is between medium and heavy displacement, favoring the chunky end, and will hold her way across calm water for a fair distance. It is this attribute that I rely on when performing maneuvers under sail alone. Keeping the wind on my beam, I make for a point about fifty yards to leeward of the first buoy in line along the shore. I pull a short ten-foot section of dock line from the locker and stroll forward to place it and the long handled boathook at the bow. One end of the line is made fast to the large anchor bollard with a bowline knot and then led down through the anchor chock and back aboard over the life lines.

With a hundred yards to go to my turning point I roll in the jib and the bow wave descends from a chuckle to a murmur. The main continues to draw well as I ponder the intricate relationship of my seven tons of mass, speed, momentum and factor in a series of tactical steps for arriving at a two-foot diameter destination without the aid of brakes. I slowly ease the main sheet to slow down a bit. She glides across the dark water with little effort. I make my turn when I am directly downwind of the ball. Throwing off the main sheet from the cleat, I pull through the blocks a half-dozen feet of slack so that the boom will be able to roam freely as we head directly into the wind. It is only with a very intimate knowledge of the boat, gained from many trials, and numerous errors, that you can judge to within a dozen or so yards the amount of time, given a variety of wind and wave conditions, when forward momentum will leave your boat and you will coast to a dead stop. It is always best, just like a putt in golf, to aim to stop just past the mark rather than right at it.

With the main sail fluttering in the light breeze, I make my way forward at the last possible moment to move without hurrying. The ball is miraculously within the reach of the boathook and I snag the mooring pennant. Hauling it up to life line level, I find the heavier loop attached to the light retrieval line, reeve my short piece of rope through the eye, and quickly drop my short rope back down and up through the anchor chock before securing the end to the bollard on top of the bowline with a few overhand loops. The boat tugs firmly against the ball, and I turn and let go the main halyard, tugging the sail down in a rush into its lazyjacks. After securing the sheet to keep the boom steady, I roughly flake the main and lash it home with a few sail ties.

One last check of the mooring line led through the chock for chafe and I am heading below to lay my head down on the pillow for forty, make it fifty, winks.

The nine little jewels that comprise the Isles of Shoals make up in juicy history for what they lack in stature, space, or vegetation. This is the home of John Smith's prophetic visions of wealth and grandeur that prompted the first English settlements in the New World. The islands also boast legends of Blackbeard's treasure, and even an axe murder or two. It has been the residence of poets, ex-presidents, scoundrels, and Godless men banished from the Pilgrim enclaves at Plymouth. It has a goodly share of colorful ghosts.

John Smith waxed so eloquently about these islands he even named them the "Remarkablest Isles." His reports claimed that two-dozen men were able to hook 60,000 fish in a month. The old adage of being "hoisted on your own petard" might be true here, for when the time came for the crown to reward Smith for all his efforts in the New World, he was granted these little shrubby islands as payment in full for his lifetime of effort. John never came back to these barren rocks to start his life in paradise.

Legend has it that the dour Pilgrims of the Plymouth Plantation were starving in the winter of 1621. They set out in boats to find food and stumbled into the Isles of Shoals where the resident fishermen fed and housed them. Of course, the staunch morals were no match for the rough and tumble "Shoalers," so they fled back to their settlement at the first opportunity lest they be infected.

It was to these lawless islands that the Pilgrims banished Thomas Morton of Merrymount for the crime of erecting a Maypole. It was also alleged Morton was guilty of corrupting the Indians by offering fair competition in the form of higher prices for the furs the colonists bought and then supplied to the European markets, and for tainting the Kingdom of Heaven in the Wilderness by dancing, singing, and throwing wild beer parties for the heathens.

Morton must have been one of our country's first political activists, and a satirist as well, having fun with the Puritans by calling their diminutive chief soldier, Miles Standish, "Captain Shrimpe," and pompous John Endicott, "Captain Littleworth." Morton, in his voluminous writings sent back to England, respected, defended, and admired the native Algonquin and their Earth-friendly and egalitarian form of government. It is a simple fact our nation would have been better served if the Merrymount Colony had survived and the rigid Puritan Roundheads had starved. Finally the Calvinists had suffered enough and sent Morton home to England in chains as the "Pagan Pilgrim." In retrospect Morton's treatment by our founding fathers was the first blatant transgression of free speech and human rights that led directly to our country's present state of worldwide compassion, tolerance, respect for other cultures. Where is our Merrymount sense of fair play?

In 1720 Edward Teach, better known as Blackbeard, brought his fifteenth and last wife to Smuttynose on their honeymoon. The noted pirate was on the run from the British fleet, but he took the time to build his wife a house on the island, and he left when the admiralty finally caught his scent. His wife remained on the shoals for the rest of her life. Many claim she was guarding the pirate's treasure that was buried somewhere nearby. Her lonely figure is still seen from time to time standing atop the rocky southeastern corner of Smuttynose on the black smudge of seaweed that looks like a nose against the granite cheeks that gave the island its name.

If ghosts are your thing, you can't toss a wet mackerel on these islands without hitting one. On March 6, 1873, three women tucked themselves down to sleep in a fishing cottage on Smuttynose to spend their first night ever, alone. Their men folk were on the mainland ten miles away awaiting a train of bait fish from Boston. By morning two of the young Norwegian fishwives had been hacked to death by an axe murderer. The third had scrambled free and hid outside among the rocks clutching her dog Ringe for warmth to escape the bloody killer. A long, bitterly cold night hiding from a bellowing lunatic allowed Maren Hontvet to escape the same fate as her sister and sister-in-law, and she was eventually able to bring the man believed responsible to justice. A side story in Anita Shreve's recent best-selling novel The Weight of Water is based on the circumstances of the murders. Louis Wagner was hanged for the crime in 1875, but 125 years later the doubts about his guilt are still a matter of debate for the mavens of fiendish history. Was it one of the surviving women? The grieving husband, who philandered his way into being a suspect? Perhaps it was a gang of thieves from the foreign workers at the nearby hotel construction site on Appledore? A passing maniac on a sail boat? The ghostly pirate with a black beard said to roam these parts?

The sun is high in the sky when I venture back on deck. Coffee perks and I rustle up a real he-man's breakfast of eggs, bacon, and muffins. Sitting in the cockpit, I watch the comings and goings at the Marine Lab. Small groups of young people scurry this way and that in the bright sunlight, their images flashing off the tall glass windows. Seagulls ride the easy glide with frozen wings. The wind has remained light and still carries from the east. I know I should not be wasting time, but I view my lethargy as reward for a long cold night. By the time everything is put away, it is noon and I had better get a shake on to make Cape Ann and the Annisquam River by dinnertime.

FOURTEEN

THE ANNISQUAM RIVER

I sail off the Marine Lab's buoy by hauling the main up its tracks; a loose main sheet allows the sail to flap ineffectively like a wind vane. Strolling forward, I let go the short line at the bow by pulling the free end back through the loop on the mooring. The boat backs down as the wind exerts its strength. I steer as we fall backwards with the tiller hard over to starboard, leading the stern away from the direction we want the bow to go. *Dog Star* slowly, but with determination, falls off to starboard as I haul in the sheet; the sail fills with a will as we begin to make way. The restraining line on the furling gear is let free to run, and the jib comes rolling out with a bang to be sheeted home. Within another minute the mizzen is cranked up the mast and drawing. The whole event encompasses just about the time it would take me to start and warm up the diesel. I get a hearty wave from a group of three students sitting on the dock with their legs dangling out over the water. I note with interest that the tide is almost low by the dark water coloration on the dock's pilings. I remind myself that to enter the Annisquam River and the Blynmann Canal we must play the tide card at the proper moment or face a push against a sizeable current.

With the boat settled in to a close reach, I duck below for my copy of *Eldridge Tide and Pilot Book* that is always ready at hand when sailing in these waters. Don't leave port without it. First published in 1875, the information contained inside was first gleaned from Captain George W. Eldridge's own observations of the time of tidal fluctuations along the coast of Cape Cod, Buzzards Bay, and Vineyard Sound. I conjure a mental image of the gentleman depicted inside the cover page in his worsted wool three piece suit and bowler sitting at the water's edge with a notebook and pencil waiting patiently for the tide to turn. I open the 131st annual edition of this remarkable publication and thumb through to the highs and lows of Boston Harbor. I am happy to see that the tide is not yet dead low, and the high mark is scheduled for just after dark. I turn to the pages that list all the ports along the coast of Massachusetts and find the Annisquam River. Coincidentally the extrapolation tables list the high water time as the exact same as Boston, and the height schedule will be 8.8 feet. Now I can relax and enjoy the sail, knowing I will be able to carry a fair incoming tide into and beyond the shallows at the very tight canal entrance.

The north shore of Massachusetts is one long beach with high sand dunes all the way from the Maine/New Hampshire border down to Gloucester. As we leave the Isles of Shoals behind, the wind begins to swing more to the south, drawn by the warm sun over land, and I harden up the sails to compensate. The waves are small and not well formed so *Dog Star* lifts her skirts and makes the miles. Hard on the wind, *Dog Star* virtually sails herself and my hand only strays to the unrestrained tiller when a wave rolls us a bit more than normal. The afternoon unfolds in haze as Cape Ann slowly grows along the horizon. In the distance a swirl of flying gulls pinpoints the location of a Gloucester fishing boat, hull mostly down and out of view, making way around the twin light towers of Thatcher Island. I set a course for nun "4" well outbound of the creeping shoal that marks the inner passage. The wind is getting stronger and I steer for the lee shore that continues to keep the swells low and manageable. This is a gentleman's beat to windward, unlike the jarring terror of some memorable homogenizing bashes in the past. A skinny, twenty-something version of myself once spent six weeks and six separate races with the wind never moving aft of a close reach. I found out fast why there are very few gentlemen after the first few days in an offshore ocean race.

The Southern Ocean Racing Conference (S.O.R.C.) traces its beginning back to the inaugural St. Petersburg to Havana, Cuba, race started by George "Gidge" Gandy in 1930. The concept was born in a bar in Havana, and the exotic destination of this race was its biggest draw. In the 1930's Havana gave nothing away to Paris in the pleasure, decadence, and lascivious nature of it casinos and waterfront nightclubs. Yachts and their crews raced fast and stayed long, before tiring of recounting every sea story to anyone who would listen. In 1934, another race, the Miami to Nassau excursion, was the brainchild of Art Bosworth of the Miami yachting fraternity and Sir Roland Symonette of the Nassau Yacht Club. Now the yachts from the elite clubs up north, stuck in the throes of a New England winter, had a couple of good reasons to head south, and many of them did, returning year after year.

By 1960 Castro had shut down the casinos and the luxury hotels. The powers that be turned their backs on the new communist regime. It was the end of an era in American ocean racing, but the St. Petersburg Club stepped up again. After a few trial balloons on the direction and course, they sponsored what was to become one of the toughest challenges for modern ocean racers, and for a while even surpassed the Newport-Bermuda Race in prestige. The St. Petersburg to Fort Lauderdale race is a three-ring circus that includes the rough and tumble Tampa Bay, the churning shallow waters of the Gulf of Mexico and finally a rounding of the "Cape Horn of Florida", Key West, and the ride on the unpredictable and dangerous Gulf Stream north to the finish.

In the late sixties the modern format of a six race series had been established, and anyone who was anyone in the small but growing world of yacht racing showed up to test their boats and crews. The old yachtsmen of the last century made of blue blood captains, wooden mega-yachts, with their old Yale and Harvard friends as crew, were suddenly facing the latest technology and youngest blood. It was a time of high energy and a quick, brutal changing of the guard. In 1965 a yacht named *Scylla* fumbled around the course, using as its primary navigation aid the stern lamps of all the boats in front of it. At the helm was a 25-year-old one-design sailor who had entered the Circuit as a joke among his friends. With a fluke of light winds and a fickle current in the Lipton Cup Race, he managed a second place, and that first piece of silver prompted a manic desire to get serious about big boats. The young skipper's name was Ted Turner, and by the time I showed up in Florida in the winter of 1971 he had turned the world's offshore racing scene on its ear.

I had left the lads of *"Chutzpah"* at the dock in West Palm Beach. I could only take so much of a good thing. My relationship with Bogart and Ahab had gone from worse to murderous. Before any blood was let, notably my own, I thought it was best to pack my duffle. It was my first time in Florida, and with over a hundred and fifty boats expected to take part in this year's S.O.R.C., I figured I could find someone who needed an extra hand. So I hitchhiked across the state to St. Petersburg and began to roam the docks at the yacht club as the fleet continued to arrive and make ready for the Venice around the buoys, and the St. Pete to Fort Lauderdale runs. *Ondine, Kialoa, Windward Passage, Bay Bea, Robin, Scaramouche, Baccara, Running Tide, Yankee Girl*, and *Dora* were lined up like stuffed shirt gold-platers on display. The most watched boat was *American Eagle*, Ted Turner's converted twelve meter, which had battled it out with the record setting *Windward Passage* for line honors the previous year. Another epic duel was anticipated. "The Bird", as she was known by the unwashed populace of testosterone addicted crews on the boats, got more dockside gawkers than all the rest combined.

Smiling, glad handing, trying to sound charming, earnest, knowledgeable, and buying a lot of beers at the club bar for people

I wanted to get to know all resulted in three days of uncomfortably and illegally sleeping under a tarp on a tired six meter on the hard in the yacht club parking lot. But, discouragement was for lesser men in boy's clothing. When my ship finally did come in, I thanked God for all of the unanswered prayers of the days past. That afternoon I saw her approaching the marina, and thought I had never seen anything so sparkling new and ready to race. Even at this point in my life I was a sucker for long legs and a pretty face. *Sorcery* was owned by Jim Baldwin, from "Down-Under," and was the largest production glass fiber boat built to date. Her black 61 ft. hull gleamed, the deck was flush with purpose, and the sparkling array of stainless gear, two large deck mounted coffee grinders, and huge winches made her look like some alien space ship that had landed from Mars. I elbowed my way down the docks and grabbed her lines as she came alongside. This boat looked like it was going sixty when tied to the dock.

L. Francis Herreshoff, known for a half century for his yacht designs and innovations in hardware, was a sailor who felt boats should be sailed by gentlemen and their well bred friends and offspring, with only the occasional hired hand to keep order and provide the odd piece of sound judgment in a crisis. Concerning the racing scene in the latter half of the twentieth century he wrote: "Modern racing is composed of gigolo yacht jockeys; that is, they are kept by the owner to sail for him." I wanted to be a "gigolo yacht jockey" in the worst way, and *Sorcery* was the object of my desire.

Before relating the chicanery that resulted in a berth aboard this dream boat, I think we should first talk a bit about boat names. I've been throwing a few of them around. The historically proven transom logos on those floating extensions of sailing's karmic goodness, which I have listed above, are classic, strong, and colorful. They just fit. The names are worthy of the sleek boats they call to mind. Let's face it; a bad boat name is a truly heinous crime against humanity. When walking around a marina, and I find a particularly "cute" or "double meaning" name such as *Foamy Sea, Party Girl, Sweet Buns, Lone Lover,* or *Bermuda Schwartz,* I can only hear Kurtz up that jungle river whispering to his heart of darkness, "The horror, the horror."

Boat names are a reflection of who we are and why we go to sea on our fragile cockles. There is a score of centuries behind us where valiant ships and brave sailors talked with reverence about their sailing homes, work platforms, and battlefields. Can you imagine Nelson triumphing at Trafalgar on a boat named *Play Station, Babes Galore* or *Happy Hooker*? Or old Josh Slocum circumnavigating alone on a boat named *The Nineteenth Hole*? Okay, okay, so I once raced on a boat named *Candy Stripper,* but it didn't make her fast on the go; as a matter of fact I did everything I could to hug the last place in the fleet, like a guy with huge hole in the seat of his pants, and I got off her as soon as I could jump for the dock.

Let me give you a few basic rules that might help in the naming of the boat ritual.

First and foremost don't ever be afraid to change the name of a boat. Don't think you have to live with someone else's linguistic

problem. The idea that getting rid of a lame moniker somehow brings about bad luck is a deep bilge full of hogwash. There are enough real live superstitions with dire consequences to pay attention to, like whistling a Broadway show tune aboard a ship at sea, without adding this bogus one to the menu. In fact, a respected old salt once gave me a sure fire voodoo rite to hold off the old name's evil spirits. When renaming your boat, on your maiden voyage, you take the old name of the boat written on a page of your log, rip it out, rip it up, and throw it over the stern. Then back up over the soggy remnants of the name. Enter a new page in the log with the new moniker and proceed ahead about your business, simple enough and guaranteed to work. My old friend's recipe also had a dead, headless chicken, a quart bottle of one-hundred-proof Everclear, and a machete involved, but I don't think those parts are really necessary.

Second rule is to never, ever, combine the letters of your whole family into some *TrisMaBoSkye* conflagration. It looks too much like the back of a basketball jersey for some big-footed galoot playing for the Kabbalakurdistani National Team. It has no class, no character, and is a serious quantitative statement on the quality of your imagination.

Third, never make a phonetic sounding "C" become a three letter word meaning a body of salt water with restricted access to an ocean. *SEAduction, SEAducer, SEArenity, SEAlestial, SEAsation,* and *SEAlebrity* are examples of a growing sickness that in my book should be illegal. The punishment for an owner who would do this to the transom of a perfectly innocent boat would be a forced name change on their driver's license, credit cards and passport to: Dum Sit, Id E. Yacht, or Mr. Ace Hole, Esquire.

Next, please don't try to be cute with something that lets us all know what you do for a living or how you made the tons of money you are floating around on. *Margin Call, Dealer Ship, Sold Short, Nip'n Tuck, Big Settlement, Heart Cutter, Soft Wear, Floss Free* and *Beef Jerky Jock* etched in gold leaf on the transom of a cobalt blue Hinckley Picnic Boat is not adding delight to another boater's day. Just when we should be enjoying the wind, waves and water we find ourselves trying to imagine a large enough self-esteem problem that would invite this sort of stupid personal promotion and somehow make it seem right. Maybe there's a tax loophole the rest of us don't know about?

Lastly, do not add Roman Numerals to a grand old name to try and make us believe that you and your family have had boats of this ancestral coinage since you were weaned from a silver cup won at Cowes during Queen Vic's Grand Jubilee. There are lots of us who can't translate the "V"s and "L"s and if you really want to impress us, don't make us feel stupid first.

Try and find a name that smacks of reality, actually means something, and one you don't mind saying three times fast just before you shout "mayday." Some of the best names I know for boats are of actual places that mean something to generations of sailors. *Finisterre, Boston Light, Flemish Cap, Breton Reef, Ithaka, Stornoway, Providence*, and hundreds of other real places whose names celebrate the ties between land and water. Other acceptable lineages are action nouns that mean something to the sailing fraternity like *Enterprise, Intrepid, Indiscretion, Tenacious, Moxie, Indefatigable, Obsession, Interloper,* and other reasonably acceptable personality disorders. Star names (celestial, not *paparazzi* bait) work sometimes, also constellations. Signs of the Astrological universe are often marginally acceptable. A schooner should always be a person's real name, have a middle initial and contain at least three a's. Don't ask; it's just the rules.

Of course, *Dog Star* is already taken, so don't go there. I'm Sirius, now!

The water is breaking lightly along the sand bar extending out from the entrance to the Annisquam River. The bright, light sand is easy to see against the dark green channel. The late afternoon is still spectacularly clear, and the sun maintains a bit of warm zing. The sail over from the Isles of Shoals has been one to remember. The entire event a perfect "10." I quickly roll in the jib and take down the mizzen and start the engine just outside of the red "4" nun. The main should still be able to draw when I weave my way inland so I leave it up as a safety option in case my internal combustion contraption suddenly develops the hiccups.

This waterway, part river and part canal, is the reason Cape Ann is really an island. The tide runs in from Gloucester Harbor and in from the entrance we are negotiating right now, meeting somewhere in the middle before reversing its course and spilling out again. The "Other Cape" as it is known by centuries of Bostonians is a mass of granite, moors, and salt marshes that stands out from the coast of Massachusetts like a solitary finger pointing east. It is the single oldest fishing port on the North American continent, dating back to 1623. In 1713 the first schooner was launched from this shore and the remarkable ability of these unique vessels quickly made New England, and Gloucester in particular, a world force in the fishing industry.

"Gloucestermen" described a new standard of tough single-minded sailors who earned their hard fought living from the sea. A man whose courage, seamanship, and determination was a poster child for this new breed was named Howard Blackburn. In 1883, although originally from Nova Scotia, Blackburn was launched from the deck of his Gloucester schooner, the *Grace L. Fears,* in a 16 foot long, two man dory to set a mile of long hooked trawl. On the Burgeo Bank, only 60 miles south of Newfoundland, deadly storms spring up in a hurry, especially in January. This particular storm came with a fury described by the schooner captain as "hellish," and although the two dorymen could see the schooner and rowed against the wind, snow, and waves knowing their lives depended on it, they were unable to make the ship before night fell. In the morning after a cruel overnight survival ordeal in the open boat, the ship was nowhere to be seen.

The veteran fishermen knew their options were slim and getting slimmer. Although half frozen, soaking wet and battling hypothermia, they struck out for the coast of Newfoundland 60 miles to the north. With no water, no food, and only the clothes they had on their back, the two rowed day and night across the worst of the storm. On the third day of the journey Blackburn's dory mate died. The survivor rowed on. When his hands lost all feeling, he let them freeze as claws to the oars so he could continue to pull. Five days after being separated from the schooner, the dory finally washed up at the settlement of Little River on the Newfoundland coast. Following months of recovery, Blackburn returned to Gloucester where his legend as "The Iron Man of the North Atlantic" became his bread and butter. Although he had lost all his fingers and most of his toes, the local merchants helped set him up in business as a tavern owner. His establishment is a long standing local tradition and still serves the less adventurous.

Not one to rest on his butt, Blackburn couldn't fade into obscurity and so returned to the sea. He sailed a schooner to the Klondike in search of gold, weathering a hurricane in the North Atlantic and massive waterspouts in the Pacific off Peru. Failing to find a pot of the yellow stuff, he attended a lecture by Joshua Slocum back in Gloucester and decided to combine his self-promotion and sailing into one grand adventure. In *The Great Western* and *The Great Republic*, both gaff rigged sloops built on Cape Ann, and much smaller than *Dog Star,* he set the world of single-handed sailing on its ear with successive transatlantic crossings despite his obvious handicaps. He became a media celebrity, touring with his story, playing for packed audiences up and down the eastern seaboard and in Europe. Howard Blackburn died at the age of 73 while busy planning a solo voyage across the Atlantic in his latest wooden gaffer, *Cruising Club*. This man went to Davy Jones' locker with enough adventure under his belt for a dozen lifetimes.

One of his favorite pastimes, his niece wrote in a biography, was for him to sail the waters of the Annisquam River and fish for dinner. I can picture his surf dory on the water ahead, leg-a-mutton sail drawing away towards home, his old derby perched on his head and his massive upper-body decked out in a black three piece wool suit with the tiller tucked under the crook of his arm and the long smoking cigar locked in his teeth.

I wiggle my fingers for luck.

Just past the white sand of Wingaersheek Beach to starboard, I throttle back and take down the main sail in the quiet confined waters of the river. Opening up to port is Lobster Cove that houses the Annisquam Yacht Club, and I hail them on Channel 68 VHF. A small Boston Whaler comes out and directs me to a mooring among a hundred other tightly packed boats. Within minutes I have the sail covers on and am settling down to a wee dram in the cockpit. The sun has ducked over the hill and the air temperature is sliding down the thermometer. A full thirty-five years of memories are waiting in the wings from the very first time I anchored here aboard the old schooner, *The Green Dragon*. I have a sneaky feeling I'll be entertaining some familiar ghosts before I get around to a second tumbler of Scotch for my head and a sweater for my body.

The real world intrudes with a sharp jangle of "Yankee Doodle Dandy."

"Hey Dad." My son's voice sounds far away over the cell phone.

"Hey yourself; where's yourself?"

"New York. Sandy Hook."

"You won't get into trouble there," I said. This is a mostly barren harbor of refuge in New Jersey across New York Harbor barely in sight of the Manhattan Skyline.

"I hear you caved on the Maine thing?"

"My joy is simply postponed," I said.

"So, it's the Cape Cod and Islands."

"Don't rub it in if you know what's good for you."

"Listen, me and a couple of my friends from the *Gammage* want to take *Dog Star* for a weekend after we get to Boston. Just get away for some boy time. Is that okay?"

The Scotch in my mouth tastes like gasoline. I swallow hard.

"Dad?"

The mere idea of turning over *Dog Star* to my son and his new found pirate/punk friends leaves me speechless.

"Dad?"

What can I say? Shouldn't I trust him? I had been passing myself off as a sailing instructor at his age with zero experience while he has been aboard since he was born. I taught him everything. He has been weaned on this boat, and he is coming off a five thousand mile voyage. He's a young man, my son. My mouth is moving but nothing is coming out.

"Okay then." Tristan, sighs dramatically, but doesn't skip a beat. "Can I just borrow some money instead?"

This I can handle, air comes back into my lungs. "You do understand that part of the borrow concept means repay?"

"Sure."

"In this lifetime," I said.

"Whatever," he said and quickly launches into the plan he has hatched to go with a watch-mate from the *Gammage* to the boy's parent's house on Nantucket and try to find a place to live and a job for the summer. The money is for initial rent, board, and ferry costs. It is a princely sum. I figure quickly that it is a small price to pay for not answering the "borrow the boat" question. I reluctantly agree. I breathe my own silent deep sigh of relief. Then it all dawns on me. I am stunned. I begin to blush.

"Thanks dad." He sounds vaguely sincere.

"You played me, right?"

"Right." He admits the bait and switch almost too fast. Smug is an awful sin. I can feel the triumphant smile through the phone.

"Well done," I said, and mean it. Being had was never so sweet.

"See you in Boston at the downtown pier in four days. I'll be the one with the big tattoo on my chest," he said and signs off.

How fast they grow up. I know he is kidding, but for the next thirty minutes I speculate about what the tattoo might say and what that would say about my son.

FIFTEEN

GLOUCESTER HARBOR

I aim straight for the Annisquam Club dock in the cool shadows early the next morning. The mission is to search for a small convenience store in the hopes of finding a loaf of not so white bread for lunch. *George* and I duck and weave around the minefield of other moored boats and, when we finally make the dock, a friendly hand takes our painter.

"Not many row no more," the compact and spry man said as he resumes his seat on a tall white five-gallon bucket. He holds a small fishing pole with an open reel that looks even older than his own seven plus decades.

"Not many fish for breakfast no more, either."

We acknowledge both these facts between us as I cleat *George* home with a full turn and two overhand hitches.

"That your wooden boat out yonder."

"That's *Dog Star*," I said with pride.

"Thought so."

"You know her then?"

"Might say so." He nods in her direction. "I burned her all up, once, a while back."

"Pardon me?"

144

"Out at the Beetle Cat shed on Smith Neck, Nonquitt. Torched her off, burned her to the ground, spread her ashes and then hosed the steaming mess down for good measure."

I am speechless.

"A fireman." He scans me with clear blue eyes and a pensive look under bushy white eyebrows. "Up Dartmouth way, for forty years, retired now."

I recover with a dunce's half smile.

"Old Waldo Howland at Concordia paid us extra to haul away the leftover crap," he said. "Still got a few pieces of melted bronze keelbolts from her innards in my basement."

My eyes stray quickly to my pride and joy resting across the quiet harbor. I could imagine the fire licking at her coachroof.

"She's a ghost," he said offhandedly with a wink and a smile. "She shouldn't be here."

The words are like handing my executioner a cold shilling.

I swallow hard, trying to imagine the dull, dreary world without her in the picture and simply couldn't. I thank him again for the help with the dinghy. Embarrassed at the tear in my eye, I hurry off to find my bread. Strange, unexpected things happen when your boat is older and has a richer past than you do.

How do you invite yourself aboard a complete stranger's boat for a six-week race circuit? The answer is you pull out all the stops, hold nothing back, and lie, cheat, bribe, coerce, blackmail, intimidate, and use subterfuge to accomplish your noble goal. Yacht Club bars have all of these attributes for success in the enterprise on call twenty-four hours a day, seven days a week. To get a berth aboard *Sorcery* in 1971, anything was within the bounds of propriety.

The trick to getting your way in life is making other folks believe that the very thing you need from them was their own idea all along. I began with this end in mind. To first desire something, you must put a name to it. While not a Dupont, Vanderbilt, Forbes, or Rockefeller, the odd spelling, ethnic question marks, and unlimited options for making a verbal hash of the thing, separates my last name from the Smiths and Joneses by a wide margin. My first plan was to capitalize on my label.

Yacht racing, before cell phones, boat phones, and the current spate of technology that makes a quiet solitary moment on your own rarer than a fair-minded Texan, information was ruled by mega sized message boards, bustling hospitality tents, and barroom camaraderie reminiscent of fraternity rush week at an Ivy League campus. Docks were an ant farm of spirited activity as final touches were added and new-fangled gear installed on high powered racing machines. At times the only way to contact members of your own crew was to hastily tack a note with a plan to meet or an update on progress in securing the essential but unavailable "skillywicket" to the message board. Sailors passed by this placard, with its hundreds of silent screams in frustration flapping in the breeze, with dread, always hoping they wouldn't see a note with their name marked by a black spot.

I began with half a dozen full sized sheets of typing paper, folded over, my name in different lettering and scrawls with a variety of pens and markers. Some labeled "Bob Rubadeau," others "Captain Rubadeau," and a variety of other variations blaring out the essential last name. Inside were cryptic messages: "Need you now. Question about the course. Come to the boat. Hurry! Ted Hood." Or, "Where the hell are you? Find *American Eagle* or be at the bar for drinks at eight. Ted Turner." Or, "Sorry about last night. I was a foppish prude. Please give me another chance? Love Always, Gina Lollobrigida."

The notes were tacked in such a way that the inside messages were almost impossible to miss. I was shameless.

Drinking is more than just a pastime at a yacht club bar during race week. Alcohol is the grease that spins the wheels of the machine. Aside from the half dozen testosterone laden junkies with bank accounts bordering on the obscene and those who could actually win a prized race cup or score well in the Conference, most of the participants were here for the social scene. Sobriety was a scarce commodity after 1600 hours, and hangovers from the night before rarely departed the bloodstream before lunch, so a lot of work was packed into the mid-afternoons. The bar was a loud, raucous cesspool of insults, questions about any skippers' manhood, and derogatory indictments of boats, their designers and builders. Everyone used their outside, schoolyard voices at all times. It is a wonder we are not all deaf.

I would go to the payphone in the lobby and call the bartenders and have them page "Captain Rubadeau" or "Bob Rubadeau." I would tell them I was the chair of the Rules Committee, or the Commandant of the Coast Guard. After the fourth or fifth time during the two-hour peak imbibing time I would have to plead with them to "please try again, it is a matter of national security." Obnoxious was not simply a word but a state of mind I was seeking with a firm resolve. I made sure the bartenders knew who I was and I tipped shamelessly.

During the day, when I could find someone working on *Sorcery*'s deck I would rush up and say, "Hey, I'm Bob Rubadeau. Is Huey Long (or Jim Kilroy, or Chuck Kirsch, or Bob Direcktor) aboard? I was supposed to meet him at his boat, but they said he might be over here. No? Well, hey, when he shows up tell him I had to run over to see Bill Ficker (or Wally Frank, or Norm Raben, or Halsey Herreschof, or Ron Holland) and I'll stop by later. Thanks a bunch. Remember its Bob Rubadeau. Rue-bah-doe, okay?" Then, I would be off at a run before they could scratch their head. I thought of it as Chinese water torture.

Three days of this and I was sure everyone on "C" dock was asking, "Who the hell is this guy anyway?" On the day before the start of the 105-mile shakedown race for the S.O.R.C. down the Florida coast to Venice, I figured I had to make my move, the *coup de grace*. With two six packs of Heinekens in tow, I cornered the crew on *Sorcery* at cocktail time and apologized for making them my message machine during the last few days and offered the "greenies" as payment. They let me aboard to deliver the goods.

Now all I had to do was stay there. When owner and Captain Jim Baldwin came aboard, I introduced myself and explained the offering.

"Oh, you're the Gina Lollobrigida guy."

Who could argue with that? It was the start of a six-week relationship. The next day I was at one of the two grinders trying to look strong and calm and stay out of the way. I learned that teamwork on an ocean racer is much like a mountaineering expedition to Everest except the competition for the summit never gets in the way of a back-breaking, gonzo good time. *Sorcery* won her very first ocean race by over two hours. I was parked in the fast lane.

With my loaf of bread stowed, I crank up the engine and maneuver back out into the Annisquam River. It is still early enough that the morning vapors hang low in the shaded alcoves under the dark steep banks to port. The tide is running with us but due to become slack in a half-hour. From long practice and association with this stretch of water, I keep well to the center channel and off the crowded docks of the marinas that crowd the waterway this side of the Route 128 bridge. Cars and trucks rumble overhead as we pass beneath the archway with plenty of room to spare.

With the railroad bridge up, I proceed into the blind corner after a short toot on my foghorn to let folks know I am on my way. The water under my keel is now slack and the Blynman Canal stretches out ahead as straight as an arrow. It always amazes me that waterways through many of New England's most heavily settled areas are often green and treed, at least as far as the eye can see. I applaud our forbearer's urban planning for green belts, knowing full well that the founding fathers probably thought the land worthless, at best, and maybe prime future breeding grounds for their clams and duck blinds.

The last bridge appears and I see that a sport fishing boat, probably in the charter business, is already pleading the case for an opening. I throttle up so that we can go through together. To the east, as we power out into Gloucester Harbor, is the statue of the Fisherman tugging at his spoked wheel. It is a tribute to all those who have gone down to the fishing grounds in ships and lost their lives at sea. It has had a supporting role in many of my favorite books to movies from Rudyard Kipling's *Captains Courageous* with Spencer Tracy and Mickey Rooney to Sebastian Yunger's *The Perfect Storm* with George Clooney and Mary Elizabeth Mastrantonio. No speaking parts, but a man with a message none the less.

Dog Star and I maneuver past the shoals and take a left towards the main town docks and the state fish pier. The tall, square red building that used to be the Wonson Paint Factory sits on the west side of Smith Neck facing the inner harbor. The Rockaway Hotel tumbles down the shallow hill to the water's edge joining the docks I used to launch my small fleet of Turnabouts for sailing classes. The small pastel colored cottages that line the narrow, twisting streets house a thriving artist's colony. The Rocky Neck Association was formed in 1878 and is the oldest artists' cooperative still surviving in the United States.

We round the point and Smith Cove opens up. During the height of summer it is jock-a-block full, but this calm early spring morning there are plenty of empty moorings. I spot a newer looking mooring ball with a fresh wand for its bridal and I slowly approach in the dead calm. I pull a dock line from the cockpit locker and bring *Dog Star* alongside at almost dead stop so that I simply have to lean out of the cockpit grab the wand, pull the spliced loop out of the water and reeve my own line through it. Holding both ends of the docking line, I then walk slowly forward along the side deck, pulling the ball with me, leading the line around the shrouds and sheets, until it finally sits just under the bowsprit. I cleat the two ends of my line firmly around the bollard. This approach beats trying to line up a target that is hidden by your own deck for the last twenty yards, running like a steeplechaser to the bow and trying to snag a wand from the highest point possible on a small craft, only to come up a few feet short and a couple of inches too late to snag the wary beast, simply because the bow is where the mooring ball must be when all is said and done.

There are many reasons not to pick up a private mooring. First, it is someone else's property, and they have an expectation that when they arrive it will be vacant for their use. Second, moorings are not all created equal. You may tether your forty-ton monster to a leash designed to hold a dinghy and end up somewhere else when the wind pipes up in the afternoon. Knowing the weight and condition of the mooring chain, anchor, and pennants is essential safety procedure for your vessel and the boats around you. However, it is an essential and historically established New England custom that empty mooring balls in crowded harbors are usually placed smack dab in the middle of those centuries old, common sense and common law, best protected anchorages. When anchoring is not an option because the Army Corp of Engineers in all their infinite nautical wisdom has created a mooring pattern that precludes any swing room whatsoever, and rental moorings are not available (or full), a transient sailor has two options: go somewhere else, or make the best use of what is available.

If you pick up someone else's mooring, I have one suggestion and one rigid rule to apply. I suggest that you examine as far down as possible below the waterline the condition of the mooring and assess from the makeup of the pennant and the boats on either side of you if the size and strength will hold your boat if a squall comes along while you are squatting. Launching your dinghy and investigating the equipment is often a grand idea. The one rigid rule is that you must be prepared to leave at a moment's notice if the rightful owner comes along. This means no short jaunts into town leaving the boat unattended, or even the occasional sitting within a stone's throw of your boat in the cockpit of a neighbor's gin palace. My rule of thumb is that the engine must be started and the pennant line cast off in under two minutes. If you can't make that happen you don't have your boat or your head in proper order to take advantage of this honored tradition.

I often leave my card in a ziplock bag duct-taped to the mooring with an explanation and an invitation that I would welcome the opportunity to return the hospitality at my mooring in a distant harbor at some future time. I have met many wonderful yachts-folk in this way.

I stretch my arms over my head on the foredeck and look around at a harbor front I have watched evolve for over thirty years. Bickford and Beacon Marinas still act as bookends for the cove, one to either side of the entrance. The old buildings and tumble down docks are vanishing slowly but surely, replaced by box like condos stacked like a child's shiny blocks. More is the pity.

This is a busy commercial harbor and doesn't apologize for the smell of diesel, oil, fish offal, and rotting pilings. I go below to make a baloney sandwich. I want to be back underway by noon in order to be in Marblehead by sundown. M. arrives late tomorrow night and I want to have everything just right. She calls this my "Queen of the Nile" complex because in the matter of squaring away most things on the boat she does a better job than I do. It takes her days to get things back to right after one of my helter-skelter cleaning jobs. But hey, if I can get her to be Cleopatra to my Mark Antony for the summer, what's a few hours of frantic wiping and cleaning in payment.

SIXTEEN

MARBLEHEAD

In 1980 Phil Weld shocked the world's solo ocean racing community by winning the Observer Single-handed Transatlantic Race (OSTAR) aboard his Dick Newick designed and Walter Greene built trimaran *Moxie*. Owner and publisher of the *Gloucester Daily Times*, Phil was not only the oldest at 65, but the first (and to date, last) American ever to have won the grueling 2,810 mile slog to windward from Plymouth, England to Newport, Rhode Island. As *Dog Star* and I drift past Ten Pound Island on our way out of the harbor, I can still remember Phil's infectious charm and drive that led to his improbable victory. As a member of the Eastern Point Yacht Club, where I learned the fundamentals of boat racing, he and his wife Anne were constantly pressing the limits with their high performance Tornado *Poseidon's Chariot*. I never did get a chance to ride the chariot but I always envied him the wails and screams of delight from those who had.

Phil's road to his victory was not an easy one. Fate, rules, capsizes, and luck, most of it bad, conspired to derail his dream. Without the same courage and pluck that made Howard Blackburn a "Gloucesterman," Phil would have gone quietly into that long, good night like the rest of us. Luckily for us who live vicariously through the exploits of great men, Phil Weld persevered, though he often must have felt kin to Job.

Weld had first tried the OSTAR, held every four years, in 1972 with his British built 44-foot trimaran *Trumpeter.* Plagued by gear problems, he finished well back in the pack, doubling the number of days the winner took to reach Newport. He came back in 1976 with a new 60-foot trimaran, designed by Dick Newick, *Gulf Streamer*, which was capsized north of Bermuda by a rogue wave on the delivery trip over to England for the start. Phil and his crew spent six days living in the overturned wreck until they were finally rescued and the boat abandoned at sea. Ironically, she was eventually salvaged by a Russian flagged freighter and by a long clandestine route became a Soviet based charter yacht out of Odessa.

Undeterred, Phil immediately built a new 60-foot Newick Tri, named her *Rogue Wave* and began the shakedown for the next race. In 1980 a surprising rule change in the OSTAR arbitrarily limited overall length to 56 feet. So, Phil went back to Newick's drawing board for a new boat. *Moxie* was launched with barely enough time to get the kinks out of her before the deadline in Falmouth. It was a tough race weatherwise, a raging nor'easterly gale in mid-Atlantic tested everyone's mettle and sent more than a few competitors scuttling back to safe harbor. It was physically demanding for any athlete let alone the oldest in the race. *Moxie* finished strong into a smokey sou'wester in just under eighteen days with her closest competitor nearly seven hours behind. To me Phil's enduring legacy is the obvious lesson to break Herculean tasks down to bite-sized chunks and keep chewing until the thing is done. You keep failure off the chart with an endless string of small successes.

I look over from my semi-reclining position in the cockpit of my own "dream machine" at Phil and Anne's lovely house peeking through the trees on Dolliver's Neck just above Freshwater Cove where Samuel Champlain filled his water kegs in the spring of 1607. Unfortunately, Phil died suddenly on election day in 1984 on his way to the polls to vote for the underdog. When he was frequently asked why he took up the dangerous hobby of world class single-handed ocean racing— so costly in money, time and effort, Weld responded, "How else can a guy my age get his name in the sports section?"

I remark aloud to the open space around the boat that I am moving pretty close to that three score age milestone myself, and I haven't seen my name in any sports pages for a long, long while. The fickle wind slats the main, and I force my "old aching bones" up to trim it in. Phil would have gagged. I resolve to get myself younger and be well insulated from this morose attitude before M. arrives. As my wise old grandfather always said, "If you want a hot, young thing, you got to be a hot, young thing." Amen, I say to that.

"Dad?"

"Is that an accusation?"

"Dad?"

"I'm not guilty. Go ahead, torture the whole truth out of your mother. Ask her about the trumpet player."

"Whatever." A huge pregnant sigh follows. "Hey, I wonder if you…"

"What does 'Whatever' mean?" I ask my daughter.

"Don't be funny."

"Me, funny?"

"WHAT-ever!"

"I hear that all the time and it doesn't make any sense."

"Dad."

"I'm a word man, I should know what it means."

"Fuh-ged-aboud-it."

"Really," I said. "I really, really need to know."

"What is what. Ever is ever." She growls into the phone.

"Do you lace it with sarcastic? Is that the key? Marinate it in ironic?"

"Dad?"

"Honest, just tell me the truth. I can handle the truth."

"Dad!"

"There you go again with the insults," I said.

"Just don't forget to pick up Mom. See you on Monday." The line goes dead.

I raise my arms to the spreaders in victory and exhale a cheering Super Bowl crowd noise. Anytime I get off the phone with my kids, and it hasn't cost me money, it is a center podium moment.

Marblehead describes itself as the Yachting Capital of the World. This is a little like the wall clinging gecko claiming he has brontosaurus on his father's side, but there is no harm in letting the claim go unchallenged. This harbor is undoubtedly the longest serving and among the most illustrious venues for yacht racing and recreational boat ownership in the United States. The venerable clubs: Eastern, Corinthian, Boston, Pleon, Dolphin, and Marblehead have long been the standard bearers for the centuries of active yachtsmen and women of Boston and New York. The impressive fleet of masts stands like a grove of Aspen as *Dog Star* and I round Lighthouse Point and pass, off to starboard, old Fort Sewall, where the well placed gun embankment saved Old *Ironsides* during the War of 1812 when a small British fleet chased her into this very same harbor.

I hail the Boston Yacht Club's tender, as my friend, Dr. Jeff Wisch, had made prior arrangements for me to hang on a club mooring for a few days while I pick up the rest of my motley crew. As I put the sail covers on and make the boat ready for the evening, which is fast dimming the western sky, I look up at the Georgian, Colonial, and Victorian houses that climb away from the waterfront. It is a town of rich history. The winding cobblestone streets look like the movie set of an English port in Sir Francis Drake's time. I am soon calling the launch back for a pick-up and having them phone for the rental car that I have scheduled to be delivered to the club. I barely have time for a drink at the bar before I am on my way to Logan Airport and a rendezvous with my marvelous Miss M.

SEVENTEEN

BOSTON HARBOR

The morning has a cold blanket of mist just barely rising off the water under the pale blue sky as I cradle a hot mug of coffee between my two hands. The harbor is slowly coming awake. A lobster boat moves out the channel, pushing the knee-deep fog blanket aside as she goes. The operator scurries about the open back deck getting the gear ready as the boat keeps a steady course. He or she is in bright yellow bib rain-pants, checkered wool shirt and a dark blue stocking cap. Beyond the lobster boat a small rubber dinghy weaves among the tightly packed forest of masts, its engine a muffled buzz. The sun is up, but still low under the green lawns and tall trees of Hovey Park to the east. Beyond that narrow strip of real estate is open water all the way to Portugal. The sun is catching the top of Old Burial Hill, a quiet park where the gravestones mark the great storm of 1846 when sixty-five men and boys from the Marblehead fishing fleet died, leaving behind forty-three widows and one-hundred and fifty-five children to find their own way in life. I turn the collar up on my fleece lined nylon windbreaker, knowing that as soon as the sun crests the treetops I'll be toasty warm all over.

I hear M. clatter around as she pours herself a cup and clicks open the hanging locker for her warm coat. Soon the tussled head fills the companionway and she comes up to join me with a smile. I am partly responsible for the tussled look and I am a proud guy for it. We snuggle against each other and watch the sun begin to peak through the branches of the trees.

"She looks beautiful," M. said.

I smile with pride. It is the annual payment I extract for all the yard work.

"How was the trip down?"

"Brutal, frightful, bloody-awful."

M. smiles knowingly.

"Cold, wet, miserable, lonely."

She pats my cheek.

"The waves, the wind, the Coast Guard harassment."

"Okay, okay, I still owe you." Her throaty laugh cuts through the morning quiet.

I smile again, knowing M. always pays her debts in spades. It's a fine and wonderful thing that the *Harvey Gamage* doesn't arrive in Boston until noon. Mentally counting the minutes before our time alone on our boat is over, I duck below for another wake-me-up slug of Java. I plan to need it.

I soon grew tired of the testosterone-laden world of Class A ocean racing during the mid 1970's. The boats I crewed were the gold-platers, always at the head of the fleet across the line, and I learned the art of sailing hard and staying safe. I was no stranger to high stakes competition, and the guys I sailed with were balls-to-the-wall racers. One major problem on the international scene was that the scorecard got pretty hard to follow. 1970 marked the last year that the S.O.R.C. was raced under the Cruising Club of America's efficient, if marginally flawed, handicapping system. The next year, my first on the circuit, was the beginning of the International Offshore Rating Rules (I.O.R.) and many of the most beautiful and powerful ocean racers were slowly, over the next few seasons, eclipsed in the standings by smaller, faster, wider, and less sea-worthy boats; ugly machines designed to find loopholes in the new time penalty rating equations.

Yacht racing became a Woody Allen farce. It would be like watching the Kentucky Derby in Louisville and finding out the winner an hour after the horses were put away, when the tote board finally whirled its numbers determining that the last horse in the race was actually the victor because he saved his time over the first nag across the line by a mathematical formula only M.I.T. professors could possibly understand. Owners, captains, and crews were forced to place the appreciation and rewards for their efforts on the ocean race courses of the world into the hands of land-bred mathematicians who bestowed the laurels for accomplishment in a dry and sterile fact sheet long after the excitement of hitting the finish line under a ballooning spinnaker was over.

Beautiful, go anywhere boats like *Windward Passage, Bolero, American Eagle, Caribbee, Scaramouche, Windigo, Ticonderoga, Dorade, Stormvogel, Escapade,* and *Figaro* were suddenly pushed over the hill and were being replaced by boats that got beamier, squatter, harder to steer off the wind, and were wet as hell going to weather. Add to the mix that fiberglass now allowed designers and rule makers to form any shape they damn well pleased. Boats began to look like the boogers L. Francis Herreshoff predicted when he called resin and glass fiber "frozen snot." It was the end of an era when function and rating nuances trumped beauty in the name of garish tin cups. I watched the Irish wake from the decks of the last great boats, whose designed beauty was only matched by their owner's old-school style and panache.

Needless to say yacht club bars became even louder and more effusive as the rules became more jumbled. The "my boat is better than your boat" conversations eventually boiled down to who could talk the new ratings jargon loudest and fastest. When confusion this profound happens in a bubbling vat of testosterone, blood sport usually follows. I learned quickly the two rules of the barroom brawl. The first solid truth is that no one ever wins; so don't choose sides. The second is that as soon as yelling progresses to shoving get behind the bar with the bartenders and duck down low.

We arrive by car at 11:30 a.m. at the designated pier in the inner harbor, the Boston skyline towering over our heads. Fifty adults, children, and pets mill about the huge, almost empty parking lot on this early Saturday morning. All eyes strain seaward to catch the first sight of the tall schooner. The muted submissive rumble of a big city is strange and unnerving. M. and I clutch each other's hands for security. The isolated mountain town of Telluride does not prepare your six senses for downtown Boston. Meeting the families of the other crewmembers is a special treat, and they have come from all over New England to be here for the end of the voyage.

Finally the unmistakable gaffs of the off-white sails become visible above the land. The crowd gives a cheer although she is still a mile or more out. Rounding the last turn by Governor's Island, the tall schooner finally squares away for the run up the harbor with the wind abaft the beam. The *Harvey Gamage* is an impressive sight. At 131 feet of sparred length and her two massive solid wooden sticks hung strangled in cordage, she has the look of the real fishing schooners from the 19th century. Her white hull shows the wear and weather of the ten thousand miles she has made since leaving New England last fall. All sails drawing, she quickly closes the distance. Sails begin to back as she comes around in a wide turn and a pair of deckhands scramble up the rigging to the trees in the mainmast to collar and tie home the uppers above the heavy gaff. I recognize Tristan hugging the heaving canvas sixty feet off the deck. I don't point him out to his mother but quietly continue to run the video camera. She has already noticed and doesn't want me freaking out so she zips her lip. He hardly slips at all.

The Ocean Classroom Foundation has three such ships on which they provide students with a unique educational experience during their high school careers. A crew of twenty or so students, young men and women, sign on for the double duty of running an old-school sailing ship and taking a full menu of course work in mathematics, English, history, geography, and science. Remember that the ship has no winches, no privacy, and prides itself on a dogged determination to cover a huge swath of ocean and a score of foreign ports of call during its four months of high seas adventure. The teenagers are divided into three watches who rotate the duties of sailing, navigation, anchor security, and maintenance for the duration of their stay under the sharp eye of three paid crew. In addition, the four professional teachers challenge them with a rigorous academic program, which will hopefully prepare most of them for a college life that is waiting off the end of the gangplank.

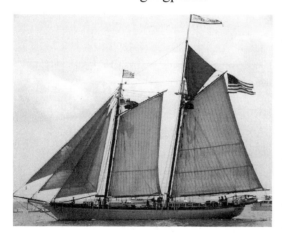
Tristan joined the *Harvey Gamage* in St. Thomas, Virgin Islands, in January. The boat headed south through the Windward Islands stopping at Martinique, Grenada, Barbados, and Aruba before shying away from the troublesome pirate activity in Venezuela and heading back across the Caribbean Sea to the Dominican Republic and Puerto Rico. From there they wove through the Bahamas before reaching the United States at Charleston. The adventure continued up the east coast with stops in the Carolinas, Maryland, New Jersey, New York and Maine, before reaching Boston.

It takes the better part of thirty minutes to furl the sails and tidy ship before they pull alongside the pier and tie her down. The scurry of the crew to the barked orders of the Captain and mate is impressive. They know their stuff. I am taking notes.

Tristan finally comes to the end of the gangplank for a hug and to issue the invitation to come aboard for the end of voyage muster. He has a new smattering of facial hair and resembles a moth eaten Lincoln. He has gotten taller, broader in the shoulders. His brown eyes have a steady sparkle. He is careful not to step a toe on the land. It is not over till it's over. I like the new visual version of my son's winsome character.

"Good trip?"

"More squid than ink," he said.

"Weather?"

"Wouldn't knock the skin off a vanilla pudding."

"A good crew?"

"They hold their course."

"Food good?"

"First Class squares, rain or shine."

"No problems?"

"None worth flapping a lip at."

"No complaints at all?"

"I'm good."

"Invasion of the Body Snatchers?"

"Have it your way," he said and smiled.

The crew gathers amidships and the rest of us gather around. The Captain starts things off with introducing the watches. He has something kind and good to say after each name. Tristan is "first to the trees, a steady hand at the helm, and a man with a ready laugh in a dark blow." To Tristan's right is a fair-haired young man, almost as tall as my son's six-feet-four-inches, who, we later learn, is Phil Weld's grandson from Gloucester. Sometimes the world seems no bigger than a postage stamp.

We tour the ship, marveling at the galley and its huge diesel fired stove that broils its way through the tropics providing three hot squares for a complement of thirty-one souls. The cook is a spry young woman with all the body fat of a piece of elk jerky. It is little wonder. Tristan's bunk is stuffed at the forepeak in a cubbyhole with two others. It must have required a shoehorn to fit the three bunkmates in at one time. With two seabags on his shoulders, our son finally says all his goodbyes and see-you-soons, and rolls down the gangplank, back into our world. It will take us months to realize all the subtle changes a semester at sea can stuff into an open mind.

Back aboard *Dog Star* we debrief with our wayward sailor. It is a treat to hear him talk about his adventures, framing them precisely in words and segments for the first time to outsiders who hadn't been there. It reminds me that there is a brief irretrievable moment in our lives when we begin to define ourselves with our own experiences. Life begins to take on patterns where each decision leads to a gestalt moment that is set to words and goes into the ledger of your life. You are no longer a voyeur, a passive observer, but a player who chooses your own path. Your family stories become simply a shared legacy while you go off to be a marquee star all on your own.

Before he goes to his bunk, as the lights of Marblehead glistened in long bright streaks across the black water, Tristan digs out his journal and hands it to his mother. With a shy smile he warns us that he isn't much of a writer yet, so just about every day of the voyage begins with the phrase: "I know I wrote this yesterday, but today the most incredible thing I have ever seen happened to us…" M. and I sit out in the cockpit for a long while this night remembering some of the same wonders we have experienced over the years during our travels. When we finally crawl into bed I can feel her wistful smile until I fall asleep with my own dreams of missed trains, lost alleyways, schedules to keep, and red sunsets that won't go naturally below the horizon.

Eighteen

MASSACHUSETTS BAY

Skye is arriving on the redeye from Seattle. Logan International Airport, under some perpetual smokescreen of construction for the last thirty years, is the absolute pits by most user friendly standards. At one a.m. on this specific summer's night, the Count of Monte Cristo could call the place home. Dirty gray linoleum stretches along the ground floor of the ticket kiosks at terminal "C", where every counter is abandoned and locked with lethal looking metal grates. Echoes of desperation bounce randomly from empty corners in the three story main hall. The few occupied chairs contain sprawled, slumped, and drooling sleepers snoring their wretched delayed-arrival hearts out. All of us are clustered around a cave-darkened corridor with double doors, under a dire message on a flashing sign warning us what carnage will happen if we try to go further and meet our party at the gate.

I grumble for my own lost sleep and M. absently responds to the softly muttered invectives tumbling from my mouth by hugging my arm as we wait for our daughter's arrival. Tristan is off spending the night with some of his friends and will rejoin us onboard *Dog Star* in the morning. I settle into an uncomfortable seat and the specters of all the comings and goings of my crazy past, through the dingy portals of this airport, queue up for a visit.

In 1973, M. and I left the United States to muddle along without us. Nixon had just been re-elected president. The finger gesture "V" took on whole new meanings. The Viet Nam war blindly raged on towards its terrible and predictable climax. Janis, Jimmy, and Morrison had taken themselves off the traveling squad. Watergate was the scandal of the hour, and I was ready to do just about anything besides race other people's million dollar boats and apologize for my country. We pooled together a few hundred dollars and flew to India on one of the very first 747 commercial airplanes. When we landed on the runway in New Delhi, the entire left hand bank of eight wheels blew out (shot out by Sikhs?) and the crippled plane had a forced evacuation on the runway. Men with guns, rakish military beanies, and a killer's look in their eyes prevented me from taking a picture of the guilty landing gear. Welcome to the far east of Kipling, Conrad, Ghandi, Mao, and Ravi Shankar.

Our goal was to go climbing and trekking in Nepal. We were running away to see the mountains. It was not to be the last time in our life that we would choose to flee to the far places in the hilly world, where no one had ever heard about the egocentric yachting world we were leaving behind. Our friend, Doug Walker from Cooperstown, New York, was in the Peace Corp stationed at a high Himalayan village only six days uphill walking from Namche Bazaar and the base camp of Everest. We were going to surprise him, but first we had to find our way north through Bengal and the Hindu Kush.

New Delhi always comes back to me late at night, either because I am already uncomfortable, or in order to use its old power to make me remember to stay uncomfortable in my now too familiar skin. The images are as fresh and vibrant as a smashed jar of raspberry jam: the harsh reality of flowing gutters along wide boulevards, loaded with cow shit and torn flowers, where street women bathe their skeletal babies; the annoyingly loud motorized rickshaws careening down the wide boulevards at reckless speeds, spewing black stink, loaded with fly covered meat and old tires held in place by random bodies with blank, sorry faces; the squalid heat bearing down, rising up, full of thundering traffic noise, stench, funeral foliage, blaring horns and endless cries for money; our cheap hotel bed of lumps and starched sheets like tin siding, with cockroaches the size of Snickers bars, and water the color of urine available down the hall from huge handles on communal spigots.

The shared toilet facilities were a plate-sized black hole behind a stained muslin sheet; a stench filled yawning vat of ooze bubbles under the broken floor tiles. The two necessary positions for your feet are worn down to mortar by five decades of squatting clients. Drunkenly lazy flies the size of marbles buzz in your hair. Nights of quiet tears for no reason other than the loss of our definition of humanity rise amid the assertive screams of terrorized victims living in the twisted alleys above the roar of un-muffled trucks, busy loading up the merchants of this chaos for the next day.

Nothing in our young lives prepared us for being suddenly vulnerable to the collision of the naked world of abject poverty and our pampered selves in the heart of New Delhi. The experience seared a new sense of life's real diversity of experience into our souls. When we traveled on north we left some of our privileged, sheltered former life behind. We never wanted it back.

The passengers from the late night Seattle flight begin to straggle out. The first ones fly out the double doors in such a rush that it could have been an old Japanese monster movie with a four-story puke-green monster running up the corridor behind them. Our daughter finally appears, laden like a war correspondent with no less than a half-dozen tote bags of various sizes on shoulder straps draped across her body. She is fashionable in a bright, ruffled maternity blouse, although her always-fit body barely shows a pregnant bulge.

"I sat in a row of three with a mother and two babies," she said with her initial hugs. "I've decided I don't want children."

"I told you so," I said, finding my first horselaugh in hours.

"Every seat was full." She begins loading me up with shoulder straps. "I was running up and down the aisles with a hundred dollar bill in my hand trying to get someone to switch seats. No takers."

"The kids were a handful?"

She staggers to make her point.

"What's wrong with our economy when I can't buy a favor for a hundred bucks?"

"The kids had obviously made an early impression on the plane."

"Each one could have starred in the *Ransom of Red Chief*."

I squeeze her shoulder.

"Or *The Omen*."

"Put it behind you," her mother said.

"Tell me truthfully." Skye is wide-eyed serious. "Were Tristan and I ever awful?"

M. and I look at our daughter with stupefied expressions, clutch each other and break down in chest humping laughter. It's a while before we can stand alone and dry our eyes.

"Oh, my, God," Skye said, realization sinking in. Her shoulders slump.

"Look at the bright side," I said, "eighteen years or so from now you and your brat will actually want to spend an airplane trip together."

A future funk is working heavy on our daughter until we load the last of her bags into the trunk of the rental car and make our getaway.

The only marginally good thing about Logan Airport is that with no traffic on Route 1 you can be in the parking lot of the yacht club at Marblehead in twenty-five minutes. *George* feels over-full and lacks a sizeable freeboard as we three (plus one in the oven) row out to the boat. Skye has recovered fully and brings us up to date on the Alaskan gossip and juicy political scandals we didn't know we had missed until we heard them. My daughter can really tell a story in hi-fi and ten spot-on voices. We laugh until our sides hurt.

I sit in the cockpit and watch, under the golden glow of the cabin's oil lamps, my daughter and her mother put away enough clothes and gear for a six-month stay. Skye feels with drumming fingers each part of the boat that finds her hands. I smile as she goes through the old treasures in the pull out drawer below her bunk one by one, giggling with her mother at the neon retainer box with the jeweled appliance inside. Her brother did the very same ritual the night before. I take a deep breath. All is finally well with my world.

G. Peabody Gardner graduated from St. Mark's School in 1906 and went on to Harvard. He was the turn of the century prototype for the gentleman yachtsman. While he had been born to both privilege and position, his finances were such that he actually had to hold a job until this or that aunt, cousin, grandmother, or great uncle passed along some of the "old'" money to which his DNA was linked. He learned to sail before he was seven in a flat-bottomed skiff named *Nancy*, and his whole life was spent in the pursuit of the next isolated harbor and next year's grand voyage with his male friends. In those days a man's boat and his hunting lodge were usually off limits to the fairer sex. I guess the only up side to our country's present homophobia is that these strict Victorian social rules have now changed for the better.

Gardner is notable for two reasons. The base of operations for his succession of yachts was right here in Marblehead, but, more importantly, the homeport for each of his boats was Roque Island, that far away goal on the coast of Maine. He called the place his "Ultima Thule."

John Lowell Gardner, G. Peabody's great grandfather, inherited Roque Island from his father-in-law, who had originally acquired the property in 1805. The collection of red and yellow houses scattered about the working farm on the northwesterly side of Shoreys Cove have provided shelter for generations of the Gardner clan. A short hop by boat from Jonesport, the island had a magical aura for Mr. Gardner, and his eloquent prose always reaches its highest tide-water mark when he speaks of his sailing into and out of the entrance to Lakeman Harbor and Great Beach.

Peabo, as he was known by friends and family, wrote a series of books about his sailing escapades. Two of my favorites are *READY ABOUT: Sailing Adventures Down East* and *HARD ALEE: Cruising Foreign*. These classy narratives are not widely known, privately printed with small runs, but have a distinctive period charm and character that sets them apart from the epic tales of high seas adventures posted by other writers. On his classic schooner *Rose* and his subsequent dream ship, *Glide*, Peabo made tidy and efficient voyages to the Canadian Maritimes including Nova Scotia, Cape Breton, Newfoundland, and the Magdalene islands. His love for the high latitudes and the lonely coasts in the North Atlantic is infectious. The skill necessary to travel these waters before any electronic navigational aids is celebrated in Gardner's writings with a dry wit, understated anxiety, and a Harvard vocabulary. Here is a sample from a chapter concerning a day in Newfoundland in 1953:

"The weather forecast mentioned 'fog in patches.' As things turned out, except for one small 'patch of sun' that came just in time to help us through a narrow short cut, we were shrouded in one great patch of fog all day. The nearer we got to Fransway Bay the thicker it got, but in due course we picked up the welcome sound of the fog signal. Closer and closer came the sound, until at last only a few yards away we saw the rocky base of a cliff – we could not see the lighthouse just above it. We swung sharply away.

"In another few seconds a most glorious sight met our eyes. We had passed in a flash from abysmal fog to sparkling sunshine. Precipitous, Norwegian-like cliffs, five hundred to a thousand feet high, rose above us on both sides, hemming in the narrow fjord that stretched before us. A mile away at the end of the fjord, clinging desperately to the steep mountain behind it, was the make-believe-looking village of Francois. Just to have the sudden sight of this fjord and toy-like town, with graceful schooners resting at anchor in the foreground, was worth our whole trip."

Peabo was old school. To read his work is like stepping into a time machine. His cruising was artful. The love for his boats and his shipmates was epic in scale. Never cease learning, never stop planning, and always "take care of your boat as you would your mother" seems to be his endearing legacy as he sailed his way well into his eighties.

Kathmandu in the early seventies was all a bustle with an international tribe of ex-patriots experiencing the various stages in a spiritual journey to the high Himalayas. The grounds and hallways of our hostel style hotel echoed a babble of exotic conversation. Aunt Jane's, serving the only hamburgers east of Afghanistan, was an oasis of western food and music in a teeming city of sounds, smells, images, and energy that were at once shocking and open armed, inviting. The temple pad for the burning of bodies on ceremonial truck engine mounts was just across the street from the tea and hashish boutique where every table had its own two-foot round, blown glass hookah for sampling the menu. Tina Turner, growling *Proud Mary,* blasted from stadium-sized speakers in the cell-sized room. The underground English language newspaper, mimeographed in smudgy blue ink, reported that the king had welcomed a new son and the boy was being swaddled in Yak dung each day for a month.

Our mountain trekking humbled us. We measured inches on the maps in days instead of hours. Destinations were weeks of walking away as we sought out our Peace Corps friend along the way to Namche Bazaar and the base camp of Everest. The steeply folded landscape translated into five miles down and five miles up eight-thousand vertical feet to go one mile "as the vulture flies" in the right direction. We learned to live on dahl (leaves), sog (lentils) and bot (rice). Taste came in the form of peanut butter.

A side expedition to Duhd Kund, the Lake of Milk, on the Tibetan Border with a group of primatologists looking for high altitude bands of monkeys opened us up to the challenges of snow filled eighteen-thousand foot passes and yak-assisted mountaineering. One night, when the wind blew outside our fortuitous cave of refuge strong enough to roll basketball sized boulders past the opening, our Sherpa porters had us listen carefully to the thunderous moaning of the wind and pick out the distinct, separate scream of the Yeti clans harmonizing close by in the pitch darkness.

Nepal, Tibet, and their perennial snow-capped mountains are surprisingly very near the equator. The temperature, which can vary a hundred degrees in a single day, is simply a matter of altitude. During a hot and muggy afternoon we trudged in a puddle of sweat up yet another endless series of steep switchbacks on a barely shoulder-width-wide trail cut from the steep mountainside by centuries of bare footed traffic. A few thousand feet of air and stunted vegetation separate us and the river valley floor. Our packs brush the uphill side of the trail as we instinctively lean away from the edge. We are careful where we put our feet.

Starting as a whisper then getting louder, we heard the eerie sound of dozens of Conch shell horns echoing down the valley from over our heads. During the last week, as we trudged on towards Everest, we had passed an extraordinary number of local people heading back down towards Kathmandu to try and secure transportation south in order to see the Dalhi Lama. He had only recently been exiled from his home country of Tibet and was to speak to the world in central India. It was expected that the crowd size at the live event would be measured in the millions. We knew the rough parameters of trail etiquette after weeks of such encounters and moved quickly, joining a pair of Nepali bearers who had sat back on a bench-sized rock ledge balancing their huge headband-supported wicker baskets against the mountainside. Two-way traffic was not a wise course on these precarious paths. From the sounds of things above our heads you had to figure the small village coming downhill had the right of way.

Our heavy packs had us perched precariously on the remaining few inches of the seat, our feet dangled in space, as the first purple-robed monks rounded the uphill turn of the trail swirling bronzed prayer wheels in their hands and chanting in a deep-throated cadence. They were followed by dozens more in a single-file parade blowing high mournful notes from huge polished shells. Finally a figure appeared with a gold and silver fabric headboard trailing a sun shade stretched out on second pike, between the two bearers walked a small man in a simple pure white robe. His face was a smooth, calm, burnished mask, and his Mongol eyes were glued to a book he held outstretched in his right arm. He passed us without a stumble or a hint of acknowledgement amidst the clatter of a following entourage consisting of dozens of women clattering finger symbols and men hooting thigh-bone whistles.

I felt a chill as this apparition passed within inches. My skin went from sweating to goose-bumps in an instant. I swear I smelled lilacs and raisins. Looking over at M., I could see her breathe as vapor

and the soft down on her cheeks showed hoar-frost as her wide eyes met mine. Our mouths simultaneously dropped open. As the sound and shock of the bizarre moment passed, and the group moved on down the hill, I once again felt the oppressive humidity and heat.

Upon relaying the details of the event later, we were provided an answer by another holy man that we visited at his mountaintop monastery. He was slowly, over a number of months, walling himself with home-made bricks into a small cave, leaving only a plate-sized opening to be passed food and water. All nourishment would be delivered through the generosity of the poor village at the base of the mountain. He was in the final stage of preparations for spending a seven-year stretch of prayer, meditation, and self-exploration. A special gift from his master, he said. He also said that on that day of strange events we had only experienced a powerful Rimpoche "taking the cool air from the mountain pass down through the valley to ease his journey." Once again we vowed never to doubt the power, determination, or possibilities of the human spirit. While we made our way slowly south through Burma and Thailand to Singapore our eyes were continually opened by kind and caring people who helped us along our journey in whatever way they could. The world is a far stranger and more wonderful place than anyone can imagine.

The club launch with Tristan aboard pulls alongside at a mite past 8 a.m. He is all in a dither and admonishes me that I have missed the morning canon for raising the colors and should properly be keelhauled before breakfast. We quickly set things right by attaching the stars and bars to its position off the stern. My son then digs out our club flag and our personal burgee on "pig sticks" to hoist up to the tops of the main truck and mizzen mast respectively. I help myself to another cup of coffee while *Dog Star* is being properly dressed.

"Feel better now?" I said.

"Vexology."

"Gesundheit," I said.

"The study of flag etiquette."

"No way."

"And you call yourself a captain." Tristan shakes his head sadly.

"Tread lightly." I lower my voice and "V" my eyebrows. How quickly respect flies out the window on the wings of a gnat of knowledge.

"The history, pride, and honor of flags on ships is really very cool."

"For this nugget I paid umpteen thousands?"

"You want your money's worth or not?"

I long ago put the "parsimony in my Yankee" and quickly shut my yapper. So I listen while my son lectures me on the proper international rules, uses, and protocols of flags aboard ships. I am surprised to learn (again, because I must have known it at one time in order to get my 100 ton license) that the International Code of Signals consists of forty flags: 26 letters, 10 numerals, 3 repeaters, and 1 code signal. With these brightly colored flapping things, Tristan informs, you can actually converse with ships of different countries at great distance without the need of a translator.

Single flag signals, a solitary flag aloft, are the lowest priority messages and each letter has one specific meaning. Some are simple and straightforward like "N" means "no," "C" means "yes," and "O" means "man overboard." Others are very specific information or instructions like "M," which means "My vessel is stopped going forward and is making no way through the water," and "L" means "You should stop your vessel instantly." I particularly liked "X" which basically means: "Stop what you are doing and damn well wait until I tell what you need to do next."

Double flags raised together are more urgent messages. "I" and "N" together mean "I am on fire," and "D" plus "X" means "I am sinking." As Tristan is rattling these off from memory I picture him and his crewmates using semaphore, like the old two-fisted, stick mounted flag waivers on the old WW II Navy movies with Robert Mitchum and John Wayne, to communicate between the wheel and the bow watch.

"No swear words?" I said.

"You have to spell them out," he said.

My son, who was not known as a detail oriented person in his life before Ocean Classrooms, then proceeds to tell me how important it was to raise signal flags "smartly." Flags only fly during daylight, except for a Yacht Club flag when the member is aboard overnight. Personal burgees and ensigns must be struck at sunset. He also returns to my transgression of this morning for not waiting at the stern for the sound of the yacht club cannon to unfurl my ensign in proper order. He was worried "people" might think we were a "slovenly ship."

I challenged him to say the last comment three times fast. He can't, but finally cracks a smile. Ah, there is my scalawag, I think.

Skye comes up into the cockpit.

"You done?" she said to her brother whose early morning lecturing voice resembles a foghorn.

"My son is sharing his words of wisdom."

"Yeah, like this family is long on words of wisdom," she said with a huff, pointing a coffee cup with herbal tea in my direction. "Remember my wedding?"

"I'm still paying it off," I said and put a sour puss on my face for her benefit.

"Remember that touching and meaningful moment as we waited alone for the organ to start my walk down the aisle and you said, 'Skye, I only have one bit of advice I can give you about what happens next.' Remember?"

I do.

"I was really excited, nervous, nauseous. It was my moment. I knew it would all be worth it once it was finally over. Now, I needed more to think about? I'd also have the truth only a father would know about married life, my future. My mind was now going a mile a minute with terrified anticipation. Yoda was going to spill the beans."

After a rather long pause Tristan finally bites the bait. "So what did he say?"

"Dad leaned in, near my veil. I held my breath, waiting for life's answers, and then he whispers, 'Don't trip!'"

We get underway on this bright sunny day by 0900 hours, bound for the farthest hook of Cape Cod and the city of Provincetown. With four sailors, all familiar with *Dog Star*'s workings aboard, I try to stay out of the way as Skye takes the tiller and Tristan casts off the mooring, constantly pointing the pennant line's position to his sister until we are well clear. This is a hard-won lesson followed religiously by our crew so that floating ropes don't get up close and personal with the spinning prop. With one eye on the paper chart, one eye on the depth sounder, and her other eye on the channel, Skye takes us slowly down through the armada of boats towards the sharp turn to starboard and the open space of Massachusetts Bay.

The wind is still non-existent as we round the point and Tristan plugs in a waypoint on the GPS a hundred yards off the outer buoy off Wood End Light, forty-eight miles away. Long, glassy swells, stretched far apart lift the bows and roll the beam in lazy arcs as the diesel pushes us along at just under six knots. The skyline of Boston stands proud, though slightly brownish, rising above the exhaust of the commuters making their way to work. I feel smug. They smell

smog. The world is in my cosmic and environmental favor.

Tristan checks his previous work with the GPS by sliding a pair of parallel rulers over the paper chart, walking a pair of dividers along the way, and comes up with the same course and distance. I am glad to see my old "belt and suspenders" method of navigation is something he hasn't lost on his latest voyage. The crew is mostly quiet, except for the odd snide, affectionate remark, and the moments pass in quiet getting-to-know-you-again body language. It is wonder full and comfort able.

When the first telltale ripple comes across the water, we all perk up our eyes and sit straighter, but no one jinxes the zephyr with a word. As the ripples fade and then come whispering back, Tristan moves slowly towards the main mast and begins to unlash the sail cover. The faint breeze is treated like a skittish wild animal that would vanish with a wrong or sudden move. I loosen the main sheet and Tristan hauls the head of the sail to the top. Soon the sail is sheeted back amidships and we motor-sail for the next twenty minutes until the wind is substantial enough to warrant the jib. Soon we are able to shut down the engine and *Dog Star* glides along at three knots in eight knots of wind just forward of the beam.

The unforced silence continues to hold us all in its wonder. It was obvious we are all lost in a past moment, scanning a similar, ancient boat memory.

"Do you think we'll see whale?" Skye said.

"Absolutely, if you're pure of heart and promise to sail me anywhere I want when I'm too old to do it myself."

This particular run across the Boston shipping lanes and just inside of Stellwagon Bank has in past years provided some opportunities to see some good-sized finback and humpback whales.

"Remember when we used to heave-to off the banks and wait watches through the night, hoping one would spray us."

"Those awful kids' sleeping bags we would get bundled in," Skye said. "They always smelled like sour milk."

M. and I let them ramble on. Those days still seemed like last week to us. I look hard to see the pint-sized versions of these two young adults as they kid each other about who actually could stay awake the longest waiting for the whales to come and visit. It all goes by so fast.

We don't see whale.

The sun is still just high enough in its westward plunge to light the Pilgrim's Monument spire, 255 feet high, which is always the very first visual aid that pops over the horizon as you approach Provincetown from the sea. Provincetown and the dunes are one of the few places on the East Coast where you can see the sun set over the ocean. We aren't worried that darkness will curtain the day closed before we make harbor, as the entrance is well lit and straightforward. We will drop an anchor well away from town across the bay along the frontage beach behind Wood End. I watch and listen while my children discuss the entrance, the lights, the duties each will have as they set the hook. I guess we didn't do it all wrong. I go below to start our dinner. Too many captains spoil the putting a-boat-to-bed brew.

NINETEEN

PROVINCETOWN

How do you explain a six foot six, mostly naked Amazon, riding a gasoline powered skateboard down the middle of the street, barely covered in black fish-net leggings, a thong, a push up bra with overflowing cleavage, penciled eyebrows, flowing shoulder length red curls, and an Adam's Apple, to a ten-year old daughter and a six-year old son?

"She is way tall," my son said.

I agreed.

"She has a bit of a beard" My barely double-digit daughter added while rubbing her own cheeks.

I agreed again.

"How about some ice cream?" I changed the subject. I had decided to let their mother explain the nuances that fall through the cracks with the normal birds and bees lecture.

We strolled further and stopped to look at the folding sidewalk billboard advertising "The Big Boned Barbies, A Musical Review." Our ice cream cones were keeping our mouths busy while we pondered the pictures of Barbra Streisand, Diana Ross, and Tina Turner wowing an overflowing raucous crowd.

"Diana's been lifting weights," my daughter said between slurps of maple-nut-crunch. I couldn't argue. We moved along down a

178

walking street full of outrageous diversity. My kids' eyes took it all in while I tried to keep us moving.

We finally made it to the general store that holds its unique place on a changing Commercial Street despite economic pressure to "go mod." It was dark and dingy, with wooden counters and bins full of the oddest and funnest stuff. Of course you could get your lime green boa and huge false eyelashes, but in the bin next door you could also score some hand carved wooden yo-yos that can still "walk the dog" and do a pretty good "sleeper in a cradle." Magic tricks of twisted ten-penny nails, black rubber daggers with painted red blood, and cat's-eyes marbles were all available for pocket change.

"Cape Cod girls, they have no combs...they brush their hair with codfish bones, pick their teeth with mussel shells, and live trussed up in sandy dells," sang my daughter as she searched for this year's (1990) skeleton hairbrush to add to her collection. Skye commemorated each trip to P-Town with a different neon color. Tristan was more of an eye-patch and cutlass kind of guy at six. A firm chip off the old blockhead.

The Wampanoaq Indians are reportedly the first people to feel the strange potential of this place, the harmonic convergence of natural eccentricity, and would venture out to the "end of the world" on occasion to celebrate the moon and harvest some clams. Portuguese fishermen followed as the potential of the Grand, Stellwagon, and Georges Banks showed their bio-mass potential. By the mid 1800's when whaling was the trade of a new breed of sea borne entrepreneurs, Provincetown, with the largest and safest natural harbor along the entire New England coast, had become one of the busiest seaports in the booming economy of the still growing United States.

By the turn of the twentieth century, front page, above the fold tourism made use of the railroad lines that in past years hauled fish and whale oil. Wealthy tourists from Boston and New York, fleeing the heat and filth of summer in the industrialized cities, came to enjoy the wind, sand, and seashore activities. They brought with them the artists and intellectual elite of their day. Charles Hawthorne, a noted impressionist, established the Cape Cod School of Art here in 1899, and the new economy was cast.

Abandoned wharves and sail lofts were soon turned into artist studios, and a band of poets, journalists, dilettantes, radicals, socialists, and theater folk made their way to this outpost of notoriety to take advantage of cheap rent, interesting neighbors, and wealthy patrons. Provincetown was called in the years before WWI the "biggest art colony in the world." Without an easel and a box of paints you were undressed. Eugene O'Neill, Tennessee Williams, John Dos Passos, Truman Capote, Norman Mailer, and a motley crew of others also produced some good literary work here down through the years.

By the mid 1960s Commercial Street had cafes, head shops, leather stores, boutiques, and the "hippies," "yippies," and future "yuppies" had found a place to call their own. The end of the spit was welcoming host to endless summers of love. By the mid 1970s the open-minded nature of the place attracted a nucleus of a talented and committed gay community, and overnight P-Town became the hottest gay tourism destination on the east coast. The eclectic nature of this bustling resort on the outer Cape must be seen up close and personal to be appreciated. Diversity is its fuel and the place virtually bubbles over with people energy. This is especially true during happy hour from Memorial Day until the Labor Day exodus.

At lunchtime we take the launch in to the floating docks off the main town pier that bisects the protected part of the harbor behind the massive stone breakwater and separates the fishing fleet to the south and the pleasure boats to the north. At the end of the pier is an enormous parking lot you must transit before hitting the mass of colorful humanity navigating Commercial Street. The four of us wander in search of minor odds and ends of a grocery list and look for a place to have lunch. The streets are narrow and crowded beyond what should be legal limits. Most folks treat all streets as "walking," cars, bikes, motorcycles, scooters, and delivery trucks do their best to claim the streets. Horns blaring, fingers flying, tempers fraying, and explosive yelling like New York cabbies are all part of the strange gender-bending scene.

Storefronts flaunt their wares. The theme is usually sexual in nature. This gets bizarrely creative at taffy shops, dry cleaning stores, and real estate offices. Hand holding and "canoodling" seem to be universal and the pairings go out of their way to explore the possibilities. Never have so many gone so far to establish shock and awe as a theme for mating. I am happy to say my kids roll along with amused appreciation, enjoying the flora and fauna with a non-judgmental confidence that is a wonder to behold. I, on the other hand, hold tight to M.'s hand and try not to look like something out of *Leave It To Beaver* reruns.

At lunch we sit in a fancy little coffee shop on the water, so crowded that four of us are crammed around a circular table barely twenty-four inches across. We are constantly scotching our chairs forward as conga lines of people continue to come in and mill around waiting for a seat. Our waitress has more piercings on her face than a Bowery bar full of Cape Horn sailors. The conversation, held at outdoor voice level because of the commotion, turns to the week ahead. Where to go? We discuss seeing friends in Quissett, Marion, and Padanarum on Buzzards Bay; maybe Falmouth, Vineyard Haven, and Edgartown in Vineyard Sound. Newport was brought up; Block Island too.

"Toasted Cheese ain't on the menu." Our waitress stands in a lopsided slouch addressing my pregnant and hungry daughter. Double tongue studs make it hard to not watch her mouth as she chewed a huge wad of something black.

"You're kidding."

"Kitchen won't do things what ain't on the menu. We're kind of busy," she said with a wave of her hand at the standing room only vultures.

The waitress hands Skye a menu and gives her eyebrows a workout doing the cha-cha from nose to the ceiling in time with her mouth.

"Can I get American cheese on your grilled Rueben?" my daughter said, all smiles and wide eyes. "On white bread?"

"You betcha" The girl muddles on back her heels.

"Great," my daughter said as the Pincushion Girl writes it down on a small pad. "Then, could you hold the corned beef? I'm a vegetarian. And scratch the sauerkraut, it gives me gas. Same on the lettuce and Thousand Island dressing, I don't like rabbit food, and bring me some mustard on the side, okay?"

"You betcha," the poor girl is still writing as she walks away on six-inch high clogs, weaving unsteadily from her perch through the crowd.

"Jack Nicholson did it better," I said, "and you just ordered a ten buck toasted cheese sandwich."

"Yeah, but I get a dill pickle,' she said with a wink.

The food takes a very troublesome forty-five minutes. We eat quickly and as soon as our chairs squeak, a throng of people are elbowing us out of the way for the right to arm wrestle for the table. I don't leave a big tip.

Swimming upstream against the current of bodies, we make our way back towards the pier. Tristan and Skye veer off to go climb the Pilgrims Monument and M. and I grab the launch back to the peace and normalcy of *Dog Star* searching for a recreational nap.

At 2 a.m. the fun starts. The discos along the beach have finally closed down and their insistent thumping techno beat is mercifully silent. I have been catching twenty-minute dozes between pumped up renditions of "Y.M.C.A." I am now willing and able to hate The Village People to their grave. I put visions of machine-gunning the one with the tool belt and hard hat out of my mind and roll over with a pillow over my head.

The first screams are enough to put a cat through a screen door. Men's and women's voices caterwaul through the crowded mooring field. It is in stereo and the numbers are more than a handful. I pull myself from my bunk and venture on deck to look around. The volume of merriment grows even louder as my head comes out of the companionway.

Three inflatable dinghies loaded to the gunnels with drunken revelers are putt-putting slowly through the boats, yelling at each other above the noise of their engines. Even the "shushes" and "quiets" from the less drunken voices are given with the decibel level of a steroid-addicted cheerleader. It's the women whose screeches sound most like claw marks on a blackboard. One female reveler in particular has a voice ideally suited to a mute button.

"I'm so wasted, take advantage honey." She repeatedly screams into the night.

Let's nickname her "Repressed."

I am about ready to let loose with a string of vitriol at the top of my own lungs when it dawns on me that I will sound a lot like the red-headed devil kids on the trawler this morning and might just rouse the few hearing challenged folks who could possibly still be sleeping from their rightful place below decks. I step into the cockpit in my starkers and pull my 10 billion candlepower spot light from its place in the port locker and point it like a Dirty Harry 44 Magnum at the dinghy closest to me, taking them from dark anonymity to light flooded center stage with the flick of a switch. They shut up in a heartbeat, trying to cover their eyes from the painful glare. Their dinghy bumps into a boat. They are blind. I start to have fun.

"Hey you, shut that off." Repressed screeches the order from somewhere off to my port. Bad mistake. I swing the beam and illuminate that boat in a nanosecond. The contents of the newly targeted dinghy cringe and squirm like vampires in the morning sun. Repressed now has every right to be, but wasn't.

Suddenly a huge boat a couple of rows out to my starboard joins me with a light even more powerful than mine. Then another, and another light trains their silent shame finger on one or the other of the gang of sleep thieves. It is an amazing part of human nature that lets one behave abominably as long as one remains incognito. The second you are found out, you succumb to the slinking guilt of an altar boy found with a playboy centerfold stuck in the folds of his cassock. Soon eight or ten lights follow the now quiet and embarrassed sailors to their respective boats. In the morning we will all know who they were and where they live. The last of the lights doesn't blink off until the final inebriated idiot disappears, stumbling in retreat below decks. Repressed and her group board a monstrous plastic boat with stubby little masts that I swear to Allah is named *In Dentured Servant*.

Then a single hand starts clapping in our reclaimed silence, and soon it is a good crowd appreciating the *quid pro quo* of our sunbeam attacks in defense of a quiet summer's night. I don't take a bow. I am still starkers. But then again I probably should, because the good lord knows nothing is shocking and anything goes, especially if you do it with a semblance of style in old, but never stodgy, Provincetown.

Twenty

PREPARING FOR SEA

After six months of trekking across Nepal, Burma, Thailand, Singapore, and Malaysia, M. and I arrived in Sydney. It was November, 1973. We had one solitary fifty-dollar traveler's check left. When we cashed it in, we had thirty-three dollars Australian in our pockets. We decided to have a beer and think things over. Stuck in the heart of downtown, we wandered in to the ritzy Wentworth Hotel to get out of the tropical heat, leaving our heavy backpacks, climbing gear, and everything we owned with the bellman. We were pretty used to being broke in foreign lands and knew our dire financial situation had nowhere to go but up. We had a second "schooner" of cold Tooheys beer to celebrate our abject lack of funds.

On my way to the bathroom I asked where the manager's office was and got an application for a job as a waiter. We sat and filled it out and I went back for a five-minute interview with the head of the service staff. I was hired. The trick monkey in the deal was that I had to have a white shirt, black pants and shiney black shoes to fit the décor. I was shown the locker room and told to be dressed and ready to go for the lunch shift the next day. Left alone, I rummaged through the abandoned broken-open lockers and found a frayed white shirt, size forty waist black pants with a well worn and glossy seat, and a pair of shoes that were black, but two sizes too large and looked like they had been used by the janitor for a decade or so. I was set. We were brazen enough to ask for an employee discount on the beers and got it. We were beginning to love this country.

During the next two weeks we dug ourselves out of a hole. Each night we would take the commuter train to the end of the line while eating doggy-bagged steak and fish saved from the garbage disposal off my customer's plates, and walk a mile and a half to a park on a beautiful tidal river just south of Botany Bay. No camping was allowed but we would set the tent up after dark. The nerve shattering screeches of the cockatoos in the trees at dawn would do the job of making sure we had the tent down before anyone in their right mind would be up. Each morning we would get on the train and head for Kings Cross for a cheap "mug-up and a grill." Tips the first day went to get M. a dress and she went looking for a teaching job. She landed three in one day. Soon we had enough money to rent a single room. When I got my own job teaching at an all-boys school, our housing got better. We bought two small second-hand motorcycles to get around. M. became the very first female "strapper" in Australia (an exercise rider for the high spirited thoroughbreds at the Randwick Raceway) bounding up each morning at 4 a.m. to get her horse fix before a long day of bending young minds. Ten months later when our schools let out for the Austral summer vacation in November, we began to make our plans to continue east across the Pacific.

The newspapers were full of the international boats arriving for the Sydney to Hobart Race, held each year on Boxing Day, December 26. The brand new 80-foot *Ondine*, Huey Long's newest Maxi, was destined to be the scratch boat in the fleet. Huey already owned the race record with the previous evolution of his baby blue racing machines and was determined to break his own mark with this newer and bigger boat. The long legged ketch, with two masts reputed to be a hundred feet tall, was straight off a record setting run from Newport to Bermuda and was the new queen of the international fleet. I began plotting and scheming and wondered who was onboard as crew. I was determined that I would find a way to not only do the race but get a lift back to the United States as well. "By hook or crook" failed to get the job done, but a bizarre technicality worked in my favor for once in this fateful tale of my sordid sailing career.

Provincetown wakes up slowly. I watch the sun catch the tip of the Pilgrims Monument before the first rays strike the tops of the houses on the small dunes to the east. As I sip my second cup of coffee Skye, once again, is the first to join me in appreciating the morning.

"Do you believe those people last night?" she said.

"They woke you up?"

"They woke up half the dead Pilgrims in the cemetery."

"Comes with the territory here on the Cape."

"I know. But, with the airplane squeeze and now the P-Town loonies, I think I'm way over the need to be where everyone else is. This part of the world is way too crowded, even if it does have warm water," Skye said with a smile and then a staged whisper, "How far away is Maine?"

"Second star to the right and straight on until morning," I said with my own un-tempered grin.

"That's got my vote." Skye gives me a one armed hug and goes down to heat some water for tea. "Right after one swim at the beach," she said from below.

I sit proud and reach for the handheld VHF. NOAA weather begins to drone on in its computerized voice shaping the days to come.

As we drop the mooring later in the new morning, after the rest of the crew voice their opinion that an overnighter to Maine is just the ticket, I make it a point to swing our boat very close to *In Dentured Servant*. Compressed air foghorns may be small but their decibel level is mighty. Revenge is my plan, but my weapon is nowhere to be found. I plead with M. for the hiding place of the noisemaker. She has easily anticipated my adolescent streak and claims she has a short-term memory loss.

"Where is the justice? Where is the outrage?" I keep shouting, a lot louder than I should. Repressed, looking like a seasick Pooka, appears in the flesh at the sun drenched opening to the cockpit. I wave and smile like a ham-boned politician. She models the look of one who is well and properly hung over. I would have tipped my hat if I were wearing one. My crew deliberately and pointedly ignores my antics by looking elsewhere.

We are now outward bound for Maine. High spirits are always part of that bargain with Neptune. Go boldly or don't go at all.

Anchored off the beach behind Long Point across the harbor from Provincetown we begin the checklist of getting the boat ready for an overnight passage. Skye and Tristan seem genuinely excited about the prospect, and I sit and read off the list of items one by one. We are in no hurry to get underway as the weather seems stable and the 165 miles of open ocean between the tip of Cape Cod and the West Passage to Northeast Harbor via Mt. Desert Rock will take *Dog Star* anywhere from 24 to 40 hours depending on the wind. Leaving in the late afternoon will make for a two-night passage with landfall in the early morning hours.

During a late lunch, the topic of who will stand what watch becomes a point of discussion. You would think this simple exercise would be a snap. Oldest to youngest; tallest to shortest; Boy-girl-boy-girl; mother-son-father-daughter, could be some of the logical orders of transition. The heated discussion immediately reminds me of one of the premier tenants of leadership: never ask a question unless you know exactly how someone is going to answer it, and you wholeheartedly agree with their opinion. The change of a watch is a critical, delicate, dangerous, and complicated business. In this family it is also the makings of a blood feud.

Picture the precision and grace of the 4 X 100 relay teams in the Olympics. The baton is the herald of command and the runners practice the smooth acceleration, the split second timing, and the "thwack" of the prize so that it appears a seamless, fluid transfer of effortless grace. A change of watch on a sailboat should be just like that. Dark of night, disgraceful weather, lack of hot food or sound sleep should not derail the well-oiled machine. On *Dog Star* the truer image to consider is that a sibling's slight, or a sarcastic aside uttered decades in the past, becomes the princess' pea under the mattress and things go to hell in a hand basket at the drop of an eyebrow. The gentle art of waking someone from a warm bunk and demanding that they go out in the cold, dark night, all alone to shiver and imagine a watery death approaching somewhere over the bow is a three stage process, but I'll get to that in a moment. Let's listen to the crew.

"I'm not following Tristan," Skye said.

"And whom would you like to follow?" I said.

"Mom," my two offspring said together in a loud "pick me" voice.

I do my best to be a grown-up and ignore the slight.

"Don't sulk," M. said and strokes my cheek.

"I'll wake up Dad," Tristan said with a gleam in his eye. He has probably learned some new tricks on the *Gammage* and intends to use them.

"I'll wake up Tristan," Skye said with a Bela Lugosi laugh.

"In your dreams, sister dearest."

"Nightmares, brother darling." Another cackle of doom escapes her lips.

"I'll post the watches before we leave," I said.

"Who elected you captain?" my son gives the question his best shot to sound serious.

"Guess who follows me?" I said.

Skye punches Tristan hard in the shoulder as he stumbles by heading below for the snack locker.

"Sissy boy," she said.

"Bully girl," he said.

I can see *Dog Star*'s three rules of engagement for calling the off-watch may undergo some brutal refinements during this next leg of the journey. Over the years we have refined the ancient mariner's art of sleep disturbance in a kinder and gentler fashion to suit the ages and temperaments of the crew. Tristan and Skye have been standing watches since the days when they thought it a privilege to sit beside their parents and drink hot cocoa to try and stay awake for a half hour or so. As teenagers they were fully vested and knew the drill: stay tethered, stay alert, stay awake.

All people wake up differently. Not one of the hundreds of people I have ever sailed with, except my wife, wakes up happy as punch to go on watch. Tagging a snoring shipmate on the shoulder at midnight is liable to get you bit, bludgeoned, or worse. The *Dog Star* rules are as follows: begin the process with a gentle call from the cockpit, something like, "times up," or "watch change," in a gentle soothing voice straight from a *Lassie* re-run. It often helps to link this gentle voice with a bit of scuttling about in the galley, setting out a snack for the new watch, or taking the hot water in the thermos and making a cup of tea or hot chocolate as a wake up gift.

If the prone figure of your relief does not move, or worse, rolls over and tucks their blankets up under their chin, it is time for an escalation to insults. Louder verbal challenges to their snores are then called for, along the lines of "Rise and shine bait breath," or "Your bunks on fire," usually does the trick. If not, approach the sleeper from the feet end and grab a big toe until they squeal.

Phase three involves a rubber sea boot and a scoop of cold seawater deposited in a bottoms-up motion to the snoring area above the shoulders. There is a phase four, but it is called burial at sea, and you can read about the entire ritual in Chapman's.

TWENTY-ONE

OFF SOUNDINGS

The normal sea breeze and its Southwest winds give up the ghost at 2100 hours and *Dog Star* cranks on the iron jib to push us through the starry night. I lie in my bunk and can just see the silhouette of Skye's wool capped head against the gentle red glow of the compass light. I have all the confidence in the world that she will have a good, safe watch. She shifts her position and her head does a quick and thorough scan of the darkness on all sides of the boat including astern.

The boat is trimmed loose and she glides up and over the long ocean swells. Sounds of a single rolling can reach my ears: the creak of the sheet through the snatch block on the rail, Skye humming a simple tune I can't quite make out. The motion is a rocking cradle, and my body presses against the leeboard I had put up and tied in place to hold me in. *Dog Star* has solid slatted and varnished lm boards that swing on hinges up from their place against the knee high foot wells between the bunks.

Late night watches are often magical. Anything is possible as the boat surges on a big swell, riding the watery skin of a lonely planet that is hurtling through space at thousands of miles an hour, sharing the vast reaches of the universe with stars whose light has not yet reached us since the Big Bang started the whole experiment. The mind at sea becomes a runaway bobsled. The switch is thrown and the best you can do is just hold on for the ride.

This is a huge part of my enjoyment of cruising with my family. Listening to the boat make the miles and the proof in the pudding of the sum total of all those lessons learned down through the years allowing each of the crew, including myself, to take a confident pride in being able to do this, and do it right. I push sleep into a back corner and resolve to really enjoy these fleeting moments of appreciation for my daughter before they become nothing more than rose-colored memories. I dress warm and go up to the cockpit.

"Is it always like this?" My daughter said.

The wind has come back at about ten knots over the port quarter, and I can't find the sleep fairy anyway. So, I put on the water for hot chocolate while I shut down the engine and get the sails up. We sit together listening to the water slide along the hull and the wind spill around the sails in the dark. Skye's hands are laced over her belly holding her little girl to be. The tiller supports the back of her knee as she steers casually downwind.

"Yeah, it's called being pregnant." I whisper conspiratorially.

"I mean the night, the stars, deep black water. Like this?" She said again softly so we don't wake up the off watch.

"Pretty much." I stretch my arms dramatically over my head. "Except when it isn't."

It is beautiful, a one in a hundred night, and I am trying to be a wise guy. Isn't that what grandfather's do? I wasn't the responsible one here.

"I don't remember the bad nights," she said.

"Brainwashing. Tricks of the ancient Chinese."

"Were there bad nights?"

"Some less than perfect ones, but none really bad." I lie.

"How did you do that?" She said, not believing my Pollyanna assessment. I am used to my family choosing not to hear what I have to say.

"Make it a game," I said. "Keep comfort the first priority and getting somewhere over the horizon a distant second. You and your brother were pretty gullible. And you slept a lot."

"Will I be able to do that with this thing?" She pats her belly.

"Sure, keeping all of the world's scary things from your kids becomes a prime motivating factor in your life. Trust me." I remembered a ton of fatherly half-truths and outright fabrications, all in the interest of good child rearing.

"So you lied," she said.

"Daily," I said.

She's quiet a long time as we sip our hot chocolate. The boat slides along gently in the rhythm of the four-foot waves rolling up astern. The Milky Way is like a glowing Frisbee, stretching from horizon to horizon.

"It works the other way to," she finally said with a chuckle.

"What does?"

"Keeping the scary parts from your parents."

Oh yeah, I forgot about that. A hundred questions I'll never ask wave their hands in the air to be first. We sit with my arm around her shoulders as the wind urges us along its way. Words would spoil it. I really don't want to know my daughter's old business. This fact surprises me. Is this a latent sign of grandfatherly maturity?

The Royal Sydney Yacht Squadron was posh. Its inner sanctums the domain of the last vestiges of imagined or invented Down-Under royalty. Doesn't it always seem that a former British Colony tries to outdo Mother England in pompous, seldom deserved, class-conscious excess whenever it can? Insufferable is to the former British Empire as arrogant is to the Parisian French. It is a descriptive word meant as an insult, but actually taken as simple, heavenly ordained, nationally embraced fact. Carrying the banner of Britain's ancestral pride into a country peopled by convicts in chains is a sizeable black hole of conundrums.

The Club, established by order of the Prince of Wales in 1862, is east of Kirribilli and just behind Wudyong Point. The sign on the massive whalebone arch over the entrance prohibited admittance under pain of prosecution. Hedgerows were twelve-feet high. A guard lounged playfully against his shack like a cowpoke gunfighter. I walked right in. The docks were full of activity. The bustle was a din. Everyone was moving along hurried straight lines in that semi-controlled state of panic days before a major ocean race. The Sydney to Hobart run was one of the sailor's triple crown: Newport-Bermuda, The Fastnet (a non-stop round trip thrash from Cowes, England to a lonely lighthouse at tip of Ireland), and this day after Christmas run to Tasmania in the 1960s and 1970s were the ultimate, most prestigious and exotic offshore challenges in the racing world. I felt right at home; like an unwanted orphan at a stranger's family reunion. Call me Oliver Twist. How the heck was I going to make this happen?

Ondine was easy to spot from a distance. Her two equally impressive matched spars towered above the fleet. Her baby blue hull was as massive and flat as an aircraft carrier, broken only by "organ grinders" and winches the size of truck tires. She towered above the dock. I gawked.

"Captain aboard?" I finally said to a curly haired giant of a Kiwi who was in the process of rebuilding a winch. Parts were scattered across the deck.

"You American?" he said.

"As apple pie." I smarmed a bit, hoping it was the right answer.

"The captain will definitely want to see you." The black, scrub-brush hair jerked in the direction of the bar. This was an unexpected turn of events. When you are expecting a slammed door and you get an appointment it is hard to re-adjust. I once again went over my pitch about my experience, the names to drop, the right touch of competent humility on my sailing skills. The whole sell was: please, like me, I don't bitch or whine, and I will pull my own weight and then some.

Thom Richardson was standing at the bar. He was tall, tan, rail thin, and blond. He looked like a movie star (maybe Stewart Granger from the 30's), very British, very upper crust. Looking down his nose at you looked swell on him. His face had been all over Rupert Murdock's shameless excuse for local newspapers for days, calling him the most eligible bachelor in years, and he was stuck here "Down Under" until Christmas.

"You American," he said after I got his attention, "U. S. Passport?"

I nodded.

"Current," he said, "like, you can go back any time, right?"

My eyebrows went up in twin paradoxes and I nodded again. What gives here?

"Don't really need an extra hand for the race, but we are sailing for San Diego mid-January after we fit out here in Sydney. You want to go?"

My mouth wouldn't work. Who cares about another damn race; I'm crossing the Pacific. "Huzzah," I say to myself. Thom frowned, looked at the ceiling, and growled in frustration.

"Okay, you can go on the race. But, you got the forepeak and the sail bag sandwich. "

I blinked, still unable to believe my good fortune. Thom's eyes got hard.

"All right, no forepeak, but I can't promise where you'll squat."

I swallowed, gulping.

"Bloody hell," his voice sank to a whisper and his hand brushed through his hair in resignation, "Right you are, go take a look and pick any bunk not occupied. I'll square it with Huey."

I was in a very fluid negotiation and I was scoring all the goals. I kept my mouth shut. I stuck out my hand, and we shook on the deal. I grabbed the bar to keep from falling faint at this chance of a lifetime.

"You do speak English, right mate?" Thom finally asked the obvious question with a worried frown.

I bought my new boss a drink. I was basking in the glow of being taken for a real sailor without my heavy sell job. The other shoe was about to fall on my run away ego.

"Fact is I got a dozen guys I know lined up for that berth. But none of the rotters is a Yank. New law says a U. S. flagged vessel must be under the command of a U. S. captain to clear into U. S. waters. Bloody morons if you ask me. Usually you can't have a yacht race without a right full plague of ball busting Americans. Now, I can't find one worth the trouble in this town for the life of me. Anyway, you get to go along if you want, but don't forget your damn passport."

Skye has crawled off to her bunk. The wind is holding and the seas are a combination of the long Atlantic swells from a storm out beyond Bermuda and the shorter waves driven by the local breeze and tide. The big round stars crowd in close about. The inky black water heaves and occasionally startles the eyes with bright explosions of white froth as a wandering wave-top tumbles headlong into its trough. The mixed sounds of the elements are only an octave or two below a Greek chorus. *Dog Star*'s long keel keeps her motion predictable as we rock along at five knots. Pulling the collar of my rain jacket up closer under my chin, I knock softly three times on the cockpit coaming as my mind tempts fate and Neptune by remarking silently how pleasant an overnight sail this is. I should have added to my penance spinning around three times and spitting into my palm, but it is a small cockpit and I am far too comfortable.

I am as modestly superstitious as the next guy, as long as he is a borderline paranoid schizophrenic with a heavy dose of '60s mysticism, a well-fired intolerance of organized religions, and a mind full of trivial, arcane good luck rituals from around the world. This odd mix, coupled with a few very *Twilight Zone* personal experiences, keeps me guessing. The grand sum of this wasted use of memory confirms in my case that we hairless apes know very little about how the magnificent universe works and what inexplicable wonders it makes happen all around us every day. Divine mismanagement is the crutch many of us depend on when seeking reasons why things are always going wrong. Those "on high" must get fairly tired of being blamed for everything. No wonder chaos is the primary rule of the universe. What can it hurt to follow the old wives' tales? At least you are being pro-active in your delusions of control.

Sailing has more ways to anger the gods than a couple of dozen vestal virgins on a spree in Vegas. Don't set sail on Friday. Don't whistle at sea. Don't remark on good fortune until the ship reaches safe port. The slightest wrinkle of pride on the part of captain or crew brings the wrath of Aeolus, God of Winds. Don't look gulls in the eye. Verbally questioning the weather in any manner is an insult to those in charge and a guarantee to make things worse in a hurry. Never shoot an Albatross. Pay tribute to Neptune when crossing the equator. Never harm a dolphin. Place a silver coin heads up under the mast. Fear "sun dogs." Never be the only one of the crew, other than the captain, who knows where the treasure is buried. Take no oaths you can't live by. And remember, above all, never take the last sip from a bottle of grog. Over the side with it and tip your hat; you proceed by the grace of Poseidon.

I let Tristan sleep into his watch. The early summer night is a riot of sight and sound. We bowl along on the edge of control, sliding downhill towards the Maine coast. First light should allow us to make landfall on Mt. Desert Rock, an island fifteen miles off the coast of Mount Desert Island. It is a remarkable whale spotting area. Could there possibly be anything more perfect, more contained, more magical than a crew at sea on a wooden boat? Even with my unlicensed and chronically juvenile enhanced imagination it is truly hard to picture. It has been just like this along this coast for others a hundred and fifty years ago.

In the summer of 1858 the heavy, gaff-rigged sloop *Helen* departed Provincetown bound for the distant shores of Mount Desert along the scarcely settled coasts leading to Maine. Robert Carter, a writer and sailor, wanted to escape the heat of an intolerable Washington D. C. summer. Our country was teetering on the brink of the Civil War. Lincoln was looking for a miracle. Carter recruited a motley crew of distinguished friends to accompany him on a voyage to the farthest reaches of coastal Maine. To protect their nascent reputations as serious personalities in the business and social world of their day, they crew are identified only as the Professor, the Artist, and, my favorite, the Thirsty Assyrian. These were aging gentlemen, backyard adventurers who did not want to be thought of as incompetent vagabonds, or spoon-fed shipboard clients off on a frivolous spree. They took great pains among themselves to portray the voyage as an expedition of hardship and discovery. The discoveries that may have been possible were certainly in the small "d"' category. But these were not small men, and they kept the illusion of industrious and worthwhile enterprise until the end of the line. One of the renowned company later founded the *Atlantic Monthly* as a clear voice for the anti-slavery movement, and Carter himself helped establish the Republican Party. To manage the thirty-three foot sloop, they engaged the ship's owner, a retired ship's captain, and another aging professional seaman. Carter called them the Pilot and the Skipper.

Their slow but steady journey up the coast was forever immortalized in the cult classic, *Carter's Coast of New England*, and this modest little book has been periodically in and out of print for a hundred and fifty years. The remarkable backdrop of the people and harbors of the working seacoast villages and cities, long before there were any tourist accommodations or attractions to draw the folks of Boston and New York, is a perfect time capsule for the day written by a confident and talented newsman. The other notable reason for this book's continuing popularity is the simple fact that not so very much has changed since the mid-19th century for a cruising sailboat and her crew plying their way along this rugged summertime coast. The havens of Marblehead, Gloucester, Rockport, the Isles of Shoals, Monhegan Island, Pulpit Harbor, and Somes Sound are all tangled up in this and subsequent stories of many a run "down east."

This was a cruise of cigar smoke, claret, and brandy in crystal decanters. Each fish caught was an epic, and ended up under the eye of the professor who promptly named it and categorized it in the log, "for lofty scientific purpose." Most specimens ended up on the sideboard at dinner. The Thirsty Assyrian was constantly warned, "to keep your mouth away from that lamp or your breath will certainly explode." They had hair raising escapes from uncharted rocks, were serenaded by a female baritone from shore at sunset; they toured light houses and public houses, lost flapjacks over the side; they challenged other boats to impromptu racing, sinned by fishing for pleasure on the Sabbath, then ran short of supplies and went to extraordinary lengths that included a cross island horse and buggy ride and a rowing ferrymen to replenish the wet and dry lockers. In essence it sounds much like any travelogue magazine article written today.

Carter writes: "The approach to Mount Desert by sea is magnificent. The island is a mass of mountains crowded together, and seemingly rising from the water. It is difficult to conceive of any finer combination of land and water than this view. Certainly only in the tropics can it be excelled – only in the gorgeous islands of the Indian and Pacific Oceans. On the coast of the Americas it has no rival, except, perhaps, at the Bay of Rio de Janeiro."

Daniel Ford, publisher of this little book, wrote that some voyages are eternal and he mentions Carter in the company of Richard Henry Dana, Darwin, and Slocum. Book promotion has lost none of its guile. I agree that some voyages are eternal, while others just seem to take that long. Maybe, in the end, all voyages are eternal to someone who found some degree of personal enlightenment while at sea. A snippet or two of Carter's prose as you retrace the path of *Helen* in your own boat is a sure-fire way to celebrate the possibilities of Maine while owning-up to being one of the proud few feckless sail-addicted adventurers who plies these waters, continuing the art form over the centuries.

TWENTY-TWO

MT. DESERT ROCK

Tasmania was right where it was supposed to be. *Ondine* did her job like the thoroughbred she was and claimed line honors but couldn't hold her time in the light airs near the end and we finished down in the pack. With twenty-four crew, divided into three eight-men watches, the possibility of long, unhappy faces was not a small matter of concern at this finish line for the nucleus of the six permanent sailors who took care of Huey Long's rocket-ship. It was our job to keep the high profile guests/sailors enjoying the heady experience of international ocean racing. We shouldn't have worried. Hobart was not a place to mope when a thousand sailors descended for a weekend party. Never have so few consumed so much for no apparent good reason. A handful of old friends surfaced from the SORC and the Bermuda races. It was a small world at this level of competition.

Back in Sydney after the race, M. and I helped the rest of the crew get the "big blue pig" (as she was commonly maligned by those who followed her transom across finish lines for nearly a decade) ready for a seven-thousand mile trip to the west coast of North America. The ship's complement was a mixture of nations. Two Brits, two Kiwis, and an Afrikaner composed the working crew.

Our cook was Kitty Slocum from Massachusetts. She claimed a direct lineage to ol' Joshua himself. She was a chain-smoking wonder who could feed an army of starving Huns in the middle of a hurricane and make it look easy. She kept to herself. Took the helm while the rest of the crew ate together, and I don't remember exchanging more than a few sentences with her for the three months that we spent on the same boat.

I was the lowest mug on the totem pole. In the beginning, my role as the added appendage, whose reason for gaining a berth was simply a passport color, had the captain and my shipmates treating me like I was a crystal vase and should be only moved towards a function if all else had failed. Even though we had raced to Tasmania and back, I was the race-day trophy crew who wouldn't go home. Luckily, a single bizarre incident helped erase many of the contributing factors to my outsider status. You won't be surprised to find out it had to do with skinny water, a new drifter, a nude beach, two five-foot steering wheels, and a Puritanical granny knot.

Prone on my bunk I watch the hot yellow glob of sunlight slide across the white enamel paint of the interior cabin-side. The first sight of the new day makes me shudder and I tuck the pile of blankets up tighter under my chin. Here's hoping the dangers of Mt. Desert Rock are off our stern and the island of the same name is growing across the horizon in a solid green band.

I can see M. tucked up under the dodger. Her eyes, under a wool ski hat, are locked on something off in the distance. The boat is still moving well, although I can feel that the wind is now more aft as we make our course and the heavy displacement hull rolls predictably from one gunnel to the other. It is dawn of our second night at sea and the waves, the wind, the sky, and the motion have all stayed fairly constant. The wind a little east of south at twelve to fifteen and a constant loping, two-foot high lazy swell, sends a lapdog chop against the rise of the bilge. The hollow taps adding a rhythmic base beat to the long rising and falling notes of the wind.

I take the decadent delight in shutting my eyes again. All is well. Worry is for those who don't trust those on watch. With a crew like this, a captain can take an extra wink. My shoulder presses against the leeboard and then back against the settee backrest as we slide through a churn cycle.

From an almost sleep, the "Prime Directive" plays a bugle timpani in my head. I don't open my eyes, but all systems are suddenly on full alert. The analysis of all the data I can absorb into my pea brain is a tsunami. Two major factors are red flagged: I can't see anything but the inside of my eyelids, and we are getting close to land. Sleep has left the building. I throw back the covers and grab my shirt. I prime the stove and finish dressing before my shivers became the Watusi. Coffee in the cockpit with my forever honey celebrating the new day is the homage I give to the necessity of the Prime Directive. M. and I have both solemnly, almost religiously, embraced this self-imposed strict first rule, the Prime Directive, from the very start of our sailing life, and it has worked for us just fine, and all the time.

Boats, debris, lobster pots, navigational buoys, whales, and the possibility of a landing meteorite must be factored into the proper anxiety level when coming from deep blue water up on to the ocean's continental shelf. Add to this obstacle course the fact that the shoreline is just over the horizon. Is it little wonder that the Prime Directive's bugle excites a sailor's attention? There will come a time when you may make the naïve assumption of mistaking the bugle for a cry of wolf. Don't. All other positive actions you can take, in almost any emergency on a boat, should follow the rigid purity of the Prime Directive. What is the Prime Directive? The Prime Directive, when navigating a boat on any body of water, is not to hit anything hard.

What I have noticed lately when sailing with others is an unhealthy tendency to cut the corners, to use navigational buoys as suggestions, and never lay down a plot line on paper. Why? Because the GPS and its cute little boat icon floating on the electronic chart screen has always been reliable and foolproof. One of my hard won observations in this life is that, when someone makes something foolproof, God makes a better fool. Building in safety margins is critical. Those margins we add on are just incremental percentages of predictability, not guarantees that something hard is just where you think it isn't. Safety margins should be a healthy percentage on the deep-water side, and please avoid the slippery slope of applying weather, schedule, crew incompatibility, babysitter, daylight, *mal de mer*, or other factors to the equation. Do you really think your peculiar set of troublesome circumstances is going to make that rock ledge quickly migrate elsewhere? And remember what I said about being prideful at sea; nothing is more humbling than waiting out a six-hour tide on the tilt during a lovely Sunday afternoon as everyone and his brother slides on by giving you the hoot.

"Steady as she g.oes there." Captain Thom Richardson bellowed the order. The crew waited at sloppy attention. The wind rips the Stars and Bars at the stern. *Ondine* ran down Sydney Harbor, past the Opera House, with a bone in her teeth, her bright blue hull slicing through the pale green water at twelve knots. The afternoon test of the newly built light drifter had gone well and now, hard on the wind under a big # 2 genoa, we were on a search and destroy mission. Search out the gear's weaknesses and destroy the weakest link while we are here in a major port where we can manage repairs.

"Right, lively now," the Captain said.

The crew scrambled shoulder to shoulder and straightened the line. Kitty, the female cook, was ashore filling out the long list of stores for the Pacific Ocean.

"Preeee-sent to starboard."

The boat was close-hauled, and I was at the lower steering station of the tandem five-foot in circumference wheels that formed a "T" at the end of the racing machines substantial cockpit. She was moving in freight train fashion. The water was barely twenty feet deep, and the boat needed all of twelve feet to stay afloat. I was told in no uncertain terms to keep the depth constant. With the seabed contours dictating the course and no sail trimmers to be had, I sometimes was forced to veer to leeward and load up the big twin sticks, each 100 feet tall, to violin string level. Think: the shower scene in the movie *Psycho*. I felt I could drag my fingers through the sand we were so close to the beach. I could smell the toasting shrimp on the "bar-bees."

The crew was lined up along the windward rail facing inboard. Five stout lads in cut off blue jeans and t-shirts that flapped competing drum solos under the southerly wind. They looked solemn. But, then again, I was just getting to know the lot and couldn't be sure they weren't enjoying the moment. It could have been the prunes and Marmite at lunch. There was definitely an earnestly sinister, military precision to their demeanor.

"Ready the volley boys." The Captain's voice fell off mute down the wind.

The rail dipped to a strong random gust and all hands steadied themselves on the deck. The Captain scanned the shore picking out the tall billboard marker that divided the beach in two: the haves and the have-nots. The boat steadied out as we rushed past the sign.

"Smartly now," he said. "Shed the togs!"

Having been at the helm and left out of the planning for this drive-by mooning, I was caught by surprise to see five men suddenly bare from the waist down angling their considerable poundage of *glutei maximi* out over the wire safety line. Now the grins were wide. Shouts, whistles and applause came upwind every time we flew by a group of beach goers spread-eagled on towels and blankets.

I was in a quandary. I needed both hands to keep this rambunctious beast from rounding up, but how could I be the only one not inflicting himself, and those around me, to the humiliation of showing private parts unasked. I reached down and began to tug at the rope belt I had put through the loops of the old jeans. I had tied them on tight. And, instead of a tidy and easily loosened square knot, I had laid the final overhand wrong and ended up with a "granny" that would not let go. I finally gave up. I imagine I must have thought of just dropping my zipper, but thankfully, rejected the half measure.

While I struggled to keep one eye on the depth and the other on the ocean out ahead, where little heads would suddenly appear amongst the waves as aging "Australian crawlers" trolled for sharks on their daily surf swim parallel along the beach. I watched the grins of my comrades begin to lose their luster. It was a long beach, and for being only one of two nude beaches in Sydney, it was decidedly scarcely populated on this January weekend. The wind was border-line chill and the initial out-of-bounds thrill of hanging out at the rail with a bunch of naked guys can only go on for so long.

"Steady there," the Captain said, "hold the line."

Captain Thom was a showman. He didn't want anyone ashore to miss the experience. After a few seconds, without a vocal response from the beach, pants came up in rapid order. The ranks broke and in full rout the crew stampeded to the cockpit. Back thumps and shriveled miseries were shared among the nautical streakers. I laughed at the jokes and agreed with their analysis of the historic significance of the spectacle. The sideways glances and winks among the others served me notice that I was still an unknown commodity. Failing to drop pants at the proper time was a factor now being put into the mix.

"Ashamed of the pecker, mate?" Nick Richardson, Thom's younger brother, recently released from the British military service (having served her Royal Majesty as an underwater demolitions expert), decided to put me on the spot. His face flushed from laughing at another joke a moment before.

"You got me," I said seriously, giving him a deer in headlights look. "But, since the sex change operation and the trademarked tattoos, I usually charge a quid or better to show the privies off. Can't go giving away the farm, can we? You know how it is."

Nick's infectious grin did a flicker, got it, shelved it, and came back strong.

"I got the bloody same problem," he said and gave me a conspiratorial wink. "They'll be lined up at the dock to get the Polaroids." The rest of the crew let it go and wandered to the windward winches to bring us on to the other tack and leave the sandy beach behind.

"Ready about," the Captain ordered. "Hard to lee!"

No one jumped to take the wheel from my hands as I put the fifty-seven ton Maxi through the eye of the wind and lined up on the vaulted white "sails" of the brand new Opera House way down harbor below the green lawns of King's Park.

"Mark." I gave the course to the grinders.

The tall mast groaned like a prod-shocked mule as it set up against the dual backstays. She began to nestle down into the groove, pulling the bow wave aft, and lifting her nose. She was stretching out fine.

"Mark." I repeated the visual course.

Nick finished at the jib "organ-grinder" with a flurry of double-armed spins and slapped me on the back as he disappeared below. Once the main had joined suit in perfect trim the rest of the crew ducked out of sight. Captain Thom gave me one long look before he disappeared. It appeared to hold no malice.

Looks like I was finally finding my place in the "pecker" order.

Mt. Desert Island is the third largest island off the coastline of the lower forty-eight, and the home of Acadia National Park. Acadia is the second most popular national park in our country. Covering 33,000 acres, it is visited by four times the population of the rest of Maine each year. Champlain first noted its beauty and potential worth in 1604. The British and the French battled over this very important part of the coast of the New World for the next hundred and fifty years. Successive settlements flew the "Red Duster" or "Bony's Handkerchief" always hoping the next ship on the horizon was not an eviction notice.

Bar Harbor used to be Eden. That was before it surrendered to the British during the Revolutionary War and was responsible for a lasting insult to Maine's fairer sex. The British sloop of war *Allegiance* had invaded the town and took a few of the residents hostage as they plied the coastline for shipping. It was reported by an English Marine sergeant in the official logs that he had been offered one of the kidnapped Yankee's daughters in exchange for his freedom. The Master Sergeant gave no reason for his declining the offer of this prize. Much is surmised by his laconic hand. Little wonder Eden hid its, I'm sure undeserved, reputation in a renaming ceremony.

Since the mid-nineteenth century the Vanderbilts, Pulitzers, Fords, Carnegies, Astors, Rockefellers, and Morgans, among a host of others, built huge summer "cottages," some with up to eighty rooms, in order to enjoy the quiet and rarified air of their chosen and exclusive summer playground.

Later, great men like George B. Dorr, Charles W. Eliot (former president of Harvard), and John D. Rockefeller (who donated almost a third of the park's present acreage) framed a vision to protect the island from both chainsaws and developers. Their dream was to preserve this dynamic granite mountain and saltwater ecosystem for the enjoyment of all Americans.

This is a much different story than the international press reported surrounding a holocaust in the playgrounds of the rich and famous. In October of 1947, the Paris newspaper *Figaro* reported as front-page headlines that a peasant uprising on Mt. Desert Island in America had set afire the grand estates built by the wealthy "Robber Barons" of the fledgling superpower. The story had legs for months. If the tabloids had their way, the whole island would have had to be renamed Libertad while the rascals fled to the mainland to hide from the enraged "peasants." The facts are that the devastating fire lasted twenty-six days and ravaged more than twenty-five square miles of the island. Two hundred and thirty homes, including sixty of the largest summer mansions, were taken down to standing chimneys and stone foundations. A full third of the woodlands of the island were gone before the fire ended at the water's edge. The lush new growth is a testament to the recuperative powers of Mother Nature.

Dog Star rounds Little Cranberry Island and rides a tailing wind, making a white moustache off the bow, to pass the white day beacon at East Bunker Ledge to starboard and line up for a run down the

Eastern Way, north of Sutton Island all the way to the narrow entrance of Northeast Harbor. The lush blue hills rise high in undulating ripples above us all the way to the distant peak of Cadillac Mountain. Clearings of hardscrabble white rock, with yellow moss outlining the major fat-bellied cracks, appear from time to time. Perhaps they are scenes of some past lightening strikes. The ageless hillsides glower with dark shadows and look the stuff of Rip Van Winkle.

I watch Tristan crane his head with the following wind and catch the tickle of the exact apparent direction on the ridge of his ear. It is an old seaman's trick, and a better telltale of the wind's fickle nature than any other. Skye stands to the jib sheets with three turns and a grip on the weather arrangement, and a lackadaisical loop with no slack on the lazy sheet. M., eyeglasses in one hand and binoculars in the other, repeatedly checks the things she sees ahead with the information on the chart.

"Put some in the bank, the current will set in," I said.

Tristan points *Dog Star* higher to give a bigger margin of space upwind and away from the shoal. Skye cranks the jib line in a scant six inches with the winch handle and reaches for the mainsheet before I can.

"Good water off to port all the way to the shore," M. said giving Tristan the all clear on the course change.

All are back in their places and doing their things. I feel like a wart on a bump on a frog on a log in the middle of the pond.

"We'll do our fuel on the way in if nobody is at the dock," I say to Tristan and he nods, never taking his eye from the world over the bow. Bear Island Light, marking our entrance to Northeast Harbor, is just gaining strength in the morning mists. Nothing in my son's body language is saying he wants me to take the tiller, although the dozens of buoys, boats, rocks, lighthouses and docks has the Prime Directive hairs on my neck coming to attention. M. is hogging the charts and electronics. Skye has every loose piece of rope-assisted control in her hands. I bite my tongue and refrain from stating the redundant warnings. I taste blood and feel slightly proud of myself. Inability at times to keep my yap shut is a recurring issue. If tongue biting doesn't work, maybe I'll try staples.

M. looks up at me, smiles, assuring me that it is all okay. After this many years she knows my creeping paranoia all too well. Breathing deep, I relax, reminding myself that all control is illusion. My mind painfully stretches to a new shape of reality and it all makes perfect sense. I conclude that here, where vigilance and mild paranoia collide, is a good place for a boat to be.

"Let me know when you want to round up," I said and step down the companionway stairs. Out of the corner of my eye I catch Tristan and Skye exchanging a look.

At 4 a.m. on occasional restless nights I awake pondering that profound, instinctual, simple communication between those two. Most times I decide it doesn't matter what was "said," only that a complete, complex, understood moment could be transmitted in that very intimate way between two separate creatures. It is a wonder. If you don't have friends who share this bond with you, stop whatever else you are doing and go nurture your truest relationships until you find that connection.

The crew leaves me below while they come into the wind and stow sails. The bangs and rattles, always amplified below decks, sound like the orchestra bullying the audience into paying attention because "the fat lady's going to sing." I stay propped in my bunk reading and re-reading a single, simple line in a book. If they need me they will call me. It is all over in a minute. The calm voices going through the flaking and tying down of the main and mizzen sails, so an errant gust can't pull a baggy pocket free at the most inopportune time, make me feel guilty for not being more relaxed when it was all so noisy.

Finally M. calls down that we are in sight of Clifton Dock and did I want to take it from here. We pass each other at the bottom of the companionway and she pats my cheek. Our eyes lock and she smiles big. My preliminary guess is that I did something right. I wonder what it was.

TWENTY-THREE

NORTHEAST HARBOR

The gas float at Clifton Dock is full, with additional circular waiting patterns of other small craft, so we proceed on down the channel. Large homes with private docks line the promenade as one pretty boat after another either passes us going in or heading out for a day on the water. I instinctively fear and dislike with malice any boat operator who intentionally, or worse yet, unintentionally, closes the distance between our respective craft. With this understood, I will share with you the scientific underpinnings of *"The Dog Star* Theory of Boat Speed in a Crowded Harbor."

Boats in a narrow channel going to and from a harbor fall into two categories. First are the foolhardy speed freaks who are demonstrating their incompetence by recklessly forging ahead at a knot or two (1 to 3 miles per hour) faster than I am, and then try to wave in a friendly manner as they pass in their rushed mindless oblivion to get to a dock a minute faster than we can.

The second group of miscreants are those who are recklessly trying to slow down the whole dad-gum world by proceeding at a knot or two slower than *Dog Star,* and are on the verge of creating a nautical catastrophe by forcing us, through our devotion to prudent seamanship, to alter our course and pass, or throttle back, to avoid having to wave at the idiot at the wheel who is holding up holy progress. Why would God, in her infinite wisdom, ever create boats that go faster or slower than mine anyway? It gives idiots a choice, and we all know where that could lead. Free-will being what it is, most folks' decisions always create problems, especially for those who don't strictly follow my lead, freely given with all the devious and self-centered devotion of a television evangelist begging for money. A word of advice to those guilty of falling into one of those two distinctive categories: slow down or speed up, and, for heaven's sake, stay out of the way.

Slowly the basin opens up like the teardrop base of a genie's bottle. An even spread of evergreen trees sweep up steep hillsides to starboard and the town dock and waterfront spreads open on a raised terrace hillock to port. The town is humming. Coming from even a few days at sea on a small boat, the sight of so many things in motion at once is a shock. Running cloud shadows move across the harbor. The wind rattles wire halyards against dozens of metal masts. There is a bite in the air. A six-inch chop keeps everything afloat bouncing joyfully. Our eyes can't take it all in.

The smiles on the crew this morning are a very special blend of pride, relief, fatigue, high doses of tension, and the joyous let down of crossing a finish line. It was a classic two-night passage, and the boat and the crew preformed flawlessly in flawless conditions. I have had the privilege of seeing smiles like this on a lot of my former racing and delivery crews. A kaleidoscope of passage-ending smiles on the growing faces of my children explodes in my head, a visual ivory trail, from swaddler to adult, etched eternal in gleaming orthodontic milestones. I know I look just as goofy, tired, and sappy as they do. Maybe my perpetual frown is sliding north as we each continue to eat up the hustle and bustle in the sheltered basin with our eyes.

The harbormaster comes back immediately on VHF channel 16 and re-directs our request for a place to hang our hat for a quick stop over to a small outboard motorboat in the mooring field. A very pleasant college-aged duo in khakis, one on each side of the gender gap, lead us to a mooring and give us the okay to use it free for "less than two hours; extensions require a night's charge," to stretch our legs and do a bit for the local economy. I call this intelligent hospitality.

In short order the dinghy is launched off its inverted position on the cabin top with the help of the main halyard. Time in port is a precious commodity when you are on a strict budget. I secure the painter to the main shrouds and go below to get my wallet. When I get back, I look down from the deck into the dinghy. It was full. A Dyer 7'11" is not an ark, but I have managed to row my whole family ashore in it for twenty-plus years. Tristan amidships, Skye in the stern, M. holding on tightly at the bow, there is no more room. Not one inch.

"Be back in a few," Tristan said.

I watch them row off without me. I feel left behind. It is becoming a central theme in my life. My melancholy is so deep I almost fail to note, for my own edification, that Tristan has an accomplished, fluid style of rowing a heavily laden small dinghy. It is a small crumb of joy in a dark void of a captain's uncertainty at being put on the shelf.

Tristan and I are walking up the street from the pier towards the grocery store, logically called Provisions, and the Shirt Off Your Back laundry. Busloads of heavy-hatted, bag loaded, poundage challenged tourists clog the sidewalk, talking on their cell phones. We use the road.

"Remember that place?" Tristan nods towards a rust sided, single story ice cream stand with a small, enclosed restaurant attached.

I did and wondered how much of it was my fault.

"I spewed some pretty hefty chunks in that establishment."

"I think you were forgiven."

"We never went back."

"They could never have cleaned it all up."

"Sea spiders, bull snot, and worm stomachs I recall."

He remembers too much. I keep my eyes on the road at my feet.

"Pretty sneaky," he said with not a small amount of grudging admiration in his voice.

"A mind is a terrible thing to waste," I said.

"What kind of pathological skinflint does it take to dine in front of his children on lobster, fresh oysters, and fried clams while calling these killer great foods "underwater spiders," "boogers from bulls" and the "stuffed rancid bellies of earthworms" just so we'd stick to a corndog and wouldn't order them?"

"One who is paying for your college education?" I said.

"But we eat organic and think tofu is a special treat all the rest of the year, and then in Maine, the fresh seafood capital of the world, we get corndogs?"

"You liked corndogs."

"I was too stupid to know the difference."

I waited for the silent rim-shot on the snare drum and finally said, "And your point is?"

It took a minute or two of testy silence before the smile comes back. A chuckle follows right along. "I'll have to remember that," he said.

The incident in question was at a time when a five-year-old Tristan ignored our descriptive names and tried everything edible (as a vehicle for ketchup) on both his mother's and my plates before Skye began a vivid play-by-play colorcast of the battle being waged by these extremely slimy and slithery beasts in the churning region of her brother's stomach acid. I recall she mentioned the chest-bursting scene from the movie *Alien* just before the eruption. Listing the vomit episode as "projectile" is understating the pressure, breadth, and scope of the pattern by a goodly margin. My boy doused our whole corner of the room. The only truly notable memory of the event was Skye wearing a goodly portion of the brew on our way home that evening in the dinghy. It follows the old sailor's adage: "Be careful in raising the tempest, lest it engulf you in its fury."

We just beat the two-hour limit at our "free-to-shop" mooring ball. All chores were accomplished efficiently in the bustling tourist town of Northeast Harbor. The larder is stocked, the icebox packed with goodies, the beer stacked deep in the bottom of the cooler. Underway, motoring out from the harbor, we stop at Clifton Dock and took on fourteen gallons of gasoline. While not the biggest sale at the pump that day the paltry number represented almost half of our total supply. Our old technology Gray Marine 4-162 gasoline engine uses about a half a gallon an hour at hull speed of five and a half knots. We harness part of the engine's fifty horsepower to crank a large alternator, a hundred and fifty amps, to charge our battery banks. We also fill our fresh water tanks and pull away from the dock in less than ten minutes. Another boat quickly fills our space.

We skirt around the rocky point to starboard, keeping well clear of Gilpatrick Cove and shortly find the buoy marking the entrance to Somes Sound. This glacier-carved river valley is unique on the eastern seaboard of the United States. It would be worth all the trouble to come to Maine if only to sail in this magnificent fjord with its tall granite cliffs, waterfalls, dark headlands, and the blue hills of Acadia on all sides. It is reputed that Viking ships filled their water casks in this estuary, which must have reminded the Norsemen of the geology of the homeland they left behind. It is like entering a movie set from of *The Lord of the Rings*. The vertical walls, five hundred feet high, slowly emerge on port and the reality is that they are so steep-to a boat could raft alongside where the granite meets the water. We decided against lying alongside in spite of the legends. Anchoring here is deep, over fifty feet, and the bottom a pile of rocks, but we head in anyway. We find our luck is flowing like the Nile during rainy season as the single guest mooring, maintained by the Acadia National Park, is open.

Everything we do is like moving through butterscotch, as the ship's company are all feeling the effects of a couple of nights at sea. Conversation is way down the list of sidebar activities as we quietly chew sandwiches and each of us retires to their bunk for a decadent mid-afternoon nap. It is quiet now, with the rising on-shore wind kept at bay by the tall cliffs. A raven tocks loudly, making an echo, in the pines. The boat is safe and once again totally ready to reverse the offshore course back to P-town. This important fact, check-listed in the logbook, truly marks the end of any single passage. My eyes close as the soft whispers of deep breathing from my crew calls for imitation, and the afternoon clouds blot out that pesky Maine sun.

TWENTY-FOUR

SOMES SOUND

It was February in 1974. Rounding out past Great Head at the entrance to Sydney harbor is assuredly one of the highly-valued rites of passage for any blue-water sailor. I was twenty-six years of age and officially listed as Captain of a world famous Class A ocean racer, a state-of-the-art, Britt Chance designed Maxi, with a new course record in the Newport to Bermuda race under her belt and a line honors victory in the Sydney to Hobart race. We are outward bound on an epic seven thousand mile delivery to San Diego via Acapulco. Meeting those first huge swells coming in from the Tasman Sea drove her bow into the air with a will to fly. M. waved goodbye from the high green bluff, and I felt like I was starring in my own movie. The boat hunkered down as the sea breeze built, and we muscled aside the heaving water in explosions of green spray. The tall twin masts were soon way less than vertical, pushed down by the malicious heavy wind swirling up the coast generated in the endless procession of low-pressure bullies pushing eastward through the Bass Straits just north of Tasmania. This was my long anticipated pinnacle of sailing perfection, the next step on my way towards a life under canvas. We all stood in the cockpit watching Australia fade into the haze off our stern.

An hour later I was driving the porcelain bus, heaving chunks, feeding the fishes, spewing the goo. Not the most auspicious beginning for my first ocean crossing. The rest of the crew probably wondered, and not for the first time, what had they taken aboard. I can only explain the onset of my very first bout with sea sickness to the fact that M. and I had made an awful lot of friends in Sydney, and each and every one wanted to give me a goodbye "shout." It was a full week of fun. During the next twenty-four hours in the Tasman Sea, the piper was paid in full. This kind of embarrassment for a twenty-six year old is unexpected, heart rendering, ego threatening, and sometimes fatal. Luckily I viewed the least likely outcome to my malaise as survival. At these first moments of *mal de mer* you pray to higher powers to let your body stop heaving and breathing.

Seasickness is a touchy subject with sailors. Henry Wheeler Shaw said: "One of the best temporary cures for pride and affectation is seasickness." The world is divided into two classes of folks, those who have been sick as dogs at sea and those who haven't found their peculiar and unique limit of gut churning motion, yet. Those macho guys and gonzo gals who smirk at the rest of us and claim they never get sick are in the second group and usually know a trick or two on how to keep their lunch where it belongs. The simple biological fact is that all of us have an inner ear that acts like a carpenter's level to give our body a hint on how to stand erect. If the bubble in our head is going back and forth, past what gravity has trained us to expect, like a ping-pong ball at the Olympics, we have a trigger mechanism that warns us to sit or lie down, or at least get off the amusement ride. This warning device is called nausea.

During World War II when America's bravest and best were taking long sea voyages on troop carriers to Europe and the South Pacific many studies were done about how to cope with this most natural reaction to being shaken not stirred. The conclusion was that about ten percent of our species are able to withstand almost anything without feeling the slightest twinge. On the other side of the spectrum are about ten percent who will feel queasy riding an escalator, will not be able to adapt to any motion, and will continue to be sick and become dehydrated to the point where their life is indeed threatened unless put ashore. The rest of us fall in between, with varying tolerances for motion, smells, anxiety, and close quarters below decks. The good news is that for the large majority of us the nausea is a short term warning alarm; our body learns to cope with the situation, and we gradually get better, adapting as time goes on.

The first word of advice I give anyone concerning motion sickness is not to let the threat of becoming ill sit in the back corners of your mind like a four hundred pound gorilla that you won't talk about. The fear that you will be laid low, unable to help yourself or the boat, until you step on dry land again is, nine times out of ten, just not going to happen. Fear is like a Petri dish for bad happenings; all sorts of ugly, squiggly things grow in the healthy imagination of your mind once you drop in a scenario. Get your arms around the boogey man. Seasickness is part of the game of offshore sailing. There will be times when your body will not let you function at 100%. It happens to us all. This is usually at the beginning of a trip. Trust in the statistics. Every hour you go forward you are becoming better equipped to handle the motion. Talk about how you are feeling with your crewmates, who likely have a twinge or two themselves. Work through your plan of combat against these dark forces, stay positive and proactive; don't try to be an idiot and offer to cook a soufflé for lunch.

There is no single silver bullet to ward off motion sickness. Staying on deck, keeping an eye on the horizon, chewing gum, wristband acupuncture machines, over the counter and prescription drugs, ginger, and all the rest work some of the time for most of the people. The best thing I have found when you face an excess of saliva, a light head, and a hint of bile at the back of your throat is to tackle the fear factor and get the damn gorilla off your back. Get sick, get better, get on with what you have to do. Don't let either potential embarrassment or a "you're better off without me" attitude keep you from getting on board that boat and going to sea. Just as a common cold sniffle doesn't always lead to pneumonia, a bout of nausea does not always lead to incapacitation in your bunk praying that God in Her infinite mercy will please drain the oceans just this once. Trust me. This brand of avoidance would be as silly as nixing the food-group chocolate because you don't like the color brown.

Ondine pressed on into the dark austral night as I stood my watches, slept with a bucket, and remained hydrated while avoiding any smell or visual sighting of food. Things slowly settled down in my stomach, but not with the weather. It got worse, lots worse. We ran east before a full gale under a storm jib and trysail. It looked as though we would make cruel short work of our first fourteen hundred mile leg to New Zealand. Then we found out about the Tasmanian Devils that had come aboard and stowed away. The hairy buggers never get sea sick.

The hike to the summit of Flying Mountain above the waters of Somes Sound wanders through a dark spruce, ash, and cedar forest on a trail softened by a deep bed of pine needles. The smells are of sweet moss and damp bark, sprinkled with a salt and iodine tang. The muffled roar of the trees, high above on the ridge standing strong against the late afternoon southerly, mixed with our huffing and puffing and sounded like a railroad steam engine.

The trail climbs steeply from the anchorage, and we could catch fleeting peeks at *Dog Star* through filtered openings in the trees. Skye and Tristan lock themselves into their obnoxiously humorous roles of eight-year-olds; verbally sparring at each other in a playful teasing banter that brought back a stadium full of rich memories. They forge on ahead. Their voices are falling down to us, clear as could be, as they speed up the switchbacks.

"You're letting an old pregnant girl beat your butt up this hill?"

"I'm using you for shade."

"Hey, there are two people in here, Mr. Beanpole."

"I was thinking a village."

"Better quit it, skinny, or I'll have the baby sit on you."

"Hey, you're off the trail."

"No way."

"Right here, sign, trash bin, arrow, everything."

"I'm not falling for that."

"I'll wait right here and show you. I won't move an inch. You're my only sister. C'mon, we gotta beat the sunset."

M. and I pause to get our breath and wait for the inevitable.

"No...wait...you...don't...damn." A thrashing of underbrush and a flash of color through the branches two turns above. The tortoise has tricked the hare.

"Now you're letting a skinny beanpole beat YOUR butt."

"That wasn't fair Tristan. I'm telling."

"Go ahead, loser."

"Mom, Tristan lied."

All four of us are still laughing hysterically at the instant replay of child antics from the past when a sedate tan-togged couple in starched shorts and binoculars comes hopping on down the trail. We all try to control ourselves but can't manage a word of greeting. We are sheepish as we got back underway. Tristan is relegated to the rear for the dual crimes of "chicanery and fibs" told to a pregnant sister.

At a slope side of round boulders and grass plots called Fernald Hill about twenty-five minutes up the trail we stop to flop on the ground and look out over the Jesuit Spring meadows where Vikings were said to have spent a time. In the low clouds and fading light we can now barely see the Cranberry Islands and the white crested Atlantic beyond. We drink hot chocolate from a thermos and munch from our stash of Girl Scout Cookies. We watch the daylight pulled westward and the electric glows of the small towns of Southwest Harbor, Northeast Harbor, and Bar Harbor to the south and east gain jurisdiction over the night sky. Around us a collective calm begs to be filled, but not with anything that could come from words. We listen to the sounds of the buzzing night as it lowered itself onto our perch. The walk down is slow and careful. We all held hands at times on the dark path to shuffle safely and capture the feeling of being lost on a grand adventure.

It is fourteen hundred tough miles between Australia and New Zealand across the Tasman Sea. This bit of "briney" is well respected for its constant gales and steep cross wave patterns as an endless parade of low pressure troughs pass just south of our route in the Great Southern Ocean. It was wet, cold, lumpy, and windy, just perfect for a thoroughbred on the hunt.

Ondine was a handful to sail. Two one-hundred foot tall masts powered her sleek hull. At seventy-three feet and change, she was a racing dinghy on steroids. Due to the amount of sail she could carry, everything was in huge proportions. The grinder winch barrels for the headsails were the diameter of fifty-five gallon drums. The number one genoa was over an acre of canvas. We sailed her with two man watches. Two crew on deck to serve her needs. We were all reluctant to call an "All Hands" for the watches in their bunks. We made do except for sail changes in rough weather. We were all young, energetic, and full of a confidence we didn't deserve. Pushing this state-of-the-art rocket to the limit was a religion. There were no labor savings devices: electrical winches, self-steering, roller furling. The boat normally raced with a crew of twenty-four. This was not a leisurely tropic cruise.

Sailing for long distances requires a method for insuring that those in charge of the vessel at any time of the day or night are rested and fully able to handle the eventual emergencies that happen at sea. On the sailing vessels of old, captains would follow tradition and divide the entire ship's company into a "port" and "starboard" watch and rotate the sleepers to the doers every six hours. This was a standard practice when your crews were twice the size you could string up in hammocks at any one time.

On *Ondine* we had a watch schedule that I believe is still pretty close to perfect for a long passage and at least six other bodies aboard your boat. Each crewmember stood a four-hour watch, but your watch mate changed after two hours. This overlapping of crew insured that at least every two hours a new set of eyes and a fresh perspective came on deck. The captain always took the dawn (4 a.m. to 8 a.m.) and dusk (4 p.m. to 8 p.m.) hours for star sights if needed. This allowed the one doing the navigation duties to sleep through the night. It also made up for the fact that sun sights for latitude were a noon occurrence that came right in the middle of your off watch. On my watch I was sandwiched between a Kiwi and the Afrikaner.

In these long gone days before satellite guidance systems, the only forms of navigation were a sextant and dead reckoning. We didn't get a lot of sun during this part of the voyage. At the end of each hour the person leaving the helm was tasked with entering into the log a set of figures on average speed, average course, sail changes, and barometer readings. These averages were compiled every morning and using the information distilled an assumed position was then placed on the charts. During those brief snippets of sun, we managed to get a few sights that leaned towards agreeing with the spot we had placed on the charts. It was my first landfall where I had a part in the celestial navigation, and I was more than a bit apprehensive until we could pick out a shoreline the morning of the ninth day out of Sydney. When it came, it jumped out of the mist and rain and wind like a troll and scared the shit out of all of us. We scrambled to change course and save ourselves from being so bloody accurate. This lucky convergence happens for celestial navigators with about the same likelihood of a Blue Harvest Moon.

We entered New Zealand through the back door at Auckland after sailing around D' Urville Island and through Cook Strait, the narrow gap between the North and South Islands, then up the eastern coast. The engine was spewing oil and overheating so we were happy to let the authorities that checked us in arrange for a diesel mechanic to arrive the next morning. It was to be a long ten days and a hefty wheelbarrow of dollars changing hands before we were able to leave Auckland with a brand new engine in the bilges.

With two Kiwis aboard we were hosted by their families and friends to a week of fast travel and social experiences that cemented in our minds that New Zealand is a small land with a huge heart. It is a magic place of rich beauty, and the inhabitants of this island country are by and far some of the friendliest and most hospitable folks on earth.

TWENTY-FIVE

CELESTIAL NAVIGATING

Skye cuddles in close, pulling a light wool blanket with her up into the cockpit. The black wall of the Viking haunted fjord only twenty yards off our stern towers in a funereal backdrop over *Dog Star*'s masts. The sky is a chaos of distant suns. The broad band of the Milky Way and its two hundred million visible stars build a white girder between the tree-lined ridges. The strong tide ripples along the rounded stones of the beach, sounding like cicadas. We talk in small voices.

"I can't remember," she said.

"Constant blunt head trauma from my butterfingers when you were a baby." I squeeze her shoulders.

"Do you ever argue with Mom?"

"Daily."

She pulls her head off my shoulder and sits back slightly to give me a scolding stare. The oil lamps from the cabin give off a faint gold light that reflects from deep in the layers of varnish on the mizzenmast. Windows on the distant shoreline flicker like fireflies in the black trees. Skye spots a lie in the low light.

"I just don't do the arguing out loud," I said so her mother won't hear.

"I heard that." M. calls up from sink duty.

"There are two theories of arguing with your Mom," I said solemnly, "and neither one works."

"How does she do that?" Skye is impressed.

"You got arguing problems?"

"Not yet." She smiles, and my sympathy goes out to her husband.

"I need to give Donavan some hard won advice," I said.

"What kind of advice?" Skye sounds suspicious.

"He needs to know what the phrases 'nothing's wrong,' 'that's okay,' and 'go ahead and do what you want,' really mean when uttered by a wife during an argument."

"Okay, so 'nothing' means 'something', big deal. You're arguing, right?"

"Let's not forget: 'don't worry about it, honey, I got it,' on trash day?"

"Hey, 'Go ahead, do what you want' sounds pretty easy to understand." Skye giggles as I strangle myself with both hands for effect.

"Yeah, but it's a dare; it is never, ever, permission. Mistake the two at your peril. Aren't these things genetically programmed in pre-natal girl school?"

"I must have missed that class."

"And the Grand Nanny of them all: 'I'll only be five-minutes'."

"I should write these down," Skye said to herself.

"And why does any argument beginning with the word 'nothing' always end up with the word 'fine'? What does fine mean in a disagreement? The dictionary says it's a state of well-being; I know better after being argued with by your mother. So, 'fine' is a critical word a husband needs to know. You're a woman, you got the secret in your bones, but us dolts haven't a clue about why a word sounding so benign carries the seven biblical plagues."

"The only defense is to zip it, Right?"

"Precisely," I said and raise a single finger to me nose. "All I have figured out in forty years with your mother is that if I ever find myself winning an argument, even the silent ones, and am about to use the word 'fine' and turn the world on its end, I will immediately apologize and shut my yap until sometime next week."

"Smart man," M. said coming out of the companionway, patting me on the knee, and nuzzles up to my unoccupied side.

"I hold those two terms to be mutually exclusive, as I shamelessly brownnose my betters." I give their shoulders a squeeze.

"You're my favorite knuckle dragger."

"Now that I finally know the rules, you don't want to argue with me?" I said.

"Fine," M. said, "That's okay. Have it your way. Say whatever you want to say. Fine. I'll get the garbage."

We all laugh until Tristan calls from his bunk to be let in on the joke. We can't explain. He just can't get the old stock phrases as punch lines. We finally give up and high-five one another for our conspiracy to keep most males in the dark about the terminal humor just the other side of a no-win argument. And they are all no-win arguments in the end.

"Go ahead," Skye said, "give my old man some smart advice."

We three cuddle under a too small wool blanket together and watch the stars that seem bright enough to warm your hands on. My gerbils are presently silent in my brainpan, but I wonder what is flying through my daughter's head as she imagines a trouble-free future without even a few whirlwind disagreements with her husband and her unborn children. The odds of that are about the same for my getting the Nobel Prize in physics, even though I have never met an imaginary number I didn't like.

Stars are wondrous gifts we mortals should open every night. We are, after all, carbon based, rumored to be conscious and intelligent beings, born from exploding novas. The galaxies are distant kin. Only isolated mountaintops and quiet boats anchored far from ambient light and pollution offer the perfect vantage point for a crystal clear night of stargazing. If the moon is late to arrive or early to depart, that is all the better. Our primal link to who and what we humans are is based on tens of thousands of years of our ancestors spending much of the time between dusk and dawn tending fires for protection from other conscious beings further up the food chain. When not trying to keep themselves off someone else's menu, they sat staring at the stars in the night sky for entertainment. They named the bright shiny ones and brought together mysticism, historic myth, and simple patterns to form constellations of gods, warriors, hunters and animal spirits. They knew instinctively to make the heavens part of their everyday life. That magic and need is locked in our DNA.

The foolish endeavor of crossing oceans before the miracle of satellite positioning technology (GPS) was a much different personal experience than it is today. To leave all solid landmarks behind and trust that, using centuries old technology once condemned by the Pope as witchcraft, you will be able to pick a course to a narrow harbor entrance thousands of miles away is much like jumping off a cliff so high you can't see the bottom, and on the way down hoping for a pile of feathers at your landing site. Paranoia is always at your side, akin to a rabid monkey on your back, but never a cozy watch-mate for extended ocean crossings.

Nathanial Bowditch penned a hernia-inducing volume of directions on how best to handle every aspect in the operation of a ship on the oceans. Everything is included, from how to tie a bowline knot to estimating the weight distribution of deck cargo on a tramp steamer so you won't turn turtle in a typhoon. A hefty poundage of the discourse is on the skills and knowledge necessary to take a measurement of a celestial body and reduce the angle you obtain to a position line on a chart. This is called "sight reduction" and requires, after Bowditch, the complete set of volumes of logarithms for each star and planet, and an up-to-date nautical almanac for yearly tweakings to the numbers.

The first part of understanding the theory is that we need to imagine the universe we see at night and all its stars, moons, and planets as fixed spots painted on the inside skin of an inflated beach ball. Suspended inside, at the very center of our beach ball experience, is a globe of the earth. Now the earth does its thing, spinning around its axis once a day, while wobbling like a top with a full dip and curtsy each year. At any split second of the day, year, or millennium, each celestial body painted on the inside of the beach ball is at a right angle, 90 degrees from the dead center of the earth, with a straight line going through only one specific spot on the curved surface of our planet. A huge set of reference volumes of jumbled figures specifically locates the sun, the moon, the planets, and some twenty navigational stars with a cryptic logarithmic identity, which represents this important vertical line by a geographic position (latitude and longitude) on the surface of the earth.

We now have a basic right triangle, and, because all of the stars and planets are all the same theoretical distance from the surface of the earth on the inside of the beach ball, we also have the "height" or length of one side. If you can find one more angle or the length of one more side, then you can solve all other angles and lengths, including the bottom leg of the triangle, which is the exact distance and direction you are from that unique geographic position on the earth's surface of the celestial body you are observing. Simple algebra and then some addition and subtraction makes the magic work. To start the process of locating yourself, you need a sexy new toy; in fact, a very specific sex toy.

It is late spring 1992 and I had just helped a dear sailing buddy, Dr. Jeff Wisch, deliver his newly purchased Stevens 47 from South Carolina to Falmouth Harbor on Cape Cod. I was hurrying away after the passage to catch a plane back to Maine and *Dog Star.* We had taken the delivery north and east outside of Cape Hatteras, using the Gulf Stream like a conveyor belt and only closed the New England coast off Gay Heads on the southwestern corner of Martha's Vineyard. Light fog kept us from seeing Buzzards Tower or No Man's Island as we passed between them. Vineyard Sound was running with us, and our speed over the ground on a broad reach was consistently ten knots. It was a classic ride.

Fifteen years later, after constantly refining and modifying this already fast modern cruising boat for the extra half knot by competing in and winning class tin in odd year Marion to Bermuda races put on by the Blue Water Sailing Club, Jeff and his youngest son Alex finished third in the highly competitive international two-handed class in the hundredth anniversary of the Newport to Bermuda classic sponsored by the Cruising Club of America in 2006.

Far offshore, in these early days, we worked to polish Jeff's sight reduction skills. He took sights with a beautiful bronze Navy issue sextant given him by his father. My own trusty and prized original Weems and Plath in its highly varnished mahogany case, about the size of a bowling ball bag, was now banging lightly against my thigh as I waved goodbye on the trot at the Hyannis air terminal doors. I checked my sea bag and found the security screening line. A polished young man, looking so starched and clean he should squeak, sporting a glowing surfer's tan and close-cropped crimson hair was operating the scanner. I passed through the metal detector and waited while he scrunched up his face, sucked on his teeth, and shifted the Mahogany box forward and back a dozen times until everyone in the waiting area was thinking either boa constrictor or bomb.

"This thing yours?" It was an accusation.

I was the only one standing within fifteen feet, holding my belt at arms length like a dead rattler, so I fessed up.

"I need to see what's inside." It wasn't a suggestion.

I inserted the stout miniature bronze key and flipped the rolled latches. The lid swung up on its oiled piano hinges. The instrument gleamed in its deep foam-padded sanctuary. The winged quadrant of polished bronze, a large spooled white control knob, short black spy glass, control shades, and the swing arm with its brightly polished silver dollar sized mirrors always took my breath away. I heaved a sigh and reached to push a swivel slide back into its proper place.

Wrong move.

"Keep your hands away from the object," he said, shoved a palm in my face and his free hand went to the mace on his belt.

Chairs skidded, people started to move away. You could smell panic in the wings.

"What is this thing?" The boy's voice broke at full volume.

"What's wrong Sean?" A voice called from the other side of the room.

"A sextant," I said.

"A what?"

"Sextant."

"Sean? Talk to me." It was a drill sergeant's bellow.

"Guy's got a sex toy here, Bert, and says he wants to carry it on the plane."

"Sex toy?" The whispered yell was a high-tension jolt. The mere idea sent a ground fault quiver through the Puritan bedrock of the senior security guard. A few of Hyannis' finest coy observers scattered about the room mouthed the words aloud, totally blowing their aloof, above-it-all cover.

"A doozy," the young man said, and, if volume was a gauge, he was going quickly towards proud for his work this early afternoon. The entire waiting room strangled itself silent for the next surprise, as each now began a slow collective shuffle forward, closing in on the varnished box on the examining table for a peek.

"What does it do?" Bert said breathlessly as he finished crossing the room through the crowd with a wake forming waddle and looked in the box. There was definite curiosity and contained excitement in his loud baritone. He was a red-faced, big-boned, middle-aged, short fellow who went to the same barber as the young man with the outside voice. Related?

His question went unanswered.

I kept my mouth shut. The hot breathing from the crowd was heavy on my neck. For the life of me, just like everyone else who was staring down at the box, I was trying to imagine a sexual act with man, woman, or beast that would be further enhanced by the glistening smooth metal instrument, its small telescope, and its dozens of silent swinging appendages. Eventually, after minutes of high drama, Bert and Sean learned from voices in the crowd that an ancient and iconic measuring device known as a sextant is, or at least was, used by seafaring men for centuries to find their way around the watery parts of our planet. The boy apologized in a whisper, admitting he was from Lowell not Hyannis. Bert offered no excuse, except a telling glare that I was obviously trying to get away with something other than making him look stupid.

The day is surely coming when the internet will probably reveal in graphic detail a remarkably inventive deviant act that includes an aging Weems and Plath and prove Bert right, but I don't need to be around for that noteworthy event in order to be proven an even worse dullard and prude than I know I am. Plausible deniability is the preferred line of defense in most good airport sex toy stories.

* * *

A sextant is simply a hand-held tool to measure an exact angle between your horizon, which at sea is barely seven miles away, and the visible object on the inside of the beach ball, whether it be the sun at noon or a star at dusk. You put an eye to a stubby telescope and your sight line passes through a circular glass that is divided in half vertically between a clear and a mirrored finish. A facing mirror rides at the hinge of the sliding arm that glides along the lower curved bar, which is marked with the precise degrees of a quarter circle. By leveling half your field of vision on the distinct line of the watery horizon and manipulating the mirrors to capture the image of the celestial body and then manually lowering that image to the visible horizon, you will have obtained the needed angle as read on the curved arch to solve the equation as to how far you are from the targeted celestial body's geographic position. With tons of practice and some luck you can pinpoint your location to within a half a mile. The trick is to always doubt your findings with a hefty safety factor when approaching anything solid. Remember the Prime Directive.

I'm up early, taking advantage of the heavy dew in the shadows of the fjord. A chamois lets you use the heavenly gift of a thick spatter of fresh condensation to remove crusted salt crystals from the varnish on the cabin sides, hatches, and cockpit coamings. I can hear M. in the galley putting the pot on to boil. I quietly raise the forward hatch to let a bit of fresh morning air into the forepeak. My two offspring are warding off the day with forty extra winks: one port, one starboard in the V berth with the varnished main mast between them at about shoulder level. Their arms are akimbo and long legs seem to fill each berth to the gills. Such a short while ago they were sacks of flour, restrained from a tumble from these same bunks by taut lee cloths that formed a safe, escape-proof crib. I look for the baby in their present.

Tristan has a scraggly goatee. Skye has her own treasure in the oven. Where did time go? Wasn't I meant to find adulthood somewhere along the way before my kids were making kids? I wring out the chamois over the side and continue to sidetrack my mind by doing the pleasant chore of taking care of the boat. I wish that life would always be as simple as doing the little things so the big things take care of themselves.

TWENTY-SIX

LITTLE CRANBERRY ISLAND

We squirt out the narrow gauntlet from Sommes Sound into the outer reaches of Southwest Harbor, home of the world famous Hinckley Yacht facility. The fringes of this half-moon bay are thickly settled with mooring balls so close together it seems impossible for a boat larger than a kayak to get to the wide wooden docks located in front of the trophy homes. Small pods of beautiful, gleaming Hinckleys in all the primary colors sit like a plastered fresco, still and fragile, against the dark clouds and shafts of sunlight moving in quickly from the southwest. *Dog Star* slows as I take the engine out of gear and we glide on the flat glass towards the bluish humps of the Cranberry Islands a few miles away off our bow.

"Looks to get a mite damp out there," I said.

"How far to Roque?" Tristan said.

"Eight wet, cold, sloppy hours."

"Wind?"

"Manageable, off the quarter, driving the rain."

"Sounds moldy," Tristan said.

"Maybe we should wait a day," I said and watch the wary look steal across my son's face. Rain alone, weighed against a fair wind, has seldom interfered with a planned excursion on his daddy's *Dog Star*.

"And do what?"

"Smell the roses, do group hugs, sing Hungarian folk songs; I'll play the bagpipes."

"Crazy-eights are always a hit," he said.

Tristan eyes me sideways. We let the boat continue to lose way. Drifting aimlessly is ten yards out ahead. My trump card will be played when momentum finally stops. Young men, stuck on a boat with their parents, will do an awful lot to avoid drifting. I keep quiet watching the weather clouds boil over the tall pines at Rings Point. I shiver once for effect.

"Not going to bite at that one."

"Bite?"

"You want me to call you a big fat, old weenie, throw out my chest and say something like: 'I'll take the helm if you can't handle it, wimpo.' And then you would let me sit out in the rain, skewered on some macho high ground while you stay warm and dry, curled up in your bunk, snickering to yourself."

"Snickering?"

"That's what it sounds like to me."

"It's prideful sighing. You're my only son."

"Sure."

Don't I just hate smart kids.

"Ain't going to do it. You're the man, oh captain, my captain. I'll stand my watch, no more, no less."

"Mutineer."

"Just a 'sea lawyer.'" He names the centuries-old biggest insult in Her Majesty's Royal Navy. This jibe references a shipmate who uses loopholes and the fine points of admiralty laws to do much less than his share. I have sailed with a few sea lawyers. Some people just can't seem to help themselves, even some pretty famous people. Sooner or later on a boat, a person's biggest flaws are exposed. It is a major cause of divorce in cruising couples. In the Royal Navy it was inevitably one less for mess after a dark and stormy night. Life is rarely that poetic.

"Why don't you work on your sister?" I dare him.

"Fish in a barrel." He winks.

"I heard that," Skye said from below.

Tristan winks again and gives me an O-kee-dok-ee thumb to pointer. I marvel at his optimism. Then again I know that Skye's biggest fatal flaw is a trusting nature. I wonder if I could leverage a good bet with their mother on the results. It's a young Donald Trump against a pregnant Mother Theresa as to which of my children, of their own free will, would sit at the tiller in the rain and think they had won a victory over their warm and dry sibling, snickering down below. Even after a couple of decades of experience with their antics I'm not totally sure of the outcome.

Clearing *Ondine* out of New Zealand had a festive atmosphere. The big baby-blue Maxi drew the constant crowds in a country where sailing is the national pastime. Different tribes of the dockside population in Auckland took it upon themselves to make sure our stay was memorable. Any reason in Kiwi lingo for a pub-crawl begins with "Hey mate, what say we…" Leading up to our departure, the gauntlet was thrown down to see which group of new friends could throw us the best (read: most outrageous) going away party. No one won; blue ribbons all around. They were each way over the top. I think even the hardest of Kiwi partiers were glad to finally see us shove off.

Our next destination on the world ocean racing circuit was over seven thousand miles away. Huey Long wanted *Ondine* delivered to San Diego via Acapulco for some major yard work before the Trans Pac Race left from San Francisco for Hawaii in about four months. The rigid formality of clearing out called for us to name our next port of call. An ocean full of possibilities presented themselves. With the vast Pacific Ocean resembling a barographic donut, with the center being a windless and desolate black hole for sailing craft, the only logical way to Mexico first led east along the Roaring Forties for nearly two thousand miles. This infamous band of water is the ancient mariner's pathway from the wharfs of Europe to the rich markets of the Far East. This stormy section of the watery realm is where the prevailing wind and weather anomalies usually come marching in from the west. It is called "roaring" because the low pressure systems that develop in these cold waters are free to spin and churn the entire way around the world before butting up against a coastline that saps their strength. It is here, south of everything except Patagonia and Cape Horn that the worst possible weather on our planet is expected most of the time.

Our entire crew had talked in loud, beer inspired voices about the possibility of "knocking off the Horn." It was a shame to our young egos that we would pass within a few thousand miles and not even attempt to scale the ultimate half-hitch on a bowline, the sailors' Mount Everest. Our plan was to go south into the mouth of the beast, use the gales and storms of the high latitudes to push us east at breakneck speed, and get to the Horn before time ran out. We'd save the time by catching hold of the Humboldt or Peruvian Current that runs like a river, flowing north, close in along the Chilean coast. We would pass through 67 degrees west longitude, backtrack, and then ride our magic carpet all the way to the equator. It seemed logical, even inspired.

"You riding east in the Forties," the port captain said.

Thom Richardson and I both nodded yes. We had simply put San Diego via Acapulco as our destination. No sense muddying the waters with our true intentions.

"Then up past Peru?"

We did the bobble-head again.

"You are going real close to Pitcairn Island, once in a lifetime," he said, "should stop."

"Might happen," I said to be agreeable.

"Okay, so I'll list that too." The port captain was happy to add to our itinerary the final stop for Fletcher Christian and the *HMS Bounty* mutineers. Thom gave me a look that has, to this day, kept me from giving anyone more information about my true sailing intentions than is absolutely necessary. This very sensible habit saves a mud-spa full of losing face to meet some arbitrary departure dates, appearing lazy or unmotivated to those who want you gone, or proving beyond a doubt that you're incompetent and don't have a clue what you are doing in the planning department, plus a dozen and more ego stripping pitfalls that go hand in hand with the vagaries of sailing boats between distant shores. This lesson came at a price.

"Would you consider hauling the mail?" The customs officer asked as an apparent aside while pausing. The approval was delayed, suspended by the question, before finishing the final dozen colorful stamps on our clearance papers.

"Sure." I said without thinking. I wasn't at all used to this captain thing, afraid to be found for the fraud I was. And it was a great country and I was just trying to be agreeable. Okay, justifications are for whiners. I goofed, hugely.

"Good-oh, mate," he said and beamed. The awed surprise was evident in his enthusiasm. "Good-oh, again." He pumped my hand vigorously. The port Captain joined him and nearly wrenched my arm off. They bordered on effusive.

My god, what had I done?

The horse was out of the gate. Refusing now would surely be an international incident. A satchel-sized bag of mail had begun an avalanche of down stream consequences in the weeks to come, including: a thinly braided hula skirt, sore armpits, a shark attack, and an arranged marriage, but that's another part of the story. When we cleared out of Auckland, *Ondine* and her crew dropped off the edge of the known world, and fell keel first down the rabbit hole.

* * *

M. finally stops the "wet seat" contest and tells the contestants to knock it off before she keel-hauls the lot of us. Orders are given to promptly head *Dog Star* for Little Cranberry Island for a walk ashore before it really started raining. Skye and M. have gone in search of legendary raspberry preserves sold by a little old church lady with a crutch. She lives, ironically, on Lamely Lane. Tristan and I have decided to walk to the ocean side of the island and take a look at what is happening out there. It is pretty obvious from the gloom and fog of the day that things over there are pretty much the same as over here, but it was a good enough reason to stretch our legs. Unexpectedly, Tristan seems almost enthusiastic for the male only sojourn in the damp mist. I am ready for the shoe to drop.

"You met mom when you were eighteen and she was seventeen, right?"

Where is this going? I nod warily at my son.

"The day after she graduated from high school, right?"

"I didn't take her across any state lines."

"Huh?"

"She talked older than her birth certificate. It was the sixties: sex, drugs, rock and roll. Of course, your mother and I were not into any of that stuff. More like holding hands, beer, corndogs, and soul music on AM radio for us."

"How did you know she was the one you were going to marry?"

"She was warm, willing, and seem to overlook the fact I was a total loser."

"Seriously," he said.

"Marry her? I just planned to sleep with her for thirty or forty years and then move on. Love 'em and leave 'em; that's me, a lone wolf. I was trapped into the marriage thing when I was drunk and agreeable at the wrong time."

"Sure."

I give him my V eye-browed "level with me or else" stare. It is ignored. I blame the low visibility.

"It's a simple question. What were you looking for in the right girl?"

"She had to be beautiful, rich, smart, full of earning potential, and with one tragic flaw."

"And that was…?"

"She had to have low expectations in men," I said.

We crest the small hill at the top of the road and looked down the way ahead at the fog that hogs all the visibility after about twenty yards.

"You guys are happy, right?"

"Deliriously."

"Really?"

"I have to believe your mother entertains herself with fantasies of the perfect homicide, but happily, for me anyway, she has restrained herself so far."

"You're such a sick dude."

" 'Sick' like 'good?'"

"No, 'sick' like 'sick.'"

"Whass'up wit chew, dawg?" I give the double fist, three-digit chest point, and loll my tongue against my chin. You don't ask your dad for chick advice unless it is past serious. I tried for laughs as a diversion.

Tristan picks up a stone and throws it ahead. It disappears before it hit the ground. I swear that thunder rolls, off in the distance. Then it comes.

"I got an offer to go do 'Yard' with the *Harvey Gamage.*"

"You mean, like, in a boat yard, painting, working, and stuff?"

"Major refit. New rigging, splice, parcel and serve, Bo' sun's gig," he said.

"Pay?"

"Maybe." His voice trails off as he makes the word a sentence.

I thought about my son slaving on a needy wooden boat that is not *Dog Star* and feel faint. It was treason. My mind is quickly connecting the dots that would lead to my son doing hard labor, for no salary, for complete strangers. This odd behavior calls for a big motivator. If it isn't the food; it has to be the company.

"I thought it was a job on Nantucket?"

"Maybe after."

"What's her name?" I said.

Tristan throws another stone. He looks to have a canary in his mouth. He chews it good before he speaks again.

"They want me there, like yesterday, to help sail her from Boston down to New Bedford."

"Whose the her?"

Tristan cracks a smile but not his lips.

I give the silence right back and try to figure out what it all means. The most obvious personal revelation crashes out of my mouth first.

"Now you're not doing Roque with us?"

"Chances are Roque is going to look exactly like this," Tristan said as his hand sweeps aside the fog that has now become thick enough to cut and stack. We stand on the white line and can't see the shoulder of the narrow roadway.

"I see different fog in different places," I said.

"Sure you do," said my son.

I'm smart enough not to start into an explanation of my inane remark, and I purposely let the embarrassment linger a bit. How else will I learn from my mistakes?

"You got a plan?"

"Not yet," he said.

I could immediately resort to playing the "but what about your mother" card, go the guilt route, but I manage to hold my tongue. The argument might be more effective with his mother around. I try to look pensive, but it probably comes off as a pout. We follow the white line back towards the dock like we are on a tethered space walk. Our two wild berry preserve foragers have been successful and in shifts we row back out to *Dog Star* and start the oil lamps to dry out things below decks. We are going nowhere until we can see the bowsprit from the cockpit. Tristan's escape is delayed. I nap and scheme on how to change my son's mind. I determine it is part of his destiny.

TWENTY-SEVEN

SHANGHAI AT SCHOODIC

William Snaith and his succession of *Figaro*'s were the absolute pinnacle of the art of the well-heeled gentlemen's amateur ocean racing addiction from the last world war well into the 1970s. He was one of the truly audacious grand characters of the blue water racing circuit. Snaith was a trained architectural draftsman, but more so the artist and inventor, a pragmatist and a dreamer with a knack for making money; his manner was one of old school charm and audacity in the face of stodgy convention. In his book, *On the Wind's Way*, Snaith recounts a transatlantic race from Bermuda to Sweden. Seventeen boats including Dick Nye's *Carinna*, who had just won a wild Bermuda Race, *Palawan*, *Ondine* (the version before the one I joined in Australia), *Constellation*, Pete Dupont's *Barlovento*, Henry Du Pont's *Cyane*, and *Anitra*, the Swedish entry, plunged into the fray. The great circle route put the boats well into the Northern stretches of the Atlantic Ocean including the forbidding and fish boat crowded Grand Banks. Snaith had an old school way with words about the ocean, the tension of being sightless, plus the normal daily challenges of wet slogging and fog:

"*Figaro* sails in an eerie environment, a world of curdled gray mist. At times the coils of curd thicken and a deeper murk settles around her. Suddenly the layers thin and the boat sails into a strangely pale, crepuscular light. Each droplet in this thinner mist hangs separately against the washed-out yellow eye of the sun; a scummy cataract of varying density veils its burning stare. The chalky green face of the ocean is seen in a short radius around the boat, its heaving surface broken by small tumbling crests. The waves come out of the mist suddenly, invisible until they are almost on the boat and then as quickly disappear ahead; a rush of energy, hurrying towards an undisclosed rendezvous...The churned air imprisoned in foaming bubbles breaks out and hisses in rage as the bubbles clutch fruitlessly at the hull slipping by. Then with a last crackle, no longer sounding angry, like the ultimate gush of gas escaping from stirred champagne or of Alka-Seltzer, the wave expires quietly into the mist leaving a wake discernable to no one but the two Mother Carey's chickens who have decided to be companions to this voyage. The bow plunges steadily on as though it, and not we, knows where we are going. It is not precisely the morning for hornpipes and chanteys."

WHO IS THE ALE MAN?

William Snaith

A MAN WITH A THIRST FOR A MANLIER BREW

Bolder, keener, more to the point

Let it make an Ale man out of you!

BALLANTINE Ale

Bill Snaith and his crew, including the racing legends Monk Farnham, Knud Reimers, Bucky Reardon, and Bermudian yachtsman of the century Bobby Symonette, took line honors and held their time among the fleet for the gold cup. This long, cold, and wet effort caused Bill Snaith to comment: "Ocean racing is made up of many bad afternoons, ugly mornings, and hard nights." The same could be said of most small boat cruising in Maine. Yet, we do it anyway. The naysayers of our sanity will often point to the fact that we are feeble-minded and only remember the good parts. I will share one more Snaith-ism to prove this is not the case.

An oft-repeated joke followed me from crew to crew in those long lost days of truly amateur ocean racing. Most of the racing boats eventually became "half-frozen swamps" after days of working to weather in the cold waters of wide heaving oceans. The anecdote was Bill Snaith's erudite first-hand description of life aboard a maxed-out sailboat in the frigid damp latitudes of our watery world: "We are all swarmy in our many layers of clothing. This morning I thought I smelled a horse. When I turned around to look, there was nobody but me."

"Swarmy" became a very "in" word of brotherhood among the small fraternity of "deck apes" that made the racers go fast. "It was majorly swarmy," described a lot of upwind passages when told at cheap beer bars in the most exotic ports in the world. Those who haven't been there will be forgiven, and probably be better people for the fact that they may never understand the visceral meaning of the term. Veteran sailors from this era are often guilty of taking inordinately long hot showers for no apparent good reason when they find themselves stuck ashore.

There is a school of thought, Snaith being one of its more vocal members, which believes, from the hard won experience and the iron stomachs of the practitioners, that a well-found boat should leave port on an extended passage in the worst weather conditions possible. The rationale is that the crew is rested and fit to handle the bad weather conditions, which sooner or later on any long passage you are going to encounter anyway. Get the chore over with early on. It is also a smart way to test the thousands of small pieces of gear in a gale near shore and if something is going to break on the boat you don't have so far to go by turning around to make repairs. This factor of breakage is a double-sized doppelganger on a one-off state-of-the-art ocean-racing machine such as *Ondine*. Weight saving is one true key to performance and speed on the water. High tech racing gear is designed to ride the delicate balance between functioning stress loads and the need to shave ounces and inches off of highly important fittings. Pushing the envelope is the key to winning, and the breaking point is usually found only through trial and error. Things break when you are going for broke. These test failures often happen when you are least ready and prepared for it. It seems illogical, but it is essential for a sailor to cherish those things that don't go bump in the night.

Ondine left New Zealand on a dark and dreary Thursday. Our planned course pointed south of east hoping to ride the tail of a massive swirling low that had just passed by and was now marching towards Patagonia. We hoped to have winds and waves behind us. We got exactly what was expected. What we didn't expect was how bloody awful and dangerous sailing in the high southern latitudes can be even if things go right. Our low was just a momentary lead pachyderm in the long line of trunk to tail, monstrous depressions that were parading around the world from west to east. Barely two hundred miles east from the South Island, we were locked into a battle with the elements that lasted for nearly a week.

The "heavy weather" rotating watch system meant that I was alone as I stumbled out of sleep, after a four-hour bunk-induced coma, into my wet foul weather gear that was hung in the sauna compartment aft and to port. Nearly every piece of clothing that was not already wringing wet was on my body as molding insulation. The cycle was tumble-wash and the floor bucked and slid like a mad bronco on ice. I tuck a wet, but not yet dripping, towel around my neck and zip the jacket up tight before tugging snug the hood over my heavy wool cap. The last watch's entry in the log book, exactly an hour ago, read: wind speed 42 to 47 knots (Force 8-9), wave height 25 to 35 ft, cresting (breaking waves), sailing with storm stay'sil sheeted amidships, speed 8.5 to 13.1, course: 110 to 165 degrees, temperature 42 degrees F. The entries were plainly written in shaky letters and were terrifying. It had been bad on my last watch. It was now a lot worse.

I paused on the second step on the companionway and listened to the chaos outside, trying to hear above the wind and the strained rigging screeching a tune, for the rush along the scuppers of solid water so that I wouldn't let a few tons of Southern Ocean down below as I scrambled on deck. The boat's movement had no rhythm. Thrown this way and that, the 50-ton boat was skidding along in a ponderous wobble, suddenly lurching past forty-five degrees from vertical before regaining her feet. I shoved open the sliding hatch over my head and popped my head out.

The scene was a Faustian hell amped up with special effects. The world was a slight shade above pitch black, and every shadowed component of the landscape was a dark heaving mass. The sea was moving like a boiling vat of tar. I could barely see the two stout five-foot wheels at the opposite outer ends of the long T-shaped cockpit. A sopping wet, huddled figure manned each one, struggling in tandem wrenches of their arms to keep the boat under control. I quickly pulled myself up and over the washboards with all the gracefulness of an elephant seal. I snapped on my shackle to the heavy wire jackline on the cockpit sole and cowered under the dodger. One of the two figures quickly left his wheel and moved in my direction like a starving refugee.

"Hate to leave all the fun," Athol shouted in my ear, "I'll let you have some of the 'sweetness' for a mite."

"A kind Kiwi gesture," I said above the wind.

"Better hurry." His voice was a serious statement.

He pressed a second safety harness and tether into my hands and was gone below, before I could ask why. Reluctantly leaving the shelter of the dodger I made the lucky mistake of turning to look forward. Thirty years later my short neck hairs still respond to this visceral memory. A twenty-five foot wall of water is imposing in the extreme. If you have the tilted perspective of heading down the face of the wave behind you and rapidly overtaking the one ahead, the perceived height of the solid thing in front of you easily doubles in size. I swear the tip of the mast in relation to the wave was only about half way up its cascading cliff face. I could feel the boat wallow as the surfing  bow slowed immediately under the impact at the base liquid crevice. She tried valiantly to lift her skirts and meet the monster head on. I fled back under the dodger wedging myself in tight. I looked up and Mark, the first mate and current helmsman, disappeared under a solid sheet of spray. I quickly pulled my arms through the heavy web strapping of the second safety harness and secured it tight across my chest. My heart was hammering loud enough to audition as a drummer for a garage grunge band.

When most of the solid water disappeared off the deck I moved aft as fast as my "Michelin Man" outfit would let me. I followed Mark's lead and, as soon as I could grab the high-side five-foot wheel, I snapped in my two tethers into the stout "D" rings on opposite sides of its pedestal. Mark gave me a stiff-armed thumbs-up and the white salt on the small amount of exposed cheeks I could see was caked like the rim of a margarita glass. He arched his eyebrows once or twice like Groucho Marx. Farce was not a usual part of his stoic image.

What was so funny?

For the next two hours I found out about *Galgen* or "gallows" humor while riding the razor's edge of disaster. The cycle would begin with the boat shaking itself off like a spaniel at a pond's edge, caught in the trough between two huge mountains of moving water. The wind was high overhead as the following sea acted as a lee windbreak. *Ondine* was shaking and shuddering from mast to keel in the erratic gusts, almost dead stopped, while Mark and I tried to tug away at each other's best guess on where to position the rudder for the surge to come. All the while, even through the layers of headgear, you can hear the approaching waterfall high over your shoulder. The tandem wheels would finally catch hold of the first rush of the wave and try to spin free from our hands as we struggled to keep the bow straight downhill. To be off by a hair meant the boat could be thrown sideways with no steerage or control, and that would mean a wave could roll the fifty-ton racing machine over as easily as a bathtub toy. Suddenly, with enough force to buckle your knees, the stern would start climbing like an express elevator and the bow would begin to plunge down at an increasingly steeper angle. Up, up, and finally the gale force winds would swarm over her stern counter and find a toe hold on the storm jib, deck gear, dodger, anything vertical, including our exposed back-ends, and the boat would be pushed over nearly sixty degrees and begin to accelerate with a neck snapping lurch. She would gain speed recklessly and begin to race the wave like a horse heading for the barn. She usually won these matches.

Surfing may be fun on a small boogey board on a sunny day at a Nantucket beach, but this was brutal, cold, and the eventual outcomes all looked bleak. Once we started outpacing the wave *Ondine* would promptly lay down the bulge in her topsides and begin to surf the 70-foot waterline. The bow wave would start growing enormous white wings and once again, because the water racing under our keel was the same speed as the boat, we would lose any grip with the rudder. We were surging along the crest of a three-story tall, crumbling, curling wave with no steerage. Then things got interesting. We would begin to hit fourteen, fifteen, sixteen knots and we were plunging down a slope and catching up to the wave ahead. The perception was that the cliff-side of solid ocean ahead was now suddenly reversing course and coming back at you. The bow would slam into the bottom of the hill and bury itself a dozen or more feet into solid black water. Mark and I were slammed forward, our chests crushed into the wheels as the boat went from careening along in the high teens to the low single digits in a split second. *Ondine* literally stops dead, lifts her bow and sends a solid wave, four feet high, back along the decks. I remember thinking how strange to see each safety line stanchion leaving a bow wake in the frothing cauldron. We held on for dear life as the cold water tried to take us with it while pouring in a waterfall off the stern. Coming up for air, we would check to see if our watch mate was still standing and *Ondine* would shake herself like a puppy, and the wave we had just outrun would begin to lift our stern again. Two hours on deck and four hours cowering in my bunk quickly wore down my enthusiasm for all of this special fun.

We made a thousand miles of easting during the first four days of our thirty-two day passage and we barely crossed the fiftieth parallel of south latitude into the "Screaming Fifties". When the weather showed signs of getting even worse, we had a brief crew meeting and decided to "leave the sweetness" behind, turn north towards the tropics, and leave the milestone of Cape Horn until another day. It was to be thirty-two years before I was able to get back down there to accomplish the scaling of "Everest Horizontal," and I wasn't disappointed with the soup of "fine weather" the second time around either.

The crescent moon, skipping between the clouds, dimly lights the small bay at Little Cranberry Island; the house windows across the East Passage along Seal Cove wink against a black wall of trees. The dense fog and steady rain that held us captive all day has finally lifted and the quiet is deafening. A single cricket ashore, rubbing its legs for a mate, stands out above the little wavelets slapping *Dog Star*'s rudder as the tide swings. I creep out of my bunk and quietly close the door to the forward cabin. I light an oil lamp, turn the wick down, and then crawl my quickly chilled body into M.'s warm cocoon.

"This better be good," M. said as she stiffens and groans with teeth clenched against the cold assault on her backside, "real good."

"It's called 'the Shanghai'," I said.

She is suspiciously quiet, speechless. After nearly four decades of my shenanigans, M. is hard to surprise.

"Ancient Chinese art of persuasion," I said.

"I'll give you marks for creativity, but I know what it means."

I notice it is getting warmer under the covers. A wiggle here, a waggle there, and my plan will be sidelined by a far greater good.

"I mean we got to get this baby going to Roque, right now. Depart while Tristan sleeps in the coma of the young at body." I shared Tristan's imminent departure plans with his mother on our way to bed a few hours ago.

"No." She said in between yawns.

"Is that, like, an 'order' no, or a rhetorical, you 'can't believe I can be this adolescent' no?"

"Both."

"Good advice. I'll log it twice in the morning."

"This is a bad idea, Brainiac. Being Shanghaied doesn't work quite like it used to a couple of centuries ago," M. gives me her school-marm voice in a stage whisper. "Today the courts call it kidnapping and it's a federal offense. Cell phones. Nine-one-one. FBI. No immunity for being a parent. I would have to testify."

"Good. Okay. I got it. Bad idea."

"It's the slammer if you do."

"Since when don't I take your advice on these things?"

I slide out from under the covers and reach for the pile of clothes at the foot of my bunk. "I just didn't want to startle you when I crank on the engine."

She sighs. I sighed louder.

"You need a hand?" she said, but not with any apparent enthusiasm.

"Naw, this way you can claim victim status."

"Been doing that since the day we met."

"Cute."

Twenty minutes later we're underway, outward bound through the West Passage, straining my eyes in the pale moonlight to see all the lobster pots with the dubious help of the blinding beam of my "trillion candlepower" floodlight sweeping the way ahead. I have the engine barely ticking over and we are making about three knots through the water with a knot or two of current steadily pushing us out to the open sea. The improvised getaway is an improbable clean break, and not a mouse is stirring below decks. The first part of my plan is working. Now I have to make up the second part.

I began my career as a big time ocean navigator by believing that Pitcairn Island was fictitious, like Key Largo and Gilligan's Island. The key ingredient in building my case against reality was the mantra: "If I can't find it; it doesn't exist." Celestial navigation, as practiced by mere mortals whose last name is not Bowditch, is like alchemy, the ancient art of turning lead into gold. A lot of old bearded "merlins" made a lot of money claiming to be expert in the illusive science of this miracle of turning a base metal to riches, but no one actually wrote down the recipe that worked. The same could be said of celestial navigation techniques. A lot of words have been written— Bowditch is over nine hundred pages—but usually they are offered in a language that defies translation into anything I can understand. My father had a word for such things: gobbledygook.

The single slim volume that boils down the cosines, transit extrapolations, convex dips, sidereal angles, and logarithms into a simple how-to is Mary Blewitt's *Celestial Navigation for Yachtsmen*. This fit-in-your-raincoat-pocket book leaves the juicy theory to the nerds and concentrates on how to take a sight, a reading from a timepiece, and turn these into a line on a chart. Not a point, mind you, a simple line, that along which you might be, if your sight was good and the clock was not off by more than a few seconds. If this line is near your dead reckoning position you are a wizard and you place your presumed location on the chart with a heavy pencil blotch and a healthy dose of old-fashioned doubtful skepticism.

There were three of us taking sights on *Ondine*. Each of us worked out our own plot lines on graph paper before going to the single paper chart. This chart incorporated about ten thousand square miles of the southern Pacific Ocean water with soundings in four figures followed by question marks. The few blue smidges of solid ground were no bigger than lady bugs. More or less, after each afternoon's confab following hours of work with number crunching, we all mostly agreed within about a ten mile circle. That was a predictable beginning, given my nascent skills in adding and subtracting. Either by peer pressure, dumb luck, or modest skill development, over a couple of weeks we began to shrink the circle of our "guestiments" to about a few miles. All sight reduction begins with an "assumed position" which is based on the cumulative mistakes of all the days past. It takes the faith of an already martyred saint and the pragmatism of a burning heretic to believe you can actually make this magic work. Constantly conjuring false confidence while not running aground on a coastline in the dark of night that, by your reckoning, should be hundreds of miles away is the mark of navigator. And now, my kids wonder why I irrationally question intangible things until they surrender from fatigue?

Ondine had been at sea nineteen days and travelled nearly three thousand nautical miles before we thought we might be pretty close to the needle in the haystack. The smart money in the crew's betting pool was not on when, but if, we would sight Pitcairn Island. One shipmate wondered if we would ever sight any land ever again (and he was one of the navigators). I was not the smart money and calmly

predicted after dinner one starry night that we would see our goal
the next day at exactly high noon. I don't think my crew stopped
laughing out loud until dawn when the morning watch (4 a.m. to 8
a.m.) happened to look behind them and spotted a humped smudge
just about to vanish below the horizon. We turned around and made
our way back to the descendents of the *Bounty* mutineers. They
quibbled when I declared it was noon somewhere; I remember I
didn't win the pool.

"Not cool, Dad."

"Surprise." I try to sound as enthusiastic as a half-drunk birthday
clown.

Dog Star is bobbing along in a light offshore zephyr that is busy
leaving the scene with the rising of the sun. The flat ocean is faultlessly
pink, pastel blue and littered with the black handles of lobster buoys
stretching ahead into a low lying mist to the east. Tristan's upper torso
is leaning out the companionway, blinking in the shafts of golden
light, under a well tumbled head of hair highlighting the peaks and
tangles.

"I got to go," he said.

"Pump the handle until nothing is waving back at you."

Tristan gives me a pretty good imitation of his mother's knock-
it-off look. His half open eyes wander past my place at the helm
and see the distinctive, tall, single birthday candle lighthouse on 'tit
Manan Island that marks Schoodic. It is a point of no return from
the civilized Maine of tourists and their SUVs. I always view it as
halfway towards the Promised Land.

"I made a commitment," Tristan said.

"And I'm holding you to it," I said.

"That's not…."

"I know."

"You're something," he said, shaking his head with a frown and heads back forward to his bunk.

"Ain't it the truth," I said softly and don't feel as happy about the fact as I should. Shanghai was definitely the wrong place to be this Maine morning. I guess I knew that even before I went there. So, what does that make me besides stubborn and stupid? I look at the chart spread next to me on the cockpit teak and know from past experience that Jonesport, just on the mainland behind Great Wass island, or Cutler, just the other side of Roque, will likely have a rental car office or bus station and my son will soon be on his way south to another of his own life's adventures. The wind dies completely and the mainsail floats slowly overhead, searching for a purpose. I start the engine. Roque Island is somewhere out there lurking beyond the morning haze and the limits of a father's control.

TWENTY-EIGHT

CHANDLER BAY

The heavily built, open, wooden, thirty-foot lifeboat tugged against *Ondine*'s rail with acrobatic twists and surges in the rough water. A dozen fifteen-foot oars lay along the thwarts. A vintage gas engine of questionable pedigree sat high on a rough hewn board lashed hard and dangling off the stern. The longboat's name was *STICK*. Disaster was fended off by twenty strong arms that held us tethered alongside for the last few moments of contact within the huge plateaus of the Pacific swell that crash against the rock cliffs a few hundred yards away.

The wide wooden seats amidship emphasized the broad beam and sweeping sheer of the sweet double-ended lines. Those planks were crammed full to the gills of the many smiling familiar faces; four distinct generations of new found friends. One gap toothed young teen was still smacking his hand under his armpit, imitating with an infectious laugh my vain but energetic attempts at grass-skirt hula dancing at the birthday party of a local sweet sixteen island girl the night before. Everyone had called me the "mailman who shouldn't dance." The entire population of the island, all 48 souls, were joined together on the joke. I waved sheepishly at the good humor.

Pitcairners, who thirty hours ago had been strangers, were bantering back and forth with us like family. Shocks of bright, unruly red hair riding over freckles were scattered among the blended diversity of the happy Polynesian faces. It was a graphic reflection of the rich mix of DNA offered by the original shipload of mutineers and their Tahitian mentors.

Suddenly one male voice broke through the chatter of goodbyes  and the boat fell silent. His first word became a note and the sentence a melody. The chorus instantly swelled when the voices of the entire congregation join in. Then, without a cue, the solo voice melded into a round where the voices of women, men, and children chased each other through the next verse. That bright, cobalt sky, dark cliffs and the white foaming crests of the late afternoon are easy to recall in vivid detail as "in the sweet by and by" was welded to my soul with hot iron rivets.

It was the age old chapel song to share aboard ships embarking out on the cruel sea. The words came to us from voices of an ancient sea faring clan thriving on a lonely rock over three thousand ocean miles from the nearest land mass. The fact our crew had before us nearly five thousand of those same open ocean miles to reach Mexico loomed pretty large in our mere mortal heads. The swelling voices rose to remind us of the yet to be sung chapters. The tune changed once again:

Now one last song we'll sing
Goodbye, Goodbye
Time moves on rapid wings
Goodbye, Goodbye, Goodbye
We part, but hope to meet again
Goodbye, Goodbye, Goodbye...

The first voice finally became the last. Only the hiss and shushing roar of the surf was left. It was now up to the old uneasy partnership between us and the gods of the sea to insure that we stick around to be part of the next chorus to be sung somewhere over the horizon.

"God speed," Steve Christian said with a solemnly raised open hand. Irma Christian kissed her open palms and held them out to us. Jay Warren mugged my hula arms once again. The boats drifted apart.

A stampeding collage of visuals ran through my head as images of the last two days washed over me like a warm rain-shower. A  frantic scene under a palm tree appeared, as a gaggle of happy kids hung off the *Bounty*'s anchor. The ten foot tall relic was an amazing heirloom of the island, which was salvaged from the bottom of the bay where the *HMS Bounty* was burned. The treasure was placed in the town square with the help of Irving and Electra Johnson and the crew of the *Yankee*. I also remember at that very moment feeling the often repeated stomach flipping moments when a lush green path ends abruptly on a toe wide ledge known locally as a "walk-a-way." Vertigo inducing vistas of the endless heaving ocean have you teetering over hundreds of feet of cliff wall falling away at your feet; huge ocean swells relentlessly pound this jagged coastline with a rhythmic determination.

We were highly honored as invited guests to witness the amazing sight of the table sagging with loads of local food and universal good wishes at the birthday gathering to honor a special young woman's new place in the community. Laughing was easy for everyone as *Ondine*'s crew tried with the dogged determination of suicidal lemmings to learn the male gyrations to a traditional hula from the elders. I couldn't remember a single frown or a moment of unease during this magical time. Visitors were never allowed to be strangers on Pitcairn.

We were all tough guys (even Kitty the cook) as the island boat handed over the mailbag stuffed with things we would post at our next port of call. They released their hold and drifted away, a steep sided swell dropped our new friends two stories beneath our still outstretched hands in a heartbeat. This departure shared common rituals and realities with ten centuries of such leavings under sail. It was final. The die was cast. As one, the six of us bent quickly to the tasks of getting the boat ready for sea and the four hundred and fifty feet of anchor rode up and stowed. There was no windlass to help with the task on the weight conscious racing machine. Leading lines back to the coffee grinder winches saved some backs and built a gnawing sore muscle appreciation for the next month of non-stop open ocean sailing.

No one looked another in the eye for a long while as we scurried about the flush deck of the big blue racing boat. No one spoke. We all carried our emotions around like a peacock feathered hat. The mast finally groaned purposefully under the pressure on behalf of us all. The running backstay took up the strain like a violin string, and the double reefed main finally, irretrievably, turned us downwind. The mountains of marching fluid energy immediately rolled us from beam end to beam end. Out of the lee of the tall island, the wind climbed to thirty knots and the long rolling swells had wind-driven waist-high breakers rolling down their flanks. We all sat cold, quiet and uncomfortable in the cockpit as the light faded slowly and the sky lit up with finger-painted red smears. We headed due north into a black starless horizon. Over *Ondine*'s stern, the tiny hump of Pitcairn Island vanished as a Brigadoon into the night.

Dog Star is busy taking her own sweet time in tracking down the safer side of the mix-master of dangerous currents at Sea Horse Ledge off the western tip of Great Wass Island. The tide is foul, running west from the Bay of Fundy and south from Moosabec Reach, and for every four knots we go forward we are taking nearly two steps back. The buoy is disgustingly coy as we try to get closer and leave it astern. I keep telling the crew the Pollyanna's side of things: it is better to buck the current here than face the beast when we turn the corner down Chandler Bay. Barely ten miles ahead we will probably be sailing like the dickens up-current while at a virtual dead stop over the ground. Schedules for arrival are painfully illusive when the tide is flushing wrong-headed in the Passamaquody.

Tristan's life view has perked up with a real "he-man's" breakfast of bacon and biscuits and eggs and home fries, plus toast and sweet homemade marmalade from coastal Maine. He is still claiming to be a kidnapped victim of a suspicious cult that thinks the devil lives on dry land. And I am labeling him officially in the log as a "stow-away", a deviant "male stalker of his sister and mother", and one who should be treated henceforth as a "pirate terrorist." Things are mostly back to normal.

The high-noon milquetoast light is unable to give any definition to the receding mainland as we lumber along in a four-foot disorderly slop, hugging the rhumb-line by motor sailing a close reach along the series of slab-sided barrier islands. Our new hazy apparitions include Wass, Head Harbor Island, and Mistake Harbor Island. They will be our close friends until we can set a course across Chandler Bay towards the almost hidden entrance to Moosabec Reach and the docks of Jonesport. These barrier islands have some colorfully named anchorages including the Cow's Yard, Mistake Harbor, and the aptly named Mud Hole that is best approached on a rising tide with room inside the tight entrance for only a couple of intimate boats. M. and Skye are below reading on the settees and Tristan is standing in the galley grazing on a smorgasbord of snacks as a warm up for a proper lunch. I am nudging *Dog Star* closer inshore, searching in vain for a back-eddy to release us from the conveyor belt of the tide.

"Have I ever been to Jonesport?" Tristan said around a mouthful of chips.

"Not since diapers."

"Yours or mine." He mumbles the punch line around a cookie.

"Depends…" I give the joke all the enthusiasm of a teenager delivering a coerced apology.

"It was the lobster boat races, right?"

"It was the sound of thunder," I said, "and you proceeded to make lobster boat engine noise whenever I rowed us anywhere for the rest of the summer."

"I was three."

"What's your point," I said.

"Statute of limitations."

"You were a real live 'motor mouth'?"

"Why do we always come to Maine?"

"No outstanding warrants," I said in a hoarse whisper.

"Really," he said.

I think about the question. It simply just feels right to turn left when we hit the Atlantic Ocean after a long winter of captivity at a boat yard. That admission, if shared, will do nothing for my reputation as a deep thinker.

"We don't always come to Maine," I said.

"More than most sane people who wander around in boats."

He has a point.

Why?

Why indeed.

"It still has an edge to it," I finally said.

"I get that," my son said, "but I've seen you get into some pretty scary messes on this boat in a lot of places that aren't Maine."

I bristle a bit about my proclivity for getting into and then out of trouble on boats, but wisely keep my yapper cinched up tight.

Tristan shovels another load of salt, starch, and fat into his mouth and crunches. The real question is like a fresh turd on the teak decks. I am on the spot. I don't want to step in it right in front of a semi-adult son, someone I am just getting to know again.

"I don't know the 'why' of it. Do I look like a guy who plans things?"

"I'm not asking for the meaning of life here."

He has a point. I grope for a man-rules metaphor.

"It's like cheese tastes really good on Italian food, but you melt it on top of Chinese and it's disgusting."

I don't get the expected guffaw. He looks confused, but thoughtful. After such an absurd statement silence is my only defense.

"So Maine is Italian food?"

"Now you've got it." I try to busy myself with the chart and ignore the train wreck of logic just around the bend.

"Everywhere else is Chinese?"

I nod. He raises his eyebrows for the punch line.

"We're the cheese," I said, regretting the necessity of being knee deep in stupid.

Tristan chews on this simple answer for a couple of mouthfuls as I try to figure out exactly how I had ever backed myself into that ridiculous rhetorical corner. My son finally nods, gives a thumbs up as if he meant it. The next time I look back from the rock ledges close off to our port, he is stretching out in the forward cabin with a bag of pretzels and an IPod dangling from his ear sockets. He is chewing to a beat and his toe is tapping air.

Who knew I am such an accomplished explainer guy?

I can attest that all my racing and offshore experience supports my favorite simple fact: sailing is mostly long hours, days, weeks of monotonous sameness punctuated by startling moments of sheer terror. Trying to maneuver *Ondine* around and through the Pacific high-pressure area and across the Inter-tropical Convergence Zone was a lesson in patience and daily speed drills at the extreme ends of ocean sailing. The "Doldrum Dash" was the exact opposite and a proving ground of the theory that only a small percentage of the trapped-like-rats, testosterone laden, adrenaline junky deck apes will go stark raving mad when trapped in a world where nothing moves but the sun and stars. I was one of that small, demented percentage.

The riveting stories of courage shared over rum toddies at yacht club bars are laden with raging winds, towering seas, and the pitiful despair of others when the gales never seem inclined to give you a break. Those chosen few who have risked sanity by tackling the big ocean in sailing craft without the fuel (or engine) necessary to power their way through the windless barrens called the Doldrums will be the only ones to fully understand when I caution sailors that screaming gales are the easy part. Harder on gear, stamina, and morale than any storm is a solid week of mid-ocean stillness. The Doldrums sound benign, but the actual experience is much worse. Think of being trapped in a cage and becoming the heart's desire of a drunken and amorous four-hundred pound gorilla; escape is the very last thing allowed.

My journal of this part of the passage is sweat stained, ink splotched, and the looping letters of my writing seem the work of a bonged-out freshman coed. The words are random, strange, and often unconnected. The temperature was well above a hundred and the sun burnt the deck until waves of heat rose in languid layers. The crew splayed around the cockpit crammed into the fast moving slivers of shade as the sun rose past local noon. *Ondine* wallowed through a pendulum motion every twenty-two seconds. I timed it. The extremes at either end pitched the twin hundred foot masts  through an arc of one hundred and twenty degrees. It was a perfect harmonic resonance of factors including the huge, slow-backed swells from the south, the natural pitching movement of the absolutely dead-in-the-water boat, the lack of any breath of wind for resistance, and a relentless momentum-induced rolling from one beam rail to the other. Holding on with both hands and a wedged leg was essential to keep from being launched like a catapult's projectile into the water or against something solid. As Hugo Vihlen, who sailed a five and a half-foot boat across the Atlantic in the early 90's, wrote: "I don't know who named them swells. There's nothing swell about them. They should have named them awfuls."

The sea was flawless. The world heaved as if the landscape was deep blue gelatin. Nothing marred the scene except the hazy white line of the horizon that never got an inch closer. I remember watching, in a heat induced stupor, the patterns of froth our boat's agitation caused along the hull. A single bubble sat in the water a few feet from my prone body. It would not go away. Sometimes the bubble would gain a foot or two; *Ondine* struggled to keep up. The recollection of the insult is vivid, the heat wilting. I hated that bubble. We were acquainted for what seemed several hours until I got up and dealt it an arching golden stream. This retributive act, on behalf of the honor of the boat and crew for ill deeds done by our opponent on the racecourse, remains the logged highlight of the week.

Calms are often punctuated by isolated cells of unstable air. Squalls along the equator are spring grizzlies on the prowl. Feeding time is random and opportunistic. During the day the horizon will blacken from the blue sky downwards. The zephyrs the boat has been struggling to catch and hold in the limp sails begin to freshen into tight little bursts from all points of the compass. The rig rattles and weaves in the sloppy sea. Sooner than you thought possible, the individual cells of the approaching front grow tall and begin to run at you above the water. Each curtain of confusion sits under a towering nimbus and rolls along on a weaving track in the fore-guard of a deep phalanx of its brothers in arms. The random movements give the tall columns of water and vapor an evil intelligence. It is easy for sailors, as sitting ducks, to give them a hunter's tenacious and treacherous nature. The on-watch points the boat towards phantom openings between the approaching dark curtains. We carry a full load of sail in order to give us the opportunity to position the boat to full advantage. This is tight-rope walking nautical style.

I used the experience to build a set of observations that seem to work most of the time. Squalls can range in wind speed from ten knots in an isolated cell to sixty-plus from a full frontal passage. Being able to judge the difference leads to less wasted effort and broken gear. The line squalls build in frequency throughout the afternoon, but are generally weaker than the ones that occur just before dawn. If you see lightening, the jig is up, expect a fair amount of wind. A frontal passage or tropical wave usually has indicators waving for your attention at least twenty-four hours before the arrival, like a mackerel sky (high streaked cirrus), increased cross wave patterns indicating wind sheer, and a falling barometer. If you can see the squall, note the angle of the leading edge of rain, and if it is slanted hard to one side, or if the forward wall looks like smoke or fog, you better batten down. If the water looks white and flattened out, it's heavy rain and little wind; if the water seems darker than the cloud, it's likely a lot of wind and little rain. And the old sailor's ditty holds true: wind before rain, you'll soon be sailing again; rain before wind, drop the jenny, reef again, hold on.

How do you dodge a squall? I have sought the answer over a good many open ocean miles and I'll share what I understand about tropical weather patterns. Squall dodging begins a long ways out from the beast that is traveling towards you at about fifteen knots. Squalls can be sighted in daylight a good twenty miles away. They are usually moving at slight angles, often to the right side of the prevailing winds in the area, like a sailboat tacking downwind. A rule of thumb is that the preferred tack to build distance between you and a squall is always going to the angle that moves towards the equator. The wind patterns bend the trades west in the northern hemisphere and east in the southern. Common sense dictates that you don't cross in front of an advancing weather line to follow this adage.

If you can feel the temperature drop like a stone, you have lost the dodge, immediately go to plan "B", which is a quick and decisive reduction in sail. The isolated cells also carry a lingering aftertaste of their passing. Behind their path is the reality of a gut churning calm with big seas and slippery decks that can last as long, or longer than the wind. The whole package is a tough experience on gear and crew morale.

Ondine suddenly heeled sharply to a sustained twenty-second blast of wet air before popping back into a becalmed state with everything shaking itself silly. A chill rode the air. Experience cued the entire crew in a single heartbeat that the next calling card was going to bowl the boat over in a mix-master for a solid forty-five minutes or so. The scramble began to get the mainsail reefed and the headsails down and secured. We were always a minute late and a couple of hands short. Turning the boat downwind saved sail battens, plus broken fingers and gear from the flapping sails, but tested the strength and agility of the deck apes to corral and hog-tie a couple of thousand square feet of sailcloth full of wind. At times in the mayhem you often find yourself hugging the bucking boom or a flailing reef line with both feet dangling out over the slipstream of charcoal gray water running aft. With the depth somewhere around two miles and the nearest land a thousand miles away, this is a bracing experience even for the adolescent of mind.

Lightning exploded like a canon blast from a dark cloud at what seemed to be mast level. The water four hundred yards off the starboard beam frothed and steamed before being torn away in the wind. Walking on a bucking boat, trying to get sail down without touching anything metal had us all staggering around like zombies on dog leashes. The old school webbed chest harnesses, caked in dried salt, chafed our skin raw. Wind driven seas, riding the backs of the hillock-sized swells grew in minutes to five feet and kept getting bigger. The wind's howl built until it made my tailbone shiver.

Everyone knew his job and what had to be done in a sequence of choreographed movements, full of priority, timing and mechanical leverage; gear on this boat was under enormous stress loads and a human error or mechanical failure inevitably meant very bad things. Everything was done by hand gestures, faith in your crewmates, and  buckets of guts. If someone held back, hesitated to act, or missed a beat, someone else would get hurt. It paid to be young, quick, and sufficiently motivated by hard won experience to keep your body in one piece and to stay alive.

No one had foul weather gear on at these "All Hands" calls. We were almost at the equator. So, the insult of the marble sized hail beating against our tee shirts and threadbare jams was undeserved and over-the-top. We then added the real injury of being tossed and shaken around by a dysfunctional gang of gray-beard bullies who seemed intent on moving the deck three ways at the same time. At night it was even more exciting as the shadows outside the deck spot lights exaggerated the rampaging elements to mythical proportions.

I always remember feeling a smudge of pride when I went off watch. Filling the log was a score sheet. Hell, I survived. The pointy ends are still up. The water is still on the outside. I'm not looking up the burial at sea procedure in Bowditch. It can't possibly get worse. Of course, in that last case, I was wrong.

It was a very long week.

TWENTY-NINE

BUNKER COVE

I know our luck is about to change for the worse. The fog comes on like a fifty foot wall of snow, advancing quickly up Moosabec Reach, swallowing the entrance buoy to Jonesport at Mark Island. In the long shadows of late afternoon, we can still see the small bluff above Bunker Cove on Roque Island a couple miles off to starboard, but tendrils of pure white fog already drift along the tops of the highest evergreens. I sit in the cockpit being petulant; feeling extremely sorry for myself with a sour puss on my face. Skye has just dropped the other shoe and left me alone in the cockpit to brood. My present ornery mood began with an innocent enough question from my favorite daughter.

"How's it going?"

This is not a good sign. In retrospect I should have created an "All Hands" emergency out of *Ondine*'s play book to delay the conversation. Skye is loath to waste time in small talk. The old sailor's saying is that you never see the dorsal fin of the shark that gets you. I answered the question.

"When I've got the three best things in life around me at the same time, how could it not be going good?"

"You mean us," she said.

"A sailboat, a fair wind, and Maine," I snort and said right back.

"Where do I fit in to the best things in life?" She settles in behind the dodger to stay out of the wind.

"Right between re-runs of Cheers and bacon."

"It could be worse."

"You have no idea," I said.

"We've been talking."

"Whispering," I said with pumping eyebrows for affect.

"Just discussing things."

"I thought you were strangling kittens for dinner."

"Sicko."

I look at the fog as it stands its ground a quarter mile off our bow.

"When am I going to show the baby off to the Syracuse relatives?"

"After it is born?" I guess the obvious and turn on the radar.

"You don't understand."

She always has me there.

"I think I'm going to go with Tristan to get the truck at Belfast, then drop him at the yard in Boston, and drive on to Syracuse to see the grandfolks."

"What about our cruise?"

"We are cruising. We've been cruising," she said with a verbal dagger held to my heart. She pauses, then, gives me back another of my cryptic adages from great sayings: "Remember, cruising is what happens on sailboats while you are busy making plans."

So near, I think, looking out towards Roque. Everything I have wished for was in place. The four of us right here, sailing up a storm. Roque Island is off the starboard bow, all's right with the world, except for the damn fog. The bigger problem is that whatever I had expected to be accomplished on this cruise hadn't happened yet, and it is now all but over. I look back at Skye.

"Better get a jacket, it's gonna get damp." I sound like a sad sack.

Okay, so I have been in absolute denial about what comes next in the evolution of old salts. It is as plain as my married daughter and "Fiona's" presence in the cockpit, busy making their own plans. My plans are just that, my plans. The important lesson to be learned from now on, I tell myself, is how to survive your obsolescence. I'm pathetic. The past is now where all my stories will take place. I am, in one blind-siding moment, a has-been story maker, just another of a tribe of story tellers in the lives of my kids. I take to frowning.

"But we all want to make Jonesport a thing for tomorrow," she said.

"Tomorrow."

"Early," she said. "After we get up and going."

I still don't get it. Skye's body language is straight from a parlor room of charades, with the waving hands helping me along a train of thought like a baby's first steps. I stumble, try, but can't catch up.

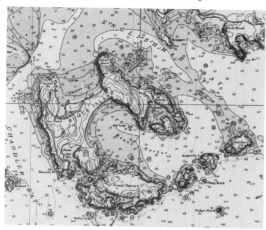

"Tonight we all want to be at Roque Island." Skye gushes the words out, tired of waiting for the light bulb to go on in my head. I finally lit up.

With nary another word, and a quick look to the chart reader, I start the long arcing turn towards the Promised Land. I still brood. Like an adolescent, I ignore the simple fact that we are finally heading exactly where I want to go, and focus entirely on the fact I hadn't gotten everything I wanted, quicker and all at once.

Skye ducks below to relay how the blood-letting had gone for the benefit and entertainment of the rest of the crew. It takes a good ten minutes on the new course and a couple of approving winks from M. through the companionway before I start seeing the delightful alternatives for the rest of the week alone on the boat with my wife. Plus, I have the entire crew on Roque Island tonight. Jamming a summer cruise centerpiece into a single evening is easy I tell myself. It is all in the attitude and follow through. By the time we are pulling down sail and starting up the engine, I'm resigned to the reality of change. My mood is almost giddy; almost.

Dog Star draws five feet. Threading the needle and entering through the back way into the great beach at Roque calls for that same number to be the depth of the channel at mean low tide. The coming journey over one particular whale-backed hump about half-way through the narrow passage is my chief concern. I know from happy past experience that the thoroughfare at Roque Island allows this boat to stay floating, and obey the Prime Directive, at almost all phases of the tide; however, the exception to the rule is my worry today. The shoreline is slab granite and angled rock, polished and tempered by four twelve-foot tidal flushes each day. Making a mistake is not an option. My apprehension over the peculiar timing of our arrival was in high gear, with the light rapidly fading, the tide barely coming on, the current swirling, and the rock with our name on it waiting to gnaw on the bone at my ankle a quarter mile away. Why do I always worry gift horses to death? Whose idea was Roque Island anyway?

The tide that has been delaying our progress most of the day has now switched to a flood, and the dark water is starting to fill into the slime-lined seams along the vertically cracked and scraggy shoreline. Although the rising tide helps if you make a mistake and go aground, the current pushing you along makes mistakes happen more quickly. We slowly come to starboard at the wide turn around the underwater ledge and sheer headland on Little Spruce Island. The engine is barely at idle and we move slowly towards the horseshoe cove, tucked against the tall backdrop of the overlapping junction of the trees of Little and Great Spruce Islands. The Bunker Cove named on the charts is behind us and is strictly shoal-water. Ahead is a familiar skyline. The ridge and sky frame our very first and one of our family's favorite anchorages at Roque Island, claimed and named by us on our inaugural family visit aboard *Dog Star* nearly twenty-five years ago. The sheer cliffs of the signature headland are still fifty-feet tall and topped by a thick rug of rough weathered spruce. The water in the anchorage, that has only adequate swing room for a single boat, is now as still as a mill pond.

I had hoped to anchor off the beautiful mile-and-a-quarter white sand beach that the island is noted for and watch the stars parade across the wide night sky without a solitary electric light to mar the view. The entrance to the narrow canal of my anxiety and access to the beach is a hard turn to port just before reaching the cove. In the dusk, I see that the fog has made the decision for me, as it is now seeping down the thoroughfare in our direction. We all see the situation and know what it means.

"Bunker Butts or the Great Beach," I said to the crew. When in doubt always ask the question you know the answer to, and agree with.

"Bunker Butts," they all said in unison.

"So, it's all on your heads." I snarled the reply like Wallace Berry as Long John Silver. "Bunker Butts t'is."

We collectively smile at the oft-told family story of getting a toddler Skye to giggle by adding "butts" to any other word in her vocabulary. So I tell the young half of the working crew to get their anchor-butts up on the bow-butt and make ready. I put the gear lever into neutral and begin the *Dog Star* anchoring ritual of anticipating every single variable of wind, tide, rock migration, and act of godly disaster.

"The Three Termites." Tristan nods his head towards a rocky ledge on Little Spruce as he leaves the cockpit for the bow and we all giggle again. The word to tag that particular place with is hermit, but the earnest mistake of a young grandchild of G. Peabody "Peebo" Gardner's, in pointing out the infamous home site to a "rusticator," has stuck solidly in the history of our travels to Roque.

Skye gives the punch line.

"Is a hermit a hermit who lives with his brothers?"

Nehemiah, Daniel, and William Ingalls were a rare breed of hermits, even by today's broad standards. They lived for fifty years in the early to mid 20th century in a shanty shack on Little Spruce Island, only yards from where we coasted, and were reported to be very proud of the fact that soap, razor, scissors, or comb were never a part of their social register. It was rumored that a disastrous marriage by the youngest brother William drove the three men to become hermits and, according to the Roque Island historian, Peebo Gardner, "women haters."

The oldest, Nehemiah was a self proclaimed "natur poet" although he could neither read nor write. In today's parlance the local gatherings where he would share his poems and stories along the wharves and in town meeting halls would be called "performance art" or a "Def Jam." Centuries before, the rhyming poet of Little Spruce would have been labeled a troubadour. Whether it was artistic jealousy, bad hygiene, or the collective personalities of caged badgers, rumor has it that the three siblings did not get along all that well. For years communication between the three brothers was usually done by the rotating odd brother, purposely left out of the feud of the month. It must have been a working model of the Three Stooges dressed up as Russian spies. To support this hunch, I offer the fact that the "spleeny" brother William once retired to the cabin for several years claiming, "sunshine was liable to leak down into a person's brain and explode if it were brought near the stove."

The Gardner family on Roque Island celebrated the uniqueness in all of the natural things around their cherished island homestead, and the Ingalls were the most strange of the local flora and fauna. It seems the Gardner matriarch at the time took it upon herself to get the estranged family back together. The local mainland paper recorded the "final" reconciliation of the Ingalls clan with the headline: "IS A SOVEREIGN……Mrs. Jack Gardner's Latest Distinction – How She Pacified Anarchy on Little Spruce Island."

"The latest news that comes up the bay from Little Spruce Island is to the effect that at last Daniel Ingalls has become reconciled to his brothers Nehemiah and William, and that the Ingalls civil government is once again firmly established. The announcement of this armistice interests all the fishermen from Petit Manan to Shackfords Head; and owing to a singular incongruity, the settlement of this Little Spruce Revolution, the re-establishment of law and order, and the reunion of this remarkable Maine family have just as much interest for the high society circles of Boston."

The ghosts of the unwashed brothers melt into the galloping mist, which is quickly gaining ground in our race to get the hook down before we go blind. The anchorage shoals sharply, the tidal current is strong, and we come up smartly under the impressive granite cliff to let go the anchor in nine feet, judging that the tide would bring this to twenty feet or more in a few hours. We let out scope and try to strike a balance between holding power and swinging room. The sun is suddenly gone behind the headland of vapor to the west, and thick fog is starting to drift down from the trees and roll along the still water. The crew goes below to light the lamps, button up against the damp, start thinking about dinner, and straighten the cabins from a day of being out hobnobbing on the coast of Maine. I stay on the bow, puttering with lines, watching the scene. Brooding is finally over, and *Dog Star* is once again smack dab in the center of my universe. The possibilities for the night are endless.

I hear the opening of cabinets and drawers, the muted sounds of conversation and bursts of contagious laughter. My hope is that my recent antics are supplying some of the "can you believe it" fodder for the jokes. I can see, through salt laced glass in the forward hatch, the bobbing of heads against the soft warm glow of the oil lamps. Music starts: Neil Young sings, *"She used to work in a diner; never saw a woman look finer; I used to order just to watch her walk across the floor..."*

The fog is thick now, packed in tight around the boat. The anchor light, hung high on the mizzen topping lift, becomes a muffled orb the size of a pumpkin only thirty-feet away. The boat is stable, pinned to the spot like a bug. Huge droplets of water begin to splat the deck from the condensation collecting from the rigging on the crosstrees. Only the soft ripple of the current running with the tide past the bow indicates any movement. It is the stillness of a primal wood. The world is purposely quiet. The smell of salted eel grass and iodine, black weed and decaying mulch is universally familiar to these higher latitudes where the water is cold and the tide deep. Everything is balanced; everything has a weight and a role. *Dog Star* being anchored right here is no small part of that whole.

This is the answer I couldn't come up with before when I was put on the spot. This is why I love Maine. The magic stuff tonight is very real. This is it, all of it. I almost call Tristan and Skye, to tell them just to get on deck and stand here and take it all in until it grabs them by the throat; demanding they become one with the rich soup of granite and spruce sailing on a vintage wooden boat with their family. I hear the rumble of laughter again from below decks and smartly decide against ordering anybody to do anything. Everything in life is timing. I'll just let the melted cheese analogy stand alone for tonight. Cold, damp, and foggy is a hard sell. I know this to be a tried and true fact.

Five hundred miles offshore in the Pacific Ocean, the colorful haze in the sunset is the wind-blown desert sand borne all the way from the coast of Central America. It was the first tangible proof that all the continents of the world had not suddenly sunk beneath the waves during the last month. *Ondine* couldn't go fast enough. The crew was pushing the envelope. Sail changes are hourly. We press on as if we were racing the devil, and the guy and his pitchfork were coming up fast from astern. "All Hands!" became a fire drill to get the job done and get back in your bunk before you came truly awake. Not a smart attitude, but it came with the territory.

We had finally crossed the equator, and I had been elevated from the realm of pollywog and ceremoniously inducted into the Royal Order of King Neptune's Shellbacks. The price of membership into the select order is crossing the zero degree of latitude by sea. It is an ancient tradition that has spanned centuries and most maritime flags. The brutality, victimizing, and hazing aspects of the earlier

versions of the ritual aboard naval vessels would not have worked well on the particular breed of scalawags along on this voyage. All of us had the ego of a debutant, the temper of a junkyard dog, and a persecution complex that could curdle milk.

Besides, my watch-mate Nick, an underwater demolitions and black-ops expert, who had just mustered out of Her Majesty's Royal Marines (and the younger brother of Tom, our de-facto captain), was my fellow inductee. Nick was good natured, played a mean three chords on the guitar, and belted out the words to every song you ever knew. He could also wipe the decks with the rest of us all at the same time without working up a sweat. I stuck close to the mean pollywog when King Neptune came aboard.

The eve of the equatorial crossing is called the Wog Up-Rising. This was where those about to be inducted could force any Shellback to reveal the secrets of their own initiation in a truth or dare sort of intimidation. In the old days this was done with a sharp knife and a heated spike; today we rely on liberal amounts of ingestible alcohol. It was interesting to hear of the other's woes and miseries. I hoped that most of what they reported was made up. Shellbacks are then sworn to secrecy on specifics of the actual ritual with King Neptune, the Royal Baby, and the always adorable Sea-Hag, except for this one instance of future inductions. Then each pollywog becomes a Shellback with the tally of secrets locked inside; gifts from the crew, never to be shared again. Only his own story can be offered up when Neptune calls. My transformation wasn't that interesting anyway, because we were getting the crap kicked out of us at the time of the equator crossing, and we did the fast-forwarded version. Nevertheless, I will never forget the event. I have conducted my share of inductions down through the years, and it always gives me the flutter-stomach heebie-jeebies to call Neptune up from his throne.

For those who like to collect titles, the U.S. Navy lists many other seagoing fraternities of record. A few from the list: the Order of the Blue Nose for those who have crossed the Arctic Circle; the Order of the Red Nose for those who have crossed the Antarctic Circle; the Order of the Ditch for those who have passed through the Panama Canal; the Order of the Golden Dragon for those who have crossed the International Date Line; the Order of the Rocks for those who have transited the Strait of Gibraltar; and, the Order of Magellan for those who have circumnavigated the globe. I particularly liked the accolade called the Realm of The Czars for those who have crossed into the Black Sea. The ultimate jeweled earbob, however, is the

Royal Diamond Shellback for those who cross the equator off the west coast of Africa at 0° 0' degrees longitude, where the Prime Meridian neatly bisects the girth of the world.

The watery sameness surrounding *Ondine* kept on for another ten days until we saw that wonderful reef of white clouds grow on the horizon, and percolating up from underneath was a brown smudge of arid land. The mirage over the water slowly grew into Acapulco. Soon, we were watching para-sailing speed boats darting around like yapping dogs, getting into the way of the huge, weaving powerboats with bikini clad girls stacked like cordwood on the foredeck and a grinning (leering) drunk high above at the fishing tower steering station. We could see the people teeming like ants on the beach, and huge jumbo jets screaming overhead landing more people by the hour. The culture shock had us all slack jawed and nervous. The first steps onto the dock were confusing as the concrete pier ducked and bounced under my feet. Both Nick and I had to sit down to cleat off the lines. Readjustment to civilization after fifty-five days from Sydney had our heads swimming in goo.

The local "costumes and intimidation" officers were not impressed with my Spanish, but my last port of call being Auckland, New Zealand got a tad of macho respect from the reception clerk as I began the unpredictable process of checking the boat and crew into Mexico. I was polite and apologetic. No ugly gringo here. My smile remained rigidly fixed as if painted by a rodeo clown. I sat with the other cruisers who all appeared to be in different stages of the unfathomable process. One gent advised it would be a few hours at the very least. I figured it was time for the next stage of cross border relation building.

I was following the sage advice of my heroes from the shelves of the nautical section in those classic books by the pioneers of cruising, specifically Allcard and Peterson. It always pays dividend to be prepared in advance to grease the wheels of bureaucracy. On the advice of my idols, I had stopped and bought three bottles of tequila, the square bottles with a genuine white and black worm at the bottom, for six bucks apiece, and stored them in my canvas shore bag right alongside my papers. I figured one for the immigration, one for customs, and one for the crew to get warmed up for a night at liberty.

I approached the reception clerk again; complimenting him on the sharp crease in his uniform, and asking how long it would be if I already had completed all the right papers. I opened my bag to let him see the passports, ship's documents, but the trio of orphaned bottles of decent tequila snagged his attention first. He became animated and friendly, ushering me in past the swinging half doors and down the hall, patting my back the whole way. He stopped and opened a door.

At the first desk I set my papers, passports, and a bottle down, backed up a pace or two and smiled. I was given the once over, twice, by the officer behind the desk. As if by magic, the entire desk was suddenly cleared with one sweep of an arm. A small uniformed back was quickly heading towards the door to an inner office. Two minutes later he re-appeared and handed me my stamped passports and pointed with a gold gapped smile to the desk across the hallway.

"Me Amigo," he said.

"Amigo," I said.

He gave my arm a knowing squeeze.

I repeated the procedure with the rotund uniform in charge of the next office. I answered a brief questionnaire through an interpreter; complimented the desktop picture of his family. Again the table was cleared magically and I was given the boat's custom clearances stamped, sealed, and signed before I could cross my legs,. The happy officer said he would look forward to my coming in to check out of Acapulco after a very pleasant stay.

I also found that word travels fast in Mexico. Another young man in a crisp uniform immediately took my arm as I exited customs, chatted away in rapid Spanish, and walked me to the very end of the hallway where an opaque glass door read COMMANDANTE in eight-inch-high gold letters. My guide was the head man's attaché. Inside I was treated to a tour of the empty office, the spotless and tidy mahogany desk the size of a ping-pong table, and the private toilet in the corner behind a standing partition. Finally, the dapper tour guide with the razor thin mustache and white pants with a crease so sharp it would put your eye out, holding my arm cradled tightly in his, indicated in no uncertain terms he was the brains behind the boss and that he felt entitled to something for his trouble. He proved he could certainly do elemental subtraction. I was glad I had bottle number three right at hand to seal the deal.

I strolled out of the main door, waving shyly at the cruising people who were there when I walked in. They really had some sour pusses on their faces as I left. I stopped for a few more bottles of the "oil that greases the wheels of bureaucracy" before getting back to the crew with their permission to go ashore. Sometime during the night, I was later told, I won a contest by doing headstands on the bar at the Hilton while someone tried to pour shots of tequila up my throat. From one sailor to another, trying to defeat gravity is a neat trick on your first night ashore.

THIRTY

CUTTING AND STACKING FOG

Dog Star's cabin is warm and full of the galloping after-dinner conversation that a family has when they haven't been together for a long while and time is too short to get it all said. Skye is holding center stage, animated in relating her own version of a scary story. The tale surrounds our family's good fortune to be spending millennium eve on Naushon Island, one of the Elizabeth Island chain just off the entrance to Wood's Hole. We had spent the week bridging the dawn of the new century on the isolated real estate between Buzzards Bay and Vineyard Sound along with twenty other friends and their children as the guests of Cindy Crofts Wisch, her husband Jeff, and the Forbes Family Trust.

The Mansion House is the huge Colonial structure, familiar to generations of New England sailors, rising from sheep shorn fields at the head of Hadley Harbor (one of the most secure and beautiful anchorages on the eastern seaboard). The icon, dating back nearly a century and a half, dominates the scene, with fourteen fireplaces, a dining table for twenty, a kitchen the size of a squash court, four parlors, and a dozen or so munchkin-sized bedrooms rambling over the three main floors. The house has hosted U. S. Presidents from Grant to Clinton. The Forbes Family Trust, that owns and manages the islands as a functioning reserve for its members, almost had Senator John Kerry, one of its own flock by marriage, as our nation's Commander In Chief.

If the dire predictions about the entire technical world shutting down because of a malfunction in roll-over digits were true, we were in the right place to step back a hundred years without a hitch. The highlight of the week, from my perspective, was sailing a Herreshoff 12 ½ in the harbor on New Millennium's morning in a blustery cold wind, wearing woolen mittens and goulashes. The incident Skye was relating happened the night before.

"There were dead faces in the attic." Skye said.

"They were plaster cast molds of dead faces," I said.

"Whatever."

"A whole big treasure trunk full," Tristan said.

"They had names written on them."

"A lot of dead people have names," I said.

"It was creepy."

"Creepy was you in a flannel nightgown," said Tristan.

"You were scared silly too," said Skye punching her brother's shoulder.

"Of the bats," he said scratching his hair as if one has taken to nest. "They were the size of pterodactyls."

"As I remember, the under-age bumping and thumping carried on until dawn," M. said.

"Who could sleep with dead faces in the attic?"

Her mother and I raise our hands.

"You guys drive me crazy," Skye said.

"It's not a long trip," I said and pour a little more red wine into my glass in order to keep up with the lively chatter that usually rolled along miles ahead of me.

Skye and her mother recall the gentrified, formal, before dinner activities when others of the Forbes Trust families, staying at one of the twenty or so houses scattered around the island, came up to the Mansion House at sundown for a cocktail and nibbles. Everyone was served holiday cheer, a pat on the back, and creamy eggnog. The eclectic group of adults, young adults, and animals gathered in front of a pair of blazing six-foot-square fireplaces, located on either end of the great room, and made polite conversation. The upper floors reverberated in the echoes of high-pitched screams as every fear ever imagined by the youngest set of our island bound visitors came out of shadowy doorways. They were being victimized by my son and the two Wisch boys. It was the homey shrieks of instigated chaos.

I change the subject when the story takes a deep breath. I am still trying again to dictate our moves and schedules. My family usually reminds me that when I get like this that there is an old 1850's cavalry saying I should pay attention to: "When the horse is dead, dismount." My fundamental problem is seldom heeding sound advice.

"How exactly are you going to introduce the beach ball under your shirt to the family in Syracuse?"

"Very carefully; I know your family."

"They'll want answers."

"It's a terrible family flaw."

"Boy or girl is going to be the question from inquiring minds."

"…always the big questions from your people, and not one single answer that is worth a quote in the whole tribe."

"So you really don't know, and don't want to know, what gender of baby you're having?"

"I was hoping for human," my daughter said without a pause.

I don't try and conjure a response.

* * *

There are times in life when your lucky star shines like there is no tomorrow. M. and I had last communicated, during the opening months of 1974 after my leaving on *Ondine,* when I phoned her from New Zealand. Mail stops were not frequent in the mid-Pacific Ocean. We had grabbed a ballpark date off the wall eight weeks ago and said we would meet up in Acapulco. Fifty-five days after I sailed out past Sydney Heads, M. hopped aboard a Quantas Airlines jet and arrived in Mexico. *Ondine* sailed into town the exact same day. M. was saved from that infamous first night ashore with six ill-mannered sailors by checking into the hotel and getting the exactly wrong information from the harbormaster concerning our arrival. We finally found each other the next morning and we have never been apart from each other that long since.

Huey Long, *Ondine*'s owner and old-school racing fanatic, sent a present to the boat upon our arrival. We met the present on the dock the next day. Two couples were going to hitch the ride to Cabo San Lucas and then up the Baja to San Diego. *Ondine* was scheduled into a shipyard for a refit before the Trans-Pac and to have the trampoline structure off her stern encapsulated with aluminum in order to add both waterline length at the heel and some mild aesthetics to the all-out speed machine. The four moved aboard immediately and at once we morphed from a muscle-bound racing sled in transit to a chartered luxury yacht. This crew of madmen, deck apes without the varnish, fresh off a long ocean passage and chock full of themselves, appeared ill-suited to the job. So, taking my normal tactful approach, I convinced Mr. Long over an expensive phone call that M. would be of invaluable assistance to Kitty, our cook turned "chef," in making the sail north a pleasure for our guests. He finally caved on his "no-woman-crew rule" when the alternative was my taking a bus north across the border and leaving Tom looking for another U.S. citizen to act as captain. It was the first time I negotiated myself into something I actually wanted.

Time was short so we provisioned and had all the necessary paperwork cleared for Cabo by virtue of the official "Tequila Alley" in a matter of days. I did note to the rest of crew the night before departure on how the wind was whistling in the rigging and the sound had been pretty constant since we had arrived. Nothing changed for the next three weeks except the wind direction that followed exactly the course we were trying to make. Having the wind dead on the nose is thrilling and fun in a racing sailboat for an afternoon in the bay. A steady diet of beating upwind for fifteen hundred miles in a high-powered rocket against a consistent twenty-plus knots of wind is not everyone's cup of tea. Any northerly trip up the Baja is a hard slog upwind with most boats hugging the coast and stopping where they can. We had a tight schedule, stopping was not an option. The wind on steroids never took a break.

Our guests retired to their cabins about twenty minutes after we cleared the sea buoy out of Acapulco. I did not see them again for three and a half days. M. was having a hard time trying to keep down her own lunch while tending to the needs of four very sick puppies below decks. It was not the leisurely cruise to write home about.

One of the male guests tried to rally and managed to get dressed, scramble on deck and sit in the cockpit.

"Some fun," he said leaning into the wind.

"You get used to it," I said over the keening in the rigging.

"Don't think so." He held on white knuckled to a nearby winch to keep from being thrown about as we launched off another wave.

The waves were eight to twelve feet and *Ondine* muscled the top third of each roller aside at the bow and the squashed water rode aft like a pair of vulture's wings. Explosions, when our tons of momentum met rolling waves, rattled our clenched teeth. The two big rigs on the boat, in spite of the reefs, kept us at hull speed and on our ear. It was a symphony of stress vibrations from backstays, wet sheets, and humming rope guys. The masts were rotating under load, causing shrill whistles and torqued groans from deep below decks.

Our guest answered my questions concerning the other guests with eyes that winced with each thunderous crash off of a wave. The rest of us quickly realized that things below decks for those stuck in the aft cabins were bad and getting worse. The only solution was to get these suffering victims of the acute sea sickness ashore. We laid a course for Cabo San Lucas and eased sheets a crack. Things aboard the boat were noticeably on the mend almost immediately. It got far better when our former guests were ensconced in a five star resort with an attending physician.

We cleared in and out of Cabo San Lucas in a single afternoon. I am sure it still stands as a record no other gringo lunatic will ever challenge. To paraphrase a Yogi Berra-ism: "You know, pesos work just like cash."

"No more Tristan stories," my son said. He points a shame finger with a definite threat in it at Skye. She grabs for it. They squirm like kids on the opposite settee.

Dinner is cleaned up and we four lounge in reclined stupor on the cushions propped around the main cabin. Candlelight still glows and flickers against the polished table top. The oil lamps are keeping the dark corners in the main cabin from getting damp and lost in the shadows. At odd intervals the cockpit canopy will spill a cup or two of condensation onto the deck with a loud smack. All else is quietly blanketed in the heavy fog that has thrown its arms around Roque Island.

"This is pretty nice," M. said. Silent agreement goes around the table. Whatever the right stuff is, we were full to the brim with it.

"Why did it feel like pulling teeth to get us here?" I said.

"It is not the destination, but the voyage," my daughter said.

I want to say "Bullshit," defend myself, demand answers, but wisely decide to think about it. The very reason the line sounded so sane and familiar is because it was one of those favorite truisms shared with my kids over the years. Idioms are the hard currency of my life. My crew is always swimming in grandma-isms.

"Nothing easily won is ever appreciated." Tristan spouts another one of my favorites.

"No matter where you go, that's where you are," M. said.

"Slow down, reef early, don't stress yourself or the ship."

"Examine a gift horse down to its tonsils."

"Sailing is the happiest time of your life."

"Never waste a fair wind or tide."

"The beatings will continue until morale improves."

"No sand on the boat. It always ends up in the captain's bunk and makes him crabby."

"Up or down in the companionway, don't be a do nothing and stand in the way of progress."

"Go rowing. You can't practice enough."

"If you want to be alone on this boat, get arrested."

"Go slow, boats don't have brakes."

"I'm always ready to compromise on my side of the issue. I'm the captain."

My children are tag teaming as many of my prophetic words and sayings as they can think of. Each new one is making their eyes water and ribcages spasm with giggles. M. is snorting right alongside her breathless children.

"Think twice, do it once."

"Dig in deep; way more in the anchor department is better."

"Paranoia is wonderful. Either you're right or pleasantly surprised."

"Adventure is the goal, life is the choice."

"I am the instrument of stinkpot Karma."

"Stop," I said.

"Be careful what you wish for," M. said as the final badda-bing that draws a howl from her offspring.

"So I hammered some things home," I said.

"With a sledge hammer and spikes," my son said.

"It was like Chinese water torture," Skye said.

"Is any of it worth anything these days?" I wonder out aloud.

"Sure, if you want to sound really old and Amish," Tristan said.

"And, when would that be?" His sister rolls her eyes to the ceiling, asking for the punch line.

"The next time we anchor in rural Pennsylvania?"

My entire complement of dinner guests is weak with all the snorting and laughing at my expense. I listen defensively as the crew picks apart, with humor and their own real-world experience, the litany of all my life's intimate lessons. They skewer those truisms I have gleaned from the strange experiences of my life, and subsequently tried to pass on to whomever would listen for the past quarter century. My philosophy of cruising and living sounded childish and dogmatic in its simplicity. The soup of my wisdom appears pretty thin.

"The one saying that makes the most sense to me," my daughter said when my long face indicates I'm not having quite as much fun as they all were, "is that 'Real happiness is not getting what you want, but wanting what you got.'" She moved her hand in a small loving circle around her mounded belly. "I'll keep using that one for sure."

Silent agreement makes a second lap around the table in the cozy warmth of our boat anchored in the fog at Roque Island. M. gives my shoulder a squeeze. Tristan smiles and winks. Skye rubs her baby. I'll take this Gestalt moment as an affirmation that decades of indoctrination are actually worth all the babble.

Ondine sped her way through the Pacific miles. Things calmed down on the weather front and the last four hundred miles were a fast paced dream with fifteen to twenty knots and we could lay our course. When M. and I had left the United States two years before, Richard Nixon had been swearing he wasn't a crook and everyone knew better. We were now busy planning our next adventure after our piecemeal circumnavigation of the world when we spotted the San Diego skyline. We decided it was fitting a drug induced fantasy to be experiencing this from behind the wheel of arguably the most famous and successful open ocean racer in the world. We were smart enough to understand how special a day this was.

The morning was layered in haze and the sun barely broke through the smog. Over the dull hum of our engine we could begin to hear the rumblings of the big city noise. We were anxious to get on with our life, see family and friends, and reconnect with our country. Our first plan was a cheap bus ride from west to east, stopping off in Steamboat Springs to see some old skiing friends and catch the spring slush.

I was able to log on my sailing resume the seven-thousand five-hundred miles as captain for the Pacific trip, and with a little book work and testing I was able to turn the *Ondine* delivery into a 100 ton captain's ticket. During the next five years M. and I managed a handful of very special boats, mostly through the Bahamas and down the Caribbean chain. We enjoyed the often humorous challenge of trying to live in paradise, on beautiful boats we could never afford, where the owner pays all the bills and our salary, while, in spite of the obstacles, remaining totally competent and professional. We managed quite well as a team. I was the weak link. On one of these charter boats the previous captain had been a smaller man and left behind the obligatory old-school white jacket with gold epilates and brass buttons. M. often wore this to greet our new guests and broke the ice aboard with a few sharp orders to me and our one-man Bahamian crew she called, for maximum stage effect, "Worthless" James. The gossipy sniping from M.'s mouth concerning our most recent bad tempered guests, the tropical antics of a boy-child husband, and a worthless "conch-headed island person" was always way over the top. She would continue to escalate the act, ranting away, until she stretched credibility beyond the audience's limits and the jig was up. Everyone had a good laugh at their own expense. At times catering to charter guests was even fun.

In 1976 we briefly came back to the States and were married. Friends, family, and sailors came from as far away as Australia and Europe to make the end of summer event. Two hundred and fifty people under a full moon dancing to a jazz trio partied until the dawn peeked over the rolling hills at my father-in-law's dairy farm in Pompey, New York. A dozen close friends had breakfast and came along on our honeymoon to Saratoga Springs for the thoroughbred horse racing. We finally left the entourage behind on a spectacular bicycle camping trip through Vermont and New Hampshire. M. and I then joined, as professional companions, a venturesome older couple aboard a spanking new Hinckley Sou'wester 50 at the Hinckley Yard in Mount Desert, Maine for a leisurely cruise south to the Virgin Islands for the winter. Life was better than alright.

The years rolled by. It was finally apparent when the sunsets and sailing the beautiful boats weren't reason enough to forget the pressures and frustrations of working to someone else's schedule and having nothing of our own but two sea-bags and a bank account. Our attitude was shot, and we needed some space from yachts and their owners. We knew it was the right time to leave running other people's toys behind. We began looking for a brand new chapter in our lives.

The story is told of the disgruntled sailor who swore on his mother's grave while struggling against a frightful rounding of Cape Horn that if he survived, just as soon as he could step ashore, he would put an oar over his shoulder and walk inland until someone asked him what that thing on his shoulder was. It was there he would spend the remaining days of his life and never go back again to the sea. Our needs were not that drastic, but a couple of years of doing anything else suddenly became a very good idea.

M. and I eventually figured northwestern Alaska would not have much of a yachting scene and decided to move to a subsistence culture of Inuits in an Inupiaq Community called Unalakleet, a couple of hundred miles south of Nome on the wind swept coast of the Bering Sea. M. was to be the first special needs teacher in the seven-hundred person village that was isolated by over a thousand miles of wilderness from  the nearest highway. I was working part time for the University of Alaska lecturing and developing technology and techniques for long distance delivery of college level courses. I was also beginning what was to be a fateful addiction to running my own string of sled dogs.

We figured we would give our Alaska hiatus two years. Twenty years later we finally moved back to the "lower forty-eight." During this time we found time for kids and careers. I also fed my sailing habit in huge bites. Between deliveries, occasional ocean racing, and annual cruises on our family's very special boat moored on the East Coast each summer, I managed to be out on the water better than three months a year. We had found our beloved Philip Rhodes' designed *Dog Star* and committed ourselves permanently to her care and well being. This is very same boat I saw in front of the Ida Lewis Yacht Club during the morning of my very first Bermuda Race. She came rather unexpectedly into our lives. The exact details of our finding this perfect match to our aesthetic and cruising needs reads like Woody Allen doing Kafka.

THIRTY-ONE

GREAT BEACH, ROQUE ISLAND

Dawn at Bunker Cove starts sloppy. Heavy condensation drips in a steady stream from every vertical pole, wire, rag and line. It takes a second cup of coffee and some slow baking cinnamon rolls before the sun finally burns a widening hole through the surface fog. On cue, the wind picks up and funnels in from the north-northwest pushing the wall of mist quickly out to sea. Columns of stark white cumulus clouds ride across the tall pine skyline, the rounded domes neatly lined up like prairie schooners at a land rush. The new air smells of fresh pine sap and granite mountain tops. Before Tristan and I can get the soggy rain awning down and shaken out the day is already showing all the indications of becoming a real sparkler. The way to Jonesport should be clear sailing on a freshening wind.

"Sorry about holding you up," I said to my son.

"You can't push the fog, it stacks itself," he said and touches the side of his nose after parroting yet another of my pet sayings.

"Hope it didn't queer the berth on the *Gamage*."

"They'll get over it. What are they going to do, fire me? I'm just a 'swabby' volunteer anyway. I'll just tell them I had to help my decrepit, aging father sail his boat."

"Thanks for not prosecuting."

"I love you too, Dad."

"You coming back aboard before you start getting ready for school?"

He shrugs and tells me he will try.

Pigs will fly first.

The Delta anchor comes up hauling a huge divot of stinking black mud flecked with a galaxy of broken shells. As father and son clean up the mess on the foredeck with brush and bucket, mother and daughter bring *Dog Star* slowly around and head back out through the narrow granite cut.

I stand at the mast with sail ties off the main and the halyard ready as the ladies round her up to face into the brisk wind. Skye, at the loosened sheet, watches closely as the sail shimmies its way up the bronze track, the breeze shaking free the long rows of reefing ties that add a discordant tapping to the deep woof-woof of the sail. The boat begins working straight uphill against the wind.

"She's there," I said as the top of the sail reaches the masthead and M. fills the sail and turns towards the distant tree topped mound of Mark Island. Skye trims the main as her mother calls out the mark. The engine rumble stops abruptly. Jib and mizzen are soon up, and our old girl bounds along like a puppy free of the pen.

Skye takes the tiller from her mother who scans the paper charts and orients them to the dim glimmer of the GPS chart plotter in the cockpit. I head below to stop the last of the coffee cups from rattling. The heavy white porcelain mugs, clamoring for attention in the sink, could probably be used as hockey pucks and survive. M. joins me below and quietly tells me she will be hitching the same soon-to-be-arranged ride to the truck in Belfast with the kids. She needs to do her seasonal visit to our shared "out-laws" and will bring the truck and herself back to Maine when Skye heads home to Alaska. I half expected the news. The curtain on our family's summer cruise is dropping faster than a lead keel heading for the bottom of the sea.

Skye calls below that the first buoy is coming up and she needs some advice. Assessing my mood as I climb on deck, I am pleasantly surprised that I am taking it all better than expected. We made it to Roque. This might be our last time on our totem island as a foursome without blood-line additions to the crew. I watch my daughter as she tries to "hold her down" on a close reach, straining against the tiller in a white knuckled gust. I ease the main a bit and *Dog Star* gains her feet again.

"Better?"

I get a smile.

"I'm glad we came to Maine," she said.

I smile back.

"It's easy to love Maine on a day like this," she said.

"It's always like this, except when the weather gets in the way."

"You're so smart," she said.

"Glad to share the wisdom."

"So, what, besides being a parent, am I going to be when I grow up?"

"I still ask myself that question every day," I said.

"Any suggestions?"

"You do what you are."

"You mean, you are what you do."

"No. I think you really don't have all that much choice in finding your way in a life. This is especially true if you are terminally stubborn, immune to embarrassment, and more lucky than good. The inner you takes over, points you in the right direction, makes it happen. You eventually become invested in that one thing that makes all the difference in your life."

"How do you know what you are supposed to be good at?"

"What brings the most pleasure to your days, keeps you awake at night dreaming about the possibilities, and seems never to be too boring to brag about."

"You mean like sailing," she said in an exasperated voice usually reserved for a badly behaved two-year-old.

"You making fun of me?"

"Constantly."

"Sailing is only the icing on the cake," I said as I point out the next mark down the channel.

"Cheese on Chinese food, and now icing on cakes?"

"I like icing."

"Your blunt and murky point is?"

I gave her the shame-on-you stare.

"Tell me the truth. I can handle the truth." She threatens above the wind.

"I find the biggest joys possible in my present life by just being your dad. Doing everything I possibly can to be the designated curmudgeon, a constant source of cash, embarrassment, and entertainment." The mizzen begins to shake and I trim it up. "I am the completely dysfunctional branch on this challenged family tree."

"So, you're saying it's not about the sailing after all."

"Of course it's about sailing," I said in mock shock. "What in life isn't about the sailing?"

She opens her mouth. She shuts it again.

"Sailing gives all the rest of it a perfect place to happen." I try to shout above the whistle of the wind.

Skye slowly shakes her head. It is a condescending waggle softened by pitying brown eyes.

"It doesn't make sense to me," she said, "yet."

"It will."

She rubs her belly and steers the boat. The smile is back.

"Dysfunctional?"

"Chronic," I said.

"Let's hope it skips a generation."

"It already has."

I slide into the cockpit next to her and give her shoulder a hug.

"You're a rare dish," she said.

"Yes, I am.

"An acquired taste." Skye and *Dog Star* boil along under the next gust.

"Why do you think I'm such a rare dish?" I ask my daughter the self serving question, feigning a polite manner, pointing to the "4" Nun, which is leaning slightly against the wind and bucking like a bronco in the following current.

"Born to it and plenty of practice?"

"Bingo," I said.

M. and I found that Unalakleet, Alaska in 1978 met our expectations about being as far from the world's yachting and ocean racing scene as possible. Our former globe-trekking life was not all that interesting to our Inupiaq neighbors. They were more concerned about why we didn't have any children. M. took them seriously and soon we were planning the mid-September arrival of Skye. That summer found us visiting our families in upstate New York to show off the unborn baby. We were also prowling the boatyards and brokerages along the New England coast looking for a boat to call our own.

Dick Scuito's brokerage office was up a long flight of stairs above a storage shed at the Concordia Company Yard in Padanarum Village, located along the waterfront of South Dartmouth, Massachusetts. The energetic, balding broker was courteous and patient as we poured through the stack of three-ringed binders of boat spec sheets looking for the needle in a haystack. We "kicked some tires" and went aboard a handful of aging wooden caskets, a few venerable plastic antiques, and found nothing that got our blood running. After a couple of days of fruitless searching, it was clear that we obviously knew what we wanted and nothing within a hundred miles was fitting our price range and expectations.

Dick was scratching his head thoughtfully as we headed down to the Rudder Restaurant for a late afternoon beer and to say our goodbyes before getting in the car and heading west. It was only then he begrudgingly admitted there was one more boat, which didn't have a page in his books, that he thought might be for sale and was just what we were looking for. He explained that a certain gentleman, a fellow member of the New Bedford Yacht Club, just the evening before had astonished the bar by announcing that he was ready to sell his boat. It seems he wasn't using her all that often, as his older brother required his added muscle to sail his larger yacht, and his parsimonious Yankee upbringing could no longer support the writing of the annual checks. By his calculations, each sail the summer before had cost him over a thousand dollars. Everyone thought he was joking, as the man and his boat had a long and colorful story. Dick thought it might be worth a shot in the dark to contact him and call his bluff.

Prescott Gustafson was a bona fide member of old New England yachting aristocracy. He was heir to a family construction business that specialized in large scale steel construction that included the labyrinth of bridges that connect the elongated fingers of land known as Rhode Island. This particular boat story begins with his post World War II courtship and marriage to his wife. It seems that his fiancée's uncle owned a lovely Philip Rhode's designed double ender where the couple's plans for a life together were defined. He later joked that he married her to have an inside track on making the vessel his. In 1948 he was able to purchase the yacht "to keep her in the family." The boat and her new owner became a vibrant fixture in Newport racing circles. As a long standing member of both the New York Yacht Club and the Ida Lewis Yacht Club, Prescott served his passion for sail as an "official measurer" for the America's Cup, insuring that the twelve meter yachts kept within their tight performance formulas throughout the nineteen fifties and sixties. *Dog Star* was honored during this period by being named "Flagship" for one of the annual New York Yacht Club "cruises"; a small, well respected gem among the two hundred foot mega-yachts of the du Ponts, Morgans, and Vanderbilts. She graced her mooring in front of the Ida Lewis Yacht Club's docks as a prime example of the very best blend of art and function for decades.

Nearly forty years after her building at the M. M. Davies & Son Yard in Solomons, Maryland, *Dog Star* was showing terminal signs of age and hard campaigning. Prescott weighed all the available options except abandonment and finally approached the venerable Waldo Howland at Concordia Yachts about the possibility of a major restoration. On close examination it was determined that a rebuild would be more costly and the result less durable than laying a new keel and starting from scratch. The die was cast and, with an upgraded set of interior plans drawn by Philip Rhode's son, a deal was struck. The Beetle Cat shed on Smith Neck, across the harbor from the yard was to be the site of the construction.

Prescott decided that he wanted the hands-on experience of shaping the new boat himself and, to the surprise and chagrin of his wife and business associates, devoted himself full time to the effort. Bill MacKenzie, recently retired foreman of the Concordia Yard, agreed to lead the project. Taking four long years in the building, using the original lead keel and bronze fittings, plus enough structural wood to keep her soul, the building of *Dog Star* proceeded at a slow but steady pace. Each fine detail, from planking to Sitka spruce spars to the bright elm interior, was labored over and treated as consummate works of old school craftsmanship. Those who watched the progress say that the words "Oh, that's good enough" were never spoken. If traditional wooden boat building is a series of compromises between time, materials, and money, this enterprise was spared any down-side of this equation.

It was rumored that Prescott's wife, miffed over the time and expense expended on his labor of love, became less than an avid sailor. Eight years after *Dog Star* was launched, to become a Padanarum Harbor and New Bedford Yacht Club poster child, nestled among the other beautiful wooden Concordia Yawls and Crocker Cats, Prescott answered Dick Scuito's phone call and, after long moments of dead silence, agreed to consider parting with the boat that had cradled his passion for nearly thirty-five years. However, certain non-negotiable conditions must be met. These details kept Dick Scuito scratching his head for months to come.

Two days later M. and I were back at the New Bedford Yacht Club docks boarding a launch to inspect the yacht broker's latest offering. Threading the way through the hundreds of boats moored and swinging around to the tide, the launch finally pointed straight as an arrow to a breathtaking dark green hulled ketch that immediately stopped the music in my head. At first glance I knew her. She was the very same boat from that long ago first-ever Bermuda Race that had captured my imagination and still turned up in Technicolor dreams during those long Alaskan winter nights. When the story unfolded over the next few months, that fateful day of my first sighting was only weeks before she was taken to the Beetle Cat shed and dismantled for her reconstruction. I was speechless as the launch pulled alongside and we stepped aboard. She curtsied to the wake of the launch and already felt like home.

Over lunch with Dick Scuito at the Club I tried not to let my enthusiasm trump whatever negotiating ploy I might fake. I knew I would have to own this boat no matter if the asking price was my right arm. It was with a contrite expression that Dick began to outline the details to consider before we talked a deal. To begin he asked us a series of questions from scribbled notes on a legal pad. Was our marriage healthy? Was our financial situation adequate and stable enough to support the boat's needs? To what use did we intend to put the boat? What was our sailing background? Could we provide references from other sailors that would attest to our skills? And stable home life? What other wooden boats had we had experience with? Each answer was written down and arrangements made to provide the necessary back-up documentation for our answers. I began to feel this was less a purchase and more of an adoption.

Then Dick dropped the other shoe. Prescott never wanted to meet us, see us, or talk with us himself. The boat must be removed from the coast of New England so that the former owner and builder would never see the boat under someone else's command. The name could not be changed. Prescott would have a binding buy-back clause in the bill of sale if any of these conditions, including proper maintenance and upkeep, were not met. Once Prescott had assured himself that our answers were verified to his satisfaction, we would make an offer, only one, and it would be accepted or rejected, bargaining was not to be part of the transaction. Dick apologized and wiped his brow before taking a Polaroid picture of us and left the table to give us time to consider the bizarre proposal. M. and I stared at each other for a long minute with confused expressions before we compared the deal to the one offered Faust and collapsed into hysterics. Life has a strange way of making dreams come true. We knew we would accept every condition and meet the devil on the down staircase if that's what it took.

In the end Prescott relented on each of his demands, and the price he agreed on was generous in the extreme. He became a wonderful friend and mentor through the next fifteen years before his passing. I still feel the loss of his wise counsel on the care and devotion needed by special boats. Each summer our family stepped aboard to the wonderful experience of cruising *Dog Star* and, for better than a quarter of a century, she has shaped and defined our lives in ways we could never have anticipated or expected. It is indeed a place where the experience of growing a family is enriched and nurtured. Nothing has changed with this past summer's cruising experience; nor should it.

The wind is still blowing steady out of the North and is liable to stay that way. The top of the mast is fielding gusts into the high twenties in the late afternoon of this extraordinary summer day in Maine. The sky is so blue against the gelatin white clouds that they look like floating icebergs drifting in from Labrador. *Dog Star* and I are tucked up close to the gleaming white sand of Great Beach on Roque Island.

Our anchor buried in deep mud in fifteen feet of transparent water. I have better than a hundred feet of chain out, adding to my secure feeling. Six-inch waves gurgle alongside, their chuckles heard above the sound of the fresh breeze moving through the tall trees four-hundred yards away. These dense pines closely rim the beach at this end and give us a welcome lee. The air is as cold, dry, and clean as a chaste kiss. I am tucked in under the dodger, with a fleece vest, propped up on cushions with my wool stocking feet straight out. I am just finishing up the log of the past few days and adding additional notes to my summer journal. While trying to report out the fairly obvious challenges and nuances of this season's epic family cruise, I had found myself wandering in circles, miles off the mark. With an abrupt and tactical course correction, riding the tide of random memories and side-bar experiences, I have finally managed to wrap it up and feel a bit self-righteous about the effort.

"I took your advice," I said to M. over the cell phone while sipping on a cold beer.

"That would be a first."

"I gave away all the 'me, me, me' parts, and tried not to be too critical or judgmental of anyone else."

"Wow, three big firsts in a row. I'm proud of you."

"Just the facts."

"Good boy."

"No forcing a cosmic reason on things."

"Never works out anyway," she said.

Skye and her mother dropped Tristan off at his new berth aboard the *Harvey Gamage* in New Bedford and are now driving on the Mass Pike heading west towards Syracuse. M. would be back aboard by the weekend, and we plan to meet in Belfast for a week of laid back cruising around Penobscot Bay.

"I got it all down on paper."

"Always knew you could."

"And I'm not going to worry it, like a dog with a bone."

"Cuts down on the drooling."

"I got it as tight as a rusted keel bolt."

"Less is more."

"I just wanted to…" I finally run out of words. It feels good.

"I know," she said.

"Of course you do."

"Stay safe and miss me like crazy," she said.

"What else would I do?"

"Be happy on our boat."

We hang up.

I am.

INDEX

AUTHOR BIOGRAPHY

R.J. Rubadeau has spent the last forty years engaged in a smoldering love affair with boats and the wonderful things they do for a person's soul. Logging over 150,000 sea miles during an amateur and professional career in the elite world of open ocean racing aboard the world's legendary yachts, the author has sailed with and against the icons of the international sailing hall of fame. He has entertained generations of sailors with his writings about the crazy trouble people can get into when they cast off dock lines and go sailing. Rubadeau has honed his communication skills in various shore-side occupations: university lecturer, grant writer, newspaper columnist, politician, speech-writer for an Alaskan governor (No, not that one!), public policy analyst, and twenty years as a professional political strategist. He is a frequent contributor to many sailing magazines and is also an award winning poet. Rubadeau and his wife Mary, best friends and partners since their teens, live with their horses and a menagerie of animals at ten-thousand feet in the Rocky Mountains near the town of Telluride, Colorado. They base *Dog Star*, their family's historic seventy-nine year old ketch and primary summer preoccupation, on Mt. Desert Island in Maine.